GROWING *in* GRACE

DESTINY IMAGE BOOKS BY PAUL AND BILLIE KAYE TSIKA

Parenting with Purpose

Get Married, Stay Married

GROWING *in* GRACE

Daily Devotions for Hungry Hearts

PAUL *&* BILLIE KAYE TSIKA
AND FAMILY

DESTINY IMAGE® PUBLISHERS, INC.
PO Box 310, Shippensburg, PA 17257-0310
"Promoting Inspired Lives"

This book and all other Destiny Image and Destiny Image Fiction books available at Christian bookstores and distributors worldwide.

For more information on foreign distributors, call 717-532-3040.
Or reach us on the Internet: www.destinyimage.com

Cover design by Eileen Rockwell
Interior design by Terry Clifton

ISBN 13 TP: 978-0-7684-0991-8
ISBN 13 Ebook: 978-0-7684-0992-5

For Worldwide Distribution, Printed in the U.S.A.
1 2 3 4 5 6 / 19 18 17 16

DEDICATION

We dedicate *Growing in Grace* to some very special people in our lives. This group of people has demonstrated time and again their desire to learn, grow, and change. Their passion to become everything that God has created them to be is not only obvious but is also contagious.

They are the dreamers who pursue life with a passion. They are the doers who will not allow themselves the luxury of excuses. They are the people who believe in their destiny and their responsibility to pass that on to the next generation. They are the IBOs of World Wide Dream Builders.

We love them, pray for them, and support them in their great adventures for success.

SPECIAL DEDICATION

On Wednesday June 1, 2016 at 10:21 A.M., the dearest friend I've ever had passed into the arms of Jesus, his Lord.

James Ronald Puryear, known to all of us in World Wide Dream Builders as "Ron Puryear" was born September 24, 1940. He and his wife, Georgia Lee, founded World Wide Dream Builders in 1978.

He was our mentor, friend, brother, and a man among men to be loved, admired, and emulated. He loved his Lord supremely, his family passionately, and the organization he and his wife founded devotedly. I will miss my precious friend the rest of my life. I know his heart was to see every IBO in WWDB grow, mature, and succeed in life.

And so this devotional is jointly dedicated to the IBO's in WWDB and this man Billie Kaye and I love deeply. Ron Puryear, a man after God's own heart.

PAUL and BILLIE KAYE TSIKA

I shake my head in disbelief
At the passing of my friend
And know by Gods assurance
It's the beginning not the end:

But even though I'm certain
He's where there is no lack
And all his hopes are realized
I still want my friend back:

I met a man many years ago
It seems like yesterday
A friendship started growing
That's in my heart to stay:

If you asked me what I think
Of this man named Ron Puryear
I'd tell you of a real mans man
Who lived with Godly fear:

He is a man of character
Of honest words & deeds
With a heart of generosity
That freed him from all greed:

His heart was not to control you
Though his leadership was strong
But to help you become your very best
By correcting what was wrong:

He sought only to empower
And believed theres but one way
By grace through faith in Christ alone
And the sacrifice HE had made:

So when I think of my dear friend
And all he meant to me
I know he loved his families
That started with Georgia Lee:

In the beginning was Jim & Brian
With Brian gone on before
To welcome Ron with open arms
When he entered Heavens door:

Jim would stay & and carry on
With the work his dad begun
And watch over all the family
Especially his precious Mom:

The other family he also loved
In which he served so well
Were those who made up World Wide
From the Diamonds to personnel:

Ron asked of me to help him
That he might hear "well done"
But the truth is he has helped me more
With the race I've watched him run:

Like all of you my heart cry's out
To try and understand
But know our God makes no mistakes
With His eternal plan:

Heaven will now be sweeter
Than for me it's ever been
To see my precious Jesus
And Ron my dearest friend:

I know that we all loved him
In our very own special way
And all have precious memories
That God knows are here to stay:

So lets continue on the work begun
By this man we won't forget
And know he's waiting for us all
In that land called No Regrets:

PAUL TSIKA
June 5, 2016

ACKNOWLEDGMENTS

Destiny Image Publishers: Once again the staff at Destiny Image has made our work a joy. Our team, Sierra White and John Martin, has been invaluable in completing this project. Visit them at: www.destinyimage.com.

Dr. J. Tod Zeiger: For several years now we have worked together with Dr. Zeiger (jtzeiger@aol.com). This has always proven to be a great blessing to our ministry.

Our children and grandchildren: Billie Kaye and I are thankful to our family for their commitment to this devotional. Desiring to encourage families to have a daily devotional time, we encouraged our family to each make a contribution with their own devotion, and many did. Family members who have shared their thoughts and beliefs include: Gretchen, our daughter; Paul, our son; Mark, our son-in-law; Melanie, our daughter-in-law; Kelley, our daughter-in-law; Meagan, our granddaughter; Marissa, our granddaughter; and Shelby our granddaughter.

We have been blessed with children, grandchildren, and one awesome great-grandson. What joy fifty-plus years of marriage has brought into our lives. Thank You, Lord!

ABOUT THE AUTHORS

Paul and Billie Kaye Tsika have been involved in ministry for more than forty-five years. Together they have authored several books including *Get Married—Stay Married* and *Parenting with Purpose*. Paul has been the pastor of a large international marketing business since 2001. Along with their staff they minister to tens of thousands of people each year and witness many coming to Christ for salvation.

Contact Information
Paul E. Tsika Ministries
5351 Hwy. 71
P.O. Box 136
Midfield, Texas 77458
361-588-7190
Website: www.plowon.org
mark@plowon.org

CONTENTS

OVERVIEW AND SUGGESTIONS FOR READING YOUR DAILY DEVOTION

You may be wondering why this daily devotional book has only 260 days instead of 365 days. After all there are seven days in a week. Our reason is simple. The majority of people we've talked to concerning daily devotionals have a tendency to become easily discouraged. Missing a day or two, a time or two has a tendency to cause them to give up with feelings of guilt and shame for not being disciplined enough.

So being the genius I (Paul) am, I've decided to look for progress instead of perfection—five days a week instead of seven. Hopefully you'll be encouraged by the idea of a two-day reprieve—not from the Lord or living right, but only from one aspect of your daily walk.

And so, we'd like to make a few suggestions for your journey. They are simple suggestions but will help you as you read your devotional five days a week.

We suggest you read:

1. Prayerfully. Before beginning your daily reading, ask the Holy Spirit to open your heart to what He is communicating to you today.

2. Thankfully. Have a grateful and thankful heart for the Word of God that is quick and powerful and sharper than any two-edged sword.

3. Personally. As you're reading, make certain you do "take things personally." God is speaking to "your" heart.

4. Practically. The Word of God is practical and applicable for your daily walk so that you may be empowered to live victoriously each day.

5. Thoughtfully. God has given you a mind for a reason, so you can think—so think about what you're reading. Fix your heart on the words of the devotion and don't let your mind wander.

6. Reflectively. Blank lines for journaling have been provided in the back of the book so that you may record your thoughts, ideas, and feelings as God speaks to you. Normally the first thoughts that

come to your mind should be recorded. This way you can reflect from year to year the changing seasons of your life and how God is speaking to you. We highly encourage you to take time daily to journal.

Suggested prayer before reading:

Heavenly Father, thank You for Your Word and the light it sheds on my daily path. I pray the Holy Spirit will open my understanding that I may live my life pleasing to You. I'm asking You to empower me today that Christ Jesus my Lord might be magnified with my words, deeds, and attitudes. Please make me a living witness of Your amazing grace, mercy, and forgiveness so that others will see Jesus in me today. I choose today to serve You and all those You put in my path with love, kindness, and patience. I ask all this in Jesus' wonderful name. Amen.

WISDOM AND WEALTH

MONDAY

CAN YOU DIG IT?

It is the glory of God to conceal a matter; to search out a matter is the glory of kings (Proverbs 25:2).

The revelation of truth has always been available to those who have experienced the new birth. You and I have all the tools necessary to "search out" the truth of God's Word. Paul told Timothy to *"Be diligent to present yourself approved to God, a worker who does not need to be ashamed, rightly dividing the word of truth"* (2 Timothy 2:15 NKJV). The King James Version says, *"Study to shew thyself approved unto God, a workman that needeth not to be ashamed, rightly dividing the word of truth."*

When our desire lines up with a willingness to search out the truth, God will reveal it to us. Whatever we are hungry for, God will see to it that we get it. That's a promise!

The words "glory" and "honor" are the same words in the Hebrew—the word *kabod*, which literally means "the splendor, benefit and reputation of God to conceal a thing, but it is the splendor, benefit, and reputation of kings to search out the matter."

The Hebrew word for "matter" is *dabar*. It means "a word inside of a word that is put there to be searched out." Who are the kings? It does not mean those who are reigning now, but those who are appointed to reign in the future (see Revelation 1:5-6).

My own interpretation reads:

> It is the splendor, benefit, and reputation of God to conceal (to hide, to provoke someone to search out) a word inside of a word to be hid until the proper time to be revealed. It is the splendor, benefit, and reputation of kings, those who have been appointed to reign in the future, to search out the word God has put inside the word that has previously been hid until the time appointed!

God's desire is for you and me to seek truth. When we seek, guess what will happen? That's right, we will find. When we knock it will be opened, and if we ask we shall receive. Showing up at church once a week, or scanning the Bible for a verse when we get in trouble will not give us Kingdom revelation.

Gold does not fall out of the tree and hit you in the head when you need a little extra money. You have to search for it with diligence, and a little sweat! Likewise, you will never receive golden nuggets of revelation from the Bible without the same effort.

Father, give me a heart to search out Your truth. I realize I cannot navigate through this world without the revelation of Your Word! Amen.

WISDOM—DON'T LEAVE HOME WITHOUT IT!

Listen, my son, to your father's instruction and do not forsake your mother's teaching (Proverbs 1:8).

The purpose of the book of Proverbs is to infuse and impart wisdom into its hearers. The theme of "wisdom" is mentioned at least 125 times. Acquiring and applying God's wisdom to the decisions and activities of everyday life is an absolute imperative. God's desires us to be wise, not wise guys. He wants us to have wise words, not make wisecracks!

I have heard it said that *"Wisdom is seeing life from God's point of view."* Proverbs 8:11 says it is better to have wisdom than rubies and nothing on earth compares with it. When a young king by the name of Solomon was asked by God the one thing he desired, Solomon asked for wisdom. God granted his request, and I believe the Father is pleased when we choose wisdom as well.

Wisdom is God's purpose for all of His children. Every right-minded father wants wisdom for his children. Solomon was no exception. Proverbs 1:8 declares, *"My son, hear the instruction of your father..."* (NKJV). I do not believe these words were meant only for Solomon's sons, but for God's sons and daughters as well.

Godly wisdom is a product of the indwelling Holy Spirit. The Holy Spirit is called the "Spirit of Wisdom." Godly wisdom is supernatural, common sense is natural. Wisdom is never a substitute for knowledge, and knowledge is never a substitute for wisdom. It takes hard work and study to gain knowledge to pass an exam in school, but it takes wisdom from above to pass the test of life. Knowledge comes by looking around, wisdom comes from looking up! To know wisdom is to know Jesus Christ. First Corinthians 1:24 says that Christ is the wisdom of God. Apart from a relationship with Jesus Christ there is no godly wisdom.

God does not withhold wisdom from those who want it. James 1:5 says, *"If any of you lacks wisdom, you should ask God, who gives generously to all without finding fault, and it will be given to you."* His wisdom is not set aside for one group or class of people. Wisdom is God's desire for all of us, including you!

Father, grant me wisdom for every decision I make. Help me to avoid the pitfalls of life by showing me Your wisdom. Amen!

GIVE A GOLDEN APPLE

Like apples of gold in settings of silver is a ruling rightly given (Proverbs 25:11).

I love the Living Bible's translation of Proverbs 25:11, it reads: *"Timely advice is as lovely as gold apples in a silver basket."* Tradition says that Solomon was referring to an ancient royal custom. The king would often host dignitaries from around the known world. During their stay he would invite them to share in a magnificent feast. The centerpiece of the banquet table was a silver basket filled with golden apples. Toward the end of the meal, the basket was passed around, and every guest was invited to select one of the beautiful, gleaming golden apples. I believe Solomon had this tradition in mind when he wrote that particular statement. He wanted the world to understand that beautiful words can be as lovely as golden apples!

From our childhood we have known the importance of words. We even learned a little rhyme to explain it: *"Sticks and stones may break my bones, but words will never hurt me."* That is a cute little saying but fundamentally false, because words can hurt you.

We live in a world of words. It was once reported that Adolf Hitler declared he would conquer more nations by the pen than by the sword. He proved his theory because he knew the importance of words. He did more damage with his negative words than any bombs that were ever dropped.

With so many negative words being spread into the atmosphere, it's time for us to fill up our silver baskets and hand out golden apples to those who are hurting among us. One of the most beautiful "golden apples" you could ever give is a word of encouragement. One of my favorite definitions of encouragement is "to inspire with courage, spirit, or hope."[1] As Christians we have a divine obligation to spread the virus of encouragement to everyone who crosses our path.

A single word can change a life. We never know what people are going through, and have no idea the impact a word of appreciation or encouragement can do. It is possible to make life richer, happier, and exciting for others when we take time to hand them a golden apple of encouragement.

Father, help me to be a conduit of encouragement to those I encounter who are hurting. Give me the right words to say, to the right person, at the right time. Amen!

I KNOW I SHOULDN'T TELL YOU THIS, BUT...

A gossip betrays a confidence; so avoid anyone who talks too much (Proverbs 20:19).

The Bible has much to say about the destructive power of words. Just as words of encouragement can build up, words of slander and gossip can destroy (James 3:5-9). Controlling our speech is a subject that is the central issue of Solomon's thinking. He wrote over 150 proverbs devoted to the subject of words. He believed that the kind of words we speak and listen to directly impact our success in life (see Proverbs 5:1-2; 10:14; 18:7; 21:23).

A gossip is a person who feels more comfortable when working secretly or undercover. You can easily identify gossips when they begin a conversation with *"I know I shouldn't tell you this, but..."* or *"Give me your word you won't quote me on this...."*

Solomon deals with the problem of gossip head-on. Every minute spent on gossip is a minute taken away from other productive activities (see Proverbs 18:8-9). Solomon issues a warning that when we give away the precious commodity of time, chattering away with someone about the juicy details of others, we are in the business of wasting time and destroying lives!

Not only is it wrong to spread gossip, but it is equally wrong to listen to gossip. There are many people who say they would never spread a rumor or gossip about their friends. At the same time they won't stop a gossip from sharing with them. Remember, the same gossip who is willing to violate another person's confidence will eventually violate yours. You would never allow your next-door neighbor to dump his garbage on your front lawn. So why would you allow the neighborhood gossip to dump garbage into your spirit?

Solomon is so adamant about the untrustworthiness of a gossip he says it twice: *"A gossip betrays a confidence, but a trustworthy person keeps a secret,"* and, *"A gossip betrays a confidence; so avoid anyone who talks too much"* (Proverbs 11:13; 20:19).

Remember, you never have to apologize for what you don't say!

Father, help me to guard my tongue and to be careful about what I say to others. Just because something may be true, give me the wisdom to know when to speak and when to keep silent. Amen!

SHARPEN YOUR BLADE

As iron sharpens iron, so one person sharpens another (Proverbs 27:17).

Have you ever tried to cut something with a dull knife? Common sense tells us it's easier to chop down a tree with a sharp blade rather than a dull blade. If it's busy work you're looking for, you might as well try to chop down a tree with a hammer. You will be busy for sure, but your frustration level will be off the charts! Let's agree, to get the job done a blade must be sharp.

To sharpen a blade you must be willing to rub it against something (like a whetstone) that creates friction and sparks. The result will be a sharpened blade. Solomon declares that our characters are honed and sharpened in the same way—through our friction and interaction with others, and allowing the Word of God to buff away any spiritual dullness. Remember, the Word of God is a *"double-edged sword"* (Hebrews 4:12), and it is with this that we are to sharpen one another—in times of meeting, fellowship, or any other interaction.

When conflict occurs, one of the first reactions is to run away and hide. Christian family counselor Gary Smalley teaches that *"Conflict is the gateway to the deepest levels of communication and intimacy in a marriage or relationship."*[2]

I find that those who run away to avoid any type of confrontation will never achieve a deep level of communication with others. Instead of viewing conflict as a dreaded enemy, view it as a necessary sharpening device for maximum achievement and success. The question is not whether conflict will come, but how we handle it when it does.

We should desire a "cutting edge" to have a more effective ministry for the Lord Jesus Christ. When the blade has been sharpened to its maximum usefulness it will shine. Left unattended a blade will become dull and useless. If a knife remains blunt, it is still a knife but less effective and useful. The more time we spend together encouraging, praying, and sharing God's Word, the sharper our blade becomes.

Father, I pray that You will open my eyes to see that You have many tools to sharpen my spirit. Help me to embrace them so that I can shine for You. Amen!

MONDAY

WORK HARD OR WORK SMART?

Do you see someone skilled [diligent] in their work? They will serve before kings; they will not serve before officials of low rank (Proverbs 22:29).

Solomon understood there is one skill everyone can learn no matter their age, background, education or IQ. Unfortunately, most people don't utilize it. When this skill is used it will ultimately produce incredible success. Moreover, when it is ignored, no matter how hard we work, the outcome will never be what it could have been.

The skill Solomon talks about is the skill of "diligence." In our modern society I have discovered diligence is a rare commodity. Most people would rather choose the path of least resistance, which oftentimes leads to shoddy work and unrealized expectations. Let's face it, we live in an instant gratification culture. We want it fast, we want it now, and the last thing we want to do is work for it.

There are those who equate working hard with working smart, and nothing could be further from the truth. The choice between the two is always up to us. The term "hard-working" is not really an accurate understanding of what it means to be persistent or diligent. For example, you can use a pair of scissors to cut your front lawn. No doubt you would be working hard, but wouldn't it be easier to buy a riding lawnmower that would get the job done in a fraction of the time?

The following is a definition of diligence that captures the meaning: "diligence is a learnable skill that combines creative persistence, a smart working effort rightly planned and rightly performed in a timely, efficient, and effective manner to attain a result that is pure and of the highest quality of excellence."[3]

Becoming truly diligent in any activity brings priceless rewards. *"The plans of the diligent lead to profit as surely as haste leads to poverty"* (Proverbs 21:5). While others are elbowing their way to the top, a diligent person will be sought out by people in positions of prominence and authority. I believe that is what Solomon is talking about when he says that people who are diligent in their work *"will serve before kings."* Applying diligence to any area of our lives, whether it be in our marriage, business, or in our relationships with other people, will bring success and profitable results!

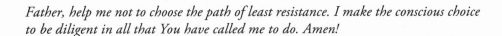

Father, help me not to choose the path of least resistance. I make the conscious choice to be diligent in all that You have called me to do. Amen!

DON'T RUN FROM REPROOF

Whoever disregards discipline comes to poverty and shame, but whoever heeds correction is honored (Proverbs 13:18).

———————⌒———————

Throughout the book of Proverbs, Solomon gives many insights on successful living. One area he puts at the top of the list is the importance of handling correction (reproof) in a positive way. He uses several words that are interchangeable—reproof and discipline. A reproof is a circumstance God brings into our lives to highlight unconfessed sin and motivate us to turn away and head in another direction. A reproof can come through difficult circumstances, words from adversaries, and even words of constructive criticism from our best friends. In a perfect world we have no issues, struggles, or difficulties to deal with. Unfortunately, we do not live in a perfect world, therefore we can expect situations in our lives that require course correction.

No matter the source, the choice is up to us how we respond to things that God sends our way to get our attention. We can choose to respond to the correction and make changes, or we can run the other way and continue our behavior. We can be smart and receive it, or we can be "stupid" (Solomon's description) and reject it. The choice is always up to us. *"Whoever loves discipline loves knowledge, but whoever hates correction is stupid"* (Proverbs 12:1).

I have often wondered why so many of us reject correction and discipline. It could be because of pride. There may be other factors involved, but pride and the fear of others are the twin killers that prevent us from a positive response to God's correction. *"Fear of man will prove to be a snare, but whoever trusts in the Lord is kept safe"* (Proverbs 29:25).

There are times when correction comes that we choose to run away and hide because it's human nature to reject anything negative. No one, at least as far as I know, enjoys correction. Let's face it, our first reaction is almost always negative. It is just the natural thing to do. It's not really our first reaction that counts but our final attitude that really matters.

Remember, we will make mistakes in life. No one is immune. God understands us, after all He is the One who created us. When we choose to respond in a positive way, God will even use our reproofs and corrections for His glory (see Psalm 103:10-12).

Father, help me to understand that when I face the reproofs of life they are for a divine purpose and not for punishment. I want to always respond in a positive way. Amen!

DREAMS ARE NOT ENOUGH

*Plans are established by seeking advice; so if you wage
war, obtain guidance* (Proverbs 20:18).

———————————◦◦◦———————————

Many years ago Billy Graham was the keynote speaker at a prestigious event honoring the delegates to the United Nations. He began his speech with the following story:

> Being here in New York reminds me of a story about Albert Einstein. Some years ago the great thinker was on a train bound for New York City. As the ticket taker came walking through the car, Einstein reached into his pocket to retrieve his ticket, but he could not find it. He frantically searched his coat pockets, turned his pants pockets inside out, but he still could not produce the ticket.
>
> The ticket taker said, "Don't worry, Mr. Einstein, we all know who you are. Forget about it." About 20 minutes later, the ticket taker came back through the car, and by this time Einstein was on the floor searching everywhere for the lost ticket.
>
> Again the ticket taker tried to reassure Einstein by saying, "I told you not to worry about the lost ticket. We trust that you purchased one, and that's good enough for us."
>
> Einstein looked up at the railroad employee and said, "Young man, this isn't a matter of trust but of direction. I need to find a ticket because I forgot where I was going."[4]

It would be fair to say that Einstein's dilemma fits the description once given by the "great philosopher" Yogi Berra who said, "If you don't know where you're going, you could end up somewhere else!" Dreams and desires are wonderful, but when it comes to getting you where you want to go in life, they are simply not enough. A dream without a plan of action is only wishful thinking. Achieving your dreams and arriving at your desired destinations in life do not happen by accident.

Solomon knew what he was talking about. He spoke from experience. His life was filled with many accomplishments not the least of which was building the temple. Solomon understood the importance of developing an action plan to accomplish any great dream. Proverbs are a collection of reminders about the importance of planning—see especially Proverbs 15:22; 16:1; 16:3; 20:18; 21:5. Put feet under your dreams and watch God do great things!

Father, thank You for my dreams, now help me develop a plan to get me there. Amen!

MAKE YOURSELF INVALUABLE

*Let love and faithfulness never leave you; bind them around your neck,
write them on the tablet of your heart. Then you will win favor and
a good name in the sight of God and man* (Proverbs 3:3-4).

Solomon describes two indispensable qualities that make us invaluable. Like a sparkling diamond, "love and faithfulness" should be such a part of our lives that they would be the first two attributes a person should notice about us. I believe the old saying is true, "You never get a second chance to make a first impression!" If we want to make a first impression that is lasting and positive, these qualities should be the first thing people notice about us. Without a doubt that is the "bind them around your neck" part of what Solomon is talking about.

He goes on to say, *"write them on the tablet of your heart."* In other words, make these qualities a central part of who we are and what we are about. As you read through the book of Proverbs you'll notice Solomon makes promises that are conditional: if you do this, then this is what God will do. The same is true with love and faithfulness. If we determine to make love and faithfulness the central issue of our lives, then we can rest assured great benefit will come to us that no amount of money can buy.

Solomon chose an interesting word for "favor." It translates as "cherished approval and preferential treatment." In other words you will be cherished, approved, and given preferential treatment by friends, peers, bosses, employees, and yes even your own family!

The good news is that these two qualities are not simply personality traits, but a choice anyone can make. Determine today to make love and faithfulness part of everyday life. Value them, develop them, and nurture them. They won't let you down.

Remember, we become invaluable not because of the amount of money we have in the bank or how many important people we have in our contact list. That's how the world system thinks. We become invaluable by demonstrating qualities that only a Christlike character can show!

Father, help me to develop these Christlike qualities in my life. Not for personal gain, but for Your glory. Amen!

YOU CAN TRUST HIM

Trust in the Lord with all your heart and lean not on your own understanding; in all your ways submit to him, and he will make your paths straight (Proverbs 3:5-6).

———◦———

Trust is a matter of the heart. The word literally means "To place confidence; to commit or place in one's care or keeping; to rely on the truthfulness or accuracy of."[5] Trust is the key in our relationship with God. Trust opens the door to God's will and growing in our potential in the kingdom.

The question is, "Can I really trust God in every circumstance I face?" The answer is a resounding, "Yes!" We can trust Him because His care is constant. He has given us a word we can stand on: *"Keep your lives free from the love of money and be content with what you have, because God has said, 'Never will I leave you; never will I forsake you.' So we say with confidence, 'The Lord is my helper; I will not be afraid. What can mere mortals do to me?'"* (Hebrews 13:5-6).

We can trust Him in the bad times. All of us are going to have bad times, bad days, and difficulties. The question is not if they come, but when. The psalmist declared, *"In God, whose word I praise—in God I trust and am not afraid. What can mere mortals do to me?"* (Psalm 56:4). We can absolutely trust Him in times of adversity because, *"The Lord is with me; I will not be afraid. What can mere mortals do to me?"* (Psalm 118:6).

Not only can we trust Him in the bad times, but also in the good times. We have a tendency to run to Him when things are going bad, and seem to forget Him when things are good. The extent to which we thank God for the blessings He provides is an indicator of our trust level. May it never be said of us that we trust more in God's instruments of provision rather than in God Himself.

In the words of the late, great preacher S. M. Lockridge, "He can satisfy all your needs, and he can do it simultaneously. He supplies strength for the week, and is available for the tempted and the tried. He sympathizes and sees, He guards and He guides. He healed the sick, and cleansed the leper. He defends the feeble, and blesses the young. He regards the aged, He rewards the diligent, and He beautifies the meek—I TELL YOU CHURCH, YOU CAN TRUST HIM!"

———◦———

Father, today I choose to trust You, no questions asked. Amen!

MONDAY

HE IS ALL I NEED

The Lord is my shepherd, I lack nothing (Psalm 23:1).

The story is told about a Sunday school teacher who challenged her first grade Sunday school class to memorize the 23rd Psalm. On a bright, sunny Sunday morning she stood before the class and said, "All right class, who can quote the first verse?" A little hand went up and young Johnny said, "I think I can." The teacher quickly replied, "Go ahead, Johnny, quote it for us." Proudly Johnny stood up and said, "The Lord is my shepherd and that is all I need!"

Young Johnny may not have quoted the verse just right, but I believe he captured the heart of the matter. Because the Lord is our Shepherd we do not lack anything, "He is all we need!" God's desire is to bring us to a place of becoming independently dependent upon Him alone.

Being in "want" is a warning signal that we are not totally dependent upon Him. We can mark it down that if anyone or anything else tries to take His place, we will never be satisfied. There are many things that clamor to be our sole provider, but at the end of it all, we are empty and restless. Whether another person, a successful business, or a hobby tries to shepherd our lives, it all ends in the same place—lives filled with disappointment and frustration.

When David used the analogy of sheep, I am reminded that is not a compliment. By and large sheep are dumb, defenseless, and directionless. It is often said that sheep literally don't know enough to go inside to get out of the rain. They may look cute in a painting, but at the end of the day sheep need a shepherd to exist.

Let's face it, we are like sheep, and we need the Shepherd to guide us, guard us, and give us all that is necessary to live godly and productive lives. Isaiah said, *"We all, like sheep, have gone astray, each of us has turned to our own way..."* (Isaiah 53:6). That pretty well sums it up. We may not appreciate the analogy and find it difficult to admit we cannot make it on our own. But, once we set aside our pride we know David is declaring an eternal truth, *"The Lord is my shepherd, and He is all I need!"*

Father, I realize like a sheep I am prone to wander on my own. Come and be my Shepherd today and lead me to the place where I can say, "The Lord is my shepherd, I shall not want."

NO FEAR

Even though I walk through the darkest valley, I will fear no evil, for you are with me; your rod and your staff, they comfort me (Psalm 23:4).

David paints a beautiful picture of the shepherd leading his sheep back to the fold. Imagine, if you will, the sheep come to a narrow gorge with shadows lying across the trail. The sheep are fearful of what lies ahead. The one thing that keeps them calm is an absolute trust the shepherd will protect them at all costs. He has protected them before, and he will again!

We have all faced times where shadows appeared as substance. Fear of the unknown can paralyze. Fear can cause us to wonder if the Lord has abandoned us in times of our greatest struggle. We need to be reminded of the Lord's promise, *"Never will I leave you; never will I forsake you."* Knowing that promise we can say with absolute trust, *"The Lord is my helper; I will not be afraid. What can mere mortals do to me?"* (Hebrews 13:5-6).

David goes on to say, *"Your rod and your staff, they comfort me."* The rod was never intended for the sheep. This heavy club was used to drive off predators. The staff was nothing more than a long pole with a little crook at the end used for helping and guiding the sheep. If the sheep wandered away, the staff would be used to hook around its leg and pull it back into the flock. The sheep had the utmost confidence that the shepherd would never use these instruments to harm or hurt them. They brought comfort and peace, not fear and intimidation.

You may feel the pressure is too great for the Lord to handle. It may seem you have just entered into your darkest valley of struggle. If so, let the words of the Great Shepherd go deep into your heart, *"I am the good shepherd. The good shepherd lays down his life for the sheep"* (John 10:11).

Jesus gives us the confidence to live free from fear no matter what comes our way!

Father, I praise You for leading me through the valley of fear. When I am tempted to abandon hope, remind me of Your never-ending love. Amen!

HOW GREAT IS OUR GOD

Lord, you have been our dwelling place throughout all generations.
Before the mountains were born or you brought forth the whole world,
from everlasting to everlasting you are God (Psalm 90:1-2).

In this "song" of Moses found in Psalm 90, he declared that God has been the dwelling place of people for all generations. A dwelling place is your home, it is where you live. The declaration is that God has been the home of humans since they have been on the earth. The apostle Paul expounded the same eternal truth when he addressed the Athenians on Mars Hill. He said, *"For in him we live and move and have our being. As some of your own poets have said, 'We are his offspring'"* (Acts 17:28). God exists as a home for people.

Three tremendous thoughts to consider:

1. Moses declared that God is great because He is the God of history. Kings live and die. Generations come and go. Despite the passing of time, there is no change in the relationship between God and the humans He created. He has been the home of people for all generations.

2. He is also great because He is the God of creation. Moses considered the creation story and declared before mountains were formed, God was. He even goes further back in time and declared before the earth was formed, God was. Moses gradually moved back in time from the formation of the mountains to the emergence of the land and finally the creation of the earth itself and declared—before all that you see, God was!

3. Finally, Moses declared God is great because He is the God of eternity. God is greater than the universe He produced, and before it came into being He was. He is above and beyond all of creation. He is from vanishing point in the past to the vanishing point in the future, thus from everlasting to everlasting God IS! The great I AM is not past, present, or future—He just IS! How great is our God!

If home is where the heart is, have our hearts found a place of rest in our true home? And where is that? In a personal relationship with God through the blood of the Lord Jesus Christ.

Father, I thank You for Your greatness. I marvel at the wonder of Your creation. Never let me take it for granted. Amen!

DON'T BE RULED BY HIDDEN FAULTS AND WILLFUL SIN

But who can discern their own errors? Forgive my hidden faults. Keep your servant also from willful sins; may they not rule over me. Then I will be blameless, innocent of great transgression (Psalm 19:12-13).

David's prayer was simple and to the point, "Don't let hidden faults and willful sins rule over me." I suspect this is a prayer we all need to pray. When we ask God to forgive hidden faults and willful sins, what do you think God will do? Do you think God will turn a blind eye, or simply say, "Forget about it?" I have discovered God does not operate that way. His method is usually to send a circumstance or a person to point out and highlight what we have done. God will cleanse us, but first He must open up the secret places.

"Forgive my hidden faults." What is a hidden fault? A hidden fault is something that may be hidden to us but not to others. The psalmist puts it this way, *"But who can discern their own errors?"* Those around us can see them plainly. Happy are the people who have someone in their lives not afraid to point out things that we are too blind to see.

"Keep your servant also from willful sins." What are willful sins? To do anything "willful" is an act of presumption and activity that stems from pride. What David is really saying, "Lord, help me to realize that without You I can do nothing." As one writer states: "Willful sins are those in which you are confident that you have what it takes to do what God wants. A prideful self-confidence is presumption, and God never asked us to do anything on that basis."[6]

David's desire was to be blameless and innocent of any and all transgression. He realized for that to happen, his hidden faults and willful sins must be dealt with. He opened up his heart and allowed the Spirit of God to expose whatever was inside and discern anything that might hinder his fellowship with God.

If we confess our sins, he is faithful and just and will forgive us our sins and purify us from all unrighteousness (1 John 1:9).

Father, give me a teachable spirit, and show me through Your Word how to be continually free from hidden faults and willful sins. Amen!

A SONG OF STEADFAST LOVE

Give thanks to the Lord, for he is good; his love endures forever (Psalm 107:1).

———✦———

The psalmist can't seem to get over the steadfast love of God. In Hebrew, the word means "an eager and ardent desire." It literally means God's love never gives up. We may give up on Him, but He will never give up on us!

The psalmist challenges us to stop and consider what the love of God means to us personally. He is not talking about an abstract concept, but a concrete reality. It is the recurring theme of this beautiful psalm. Even if we find ourselves in the middle of a tremendous setback or struggle, stop and consider the great steadfast love of God: *"Let the one who is wise heed these things and ponder the loving deeds of the Lord"* (Psalm 107:43).

One of the reasons so many give up on life from a feeling that no one cares. You may be feeling fearful and unaccepted by those around you. Before you "check out of life," stop and think about how God has accepted you, and how much He loves you. You have His word that He will meet you right where you are and take you just as you are. He is not moved by your failure or success; it makes no difference to Him at all. We have His assurance of unqualified acceptance, which is the meaning of a real love. We sometimes give love based on conditions. We have a tendency to say, "If you do this, I'll do that," or "If you love me, I will love you back." Worse yet, we may say, "If you hurt me, I'll hurt you back."

God loves us, and has already given us all He can give in Jesus Christ. So no matter what is swirling around us, we can rejoice in that fact! We can face a thousand tomorrows confident in the fact that we are "accepted in the beloved" through the blood of Jesus.

> *But because of his great love for us, God, who is rich in mercy, made us alive with Christ even when we were dead in transgressions—it is by grace you have been saved. And God raised us up with Christ and seated us with him in the heavenly realms in Christ Jesus* (Ephesians 2:4-6).

———✦———

Father, I give You thanks and praise today for Your steadfast and unqualified love. I know that Your love can give me the freedom to face every situation in my life. Amen!

MONDAY

WHAT'S YOUR VIEW?

Until I entered the sanctuary of God; then I
understood their final destiny (Psalm 73:17).

The psalmist had an envy problem. He seemed to be more concerned about the prosperity of the wicked (see Psalm 73:3) than he did about his own relationship with God. But as we read through Psalm 73, we discover he gained a new perspective on life, his enemies, and even himself. What changed? Did he all of a sudden decide that it didn't matter what happened to other people? Did he take matters into his own hands? No, not at all. His perspective and outlook changed when he *"entered the sanctuary of God"* (Psalm 73:17).

When he speaks of entering the sanctuary, he is talking about coming before the presence of God. It was in the temple that God made provision to meet with His people. When he spent time in the sanctuary before the presence of God, a new point of view emerged. He started seeing things from God's point of view—not his own.

We always have a choice when it comes to our viewpoint. The psalmist experienced a shift from thinking with the natural mind to thinking from Heaven's viewpoint. To view circumstances from the natural point of view is to become reactive and not proactive. Our vision is narrow, based on only what we see, and not on what God says about it. Spiritual thinking always focuses attention on God, allowing Him to be in control, and not our emotions. The natural mind will always say, "Me first," while the spiritual mind will always say, "God first."

How do we enter the sanctuary today? According to the New Testament, we ourselves are the sanctuary, *"And in him you too are being built together to become a dwelling in which God lives by his Spirit"* (Ephesians 2:22). God lives inside of each of us, therefore we have access to Him on a daily basis.

We no longer have to be limited to a single viewpoint when it comes to our circumstances, whether good or bad. He has given us His Holy Spirit, the written Word, and the counsel of other believers to ensure our vision is broadened. The good news is we no longer have to live *under the circumstances*—but above them! The choice is up to us. So, what's your view?

Father, help me to understand that Your viewpoint of my circumstances is more important than anything else in my life. I choose today to live above my circumstances, not to live beneath them. Amen!

THE PASSWORD INTO HIS PRESENCE

*Enter his gates with thanksgiving and his courts with praise;
give thanks to him and praise his name* (Psalm 100:4).

We live in a digital age. Almost everything we have is controlled by a term that has ingrained itself into our cultural psyche. The term I'm referring to is password. We protect our passwords with our very lives. Why? Because our passwords open the doors to everything in our lives—our phones, bank accounts, etc. Without passwords we have no access.

Psalm 100 is a beautiful hymn of praise. I am convinced this brief but beautiful psalm is more than something to be read around the Thanksgiving table. The psalmist gives us the "password" that opens the gates to the throne room of God. How is it possible to gain access to the One who created the heavens and the earth? He is surrounded not only by ministering angels but the beauty and splendor of the universe. Is there a password that gives us access?

The password that opens the gate is *thanksgiving* and our praise transports us into His courts! We are told in Psalm 22:3 that God inhabits the praises of His people.He is worthy of our praise and thanksgiving not because of what He has done for us, but simply because He is God.

By our praise we acknowledge that He is the One who has made us and we owe our love and gratitude to Him who has given us life, *"Know that the Lord is God. It is he who made us, and we are his; we are his people, the sheep of his pasture"* (Psalm 100:3). As His people we are called sheep, which means we are totally dependent on Him for protection, guidance, and provision. Our focus of praise, worship, and thanksgiving is directed toward Him because He is good, His love endures forever, and His faithfulness is unending to all generations.

Without the correct password you cannot access things that are important to daily living. Psalm 100 is a valuable reminder of how we approach God and come into His presence. Without the proper "spiritual password" we cannot access the most important thing for time and eternity.

Whatever you do, protect your password!

Father, thank You for this beautiful psalm. It reminds me of the importance of thanksgiving and praise. It also reminds me that I am God-made, not self-made. Amen!

LET GOD HANDLE IT

But you, Sovereign Lord, help me for your name's sake; out of the goodness of your love, deliver me (Psalm 109:21).

Most of us can relate to the experience David is talking about. He is under attack and falsely accused. Wicked men have determined evil upon David, and it did not matter how much it hurt. Their objective was simple—we must destroy him!

It is a painful thing to discover that someone has cast a shadow over your character and in the process tries to ruin your reputation. If you have ever been falsely accused, you know how David felt. David declared that their accusations and evil words were, *"without cause"* (Psalm 109:3). In other words, he could not see any reason for their actions.

David teaches us a tremendous lesson when evildoers attack. The first thing he did is commit the whole matter to God, *"But you, Sovereign Lord, help me for your name's sake."* Allowing God to handle the situation is also reflected in Paul's admonition in Romans 12:19, *"Do not take revenge, my dear friends, but leave room for God's wrath, for it is written: 'It is mine to avenge; I will repay,' says the Lord."* You see, trying to get even or taking matters into your own hands only makes things worse. The Lord is the only One who has the wisdom to adequately discern the situation. David had enough spiritual sense to recognize that and commit the situation to God.

The second thing David understood is the slanderous words were actually against God's name, *"Help me for your name's sake"* (Psalm 109:21). When the righteous are attacked for an unrighteous reason, God takes it personally. Make no mistake, God is involved in what happens to His people.

David is saying, "God You handle it. It is Your problem because Your name is involved!" Allowing God to handle the situation may be one of the most difficult things a Christian can do. Why? We want to defend ourselves at all cost and take revenge on those who hurt us. The lesson we must learn: Let God handle it—in His way, in His time, and the results will be righteous!

Father, forgive me for trying to handle difficult situations in my own wisdom. Help me to always commit the situation to You. Amen!

WHEN GOD LAUGHS

The One enthroned in heaven laughs; the Lord scoffs at them (Psalm 2:4).

On any given day you can turn on the news and see the world is in a mess. Psalm 2 begins with nations conspiring and the people plotting in vain. The kings are taking a stand, and the rulers have another summit. Sound familiar? The difference is in Psalm 2 we are told that these people are in open rebellion against the restrictions of God's "anointed."

Although not as obvious today, rebellion against God's law is the rotten core of the mess we find ourselves in. You don't have to be a theologian or a Rhodes scholar to figure out the world is on fire! All the "water" of the world's wisdom cannot put it out. Fallen humanity has taken every step to distance itself from God.

What is God's reaction when wicked nations plot to overthrow His anointed? Does God panic? Does He convene Congress and ask for their opinion? Does He call a summit of the world's leaders to ask how He has offended them? No! He sits in the heavens, calm and unthreatened. He doesn't even bother to get off His throne; He just laughs! Psalm 37:13 says, *"But the Lord laughs at the wicked, for he knows their day is coming"* and Psalm 59:8 declares, *"But you laugh at them, Lord; you scoff at all those nations."*

His laughter is not cruel or heartless. The same God who mocks humankind's rebellion and defiance is also compassionate toward us in our lost condition. He takes no pleasure in the death of the wicked (see Ezekiel 33:11). He is righteous in judgment, but also generous in compassion.

What does God's laughter mean for us? It is the assurance that Christ will ultimately triumph over evil. Defiance and rebellion against Him is useless. The message is clear—instead of opposing His Son, we should embrace and submit to Him. David gives practical wisdom at the close of this Psalm. It is not just for the leaders of the world, but for all humankind: *"Blessed are all who take refuge in him"* (Psalm 2:12).

Father, I choose not to focus on the darkness around me, but the light of Your love within me. Keep my feet from stumbling, and my heart from fear. Amen!

CAN YOU HEAR ME NOW?

For he is our God and we are the people of his pasture, the flock under his care. Today, if only you would hear his voice, "Do not harden your hearts as you did at Meribah, as you did that day at Massah in the wilderness (Psalm 95:7-8).

One of the most popular questions asked today is, "Does God still speak to His people?" This psalm tells us essentially what He wants—He wants us to listen to His voice. He wants us to hear Him, not just come together as in a worship service, and talk about Him! The answer to the question is "Yes!" He is speaking, but are we listening? The central issue of worship is to listen to the voice of God. *"Come, let us bow down in worship, let us kneel before the Lord our Maker"* (Psalm 95:6). God's desire is that whatever else we may do in service, when His Word is speaking, our hearts are open to listen. To "hearken" means to heed the Word, and then do something about it.

God issued a warning about the disregard of His Word: *"Do not harden your hearts."* Hardening the heart is a dangerous proposition. It is the exact opposite of hearing. The two things are mutually exclusive. He reminded them of the time the Israelites had come through the Red Sea and journeyed into the wilderness (see Psalm 95:9-11). The people began to complain because they had no water. The people accused Moses of leading them to their death. They demanded that God must prove Himself again. That is a picture of what it means to harden our hearts. In essence, God is saying, "Don't do what they did!"

God wants us to trust Him in every situation. It is impossible to trust someone you never listen to. In order to trust Him we must learn to listen to His voice, even when things are falling apart.

It is not enough to attend a public service once a week and expect to develop a keen sense of "hearing." Developing a keen sense of hearing is not a theoretical exercise, it is something we must put into practice. *"Whoever has ears, let them hear what the Spirit says to the churches"* (Revelation 2:29).

Father, help me avoid the mistakes of the past of those who hardened their hearts. Today, I will listen to the still, small voice and obey. Amen!

MONDAY

STAY HUNGRY

Not that I have already obtained all this, or have already arrived at my goal, but I press on to take hold of that for which Christ Jesus took hold of me (Philippians 3:12).

If you were to take a poll, I believe you would discover the majority of believers want to fulfill God's plan for their lives. Living by design, not by default is the goal. Everyone wants to be on the winning team!

Some have said Philippians chapter 3 is one of the most important portions of Paul's writings. In this brief chapter he looks at things on earth from God's point of view. As a result, he is not upset about the things of his past or the problems around him, but is concerned about the challenges before him. He is determined not to allow anything to rob him of his joy.

In these verses, Paul lists certain essentials for winning the race and unlocking a successful future. *"Not that I have already obtained all this"* is a statement made from the lips of a "hungry" man. He is hungry not haughty. Paul is careful not to compare himself with others in the race. If he had, he may have developed an attitude of self-attainment. Paul compared his life with God's standards, not the standards set by the religious crowd, or even other Christians.

Paul demonstrated a "sanctified dissatisfaction," which is the first essential to progress in the Christian life. He certainly was not dissatisfied with Christ. That is not what he was talking about. He was determined *"to know Christ—yes, to know the power of his resurrection and participation in his sufferings, becoming like him in his death"* (Philippians 3:10).

Paul was painfully honest about himself. He is *"pressing on"* in order to *"take hold of that for which Christ Jesus took hold of me."* On one hand Paul realized he had not reached his goal, and yet later on he said he was perfect (see Philippians 3:15 KJV). Isn't that a contradiction? No, the meaning of the word "perfect" is mature, not sinless. The mark of a mature Christian is the knowledge that he or she is not perfect! A holy hunger is required for progress. How hungry are we?

> *As the deer pants for streams of water, so my soul pants for you, my God. My soul thirsts for God, for the living God. When can I go and meet with God?* (Psalm 42:1-2).

Father, I realize You have a wonderful plan for my life. I will determine to stay hungry and keep pressing forward, not looking behind. Amen!

STAY FOCUSED

Brothers and sisters, I do not consider myself yet to have taken hold of it. But one thing I do: Forgetting what is behind and straining toward what is ahead (Philippians 3:13)

───────────◦∼◦───────────

Paul compared the Christian life to an athlete pressing toward the finish line. It is important to remember he is not telling us how to be saved. Rather, we have an awesome responsibility to live a life that is pleasing to God. No runner ever started a race with the idea of coming in last!

The "one thing" statement of the apostle Paul may be one of the most important things he said. It is not an uncommon phrase. Jesus said to the rich young ruler *"One thing you lack"* (Mark 10:21). To Martha, who was complaining about the workload, He explained, *"One thing is needed"* (Luke 10:42 NKJV). *"One thing I know!"* shouted the man who had received his sight by the power of Christ (John 9:25 NKJV). The psalmist testified, *"One thing I ask from the Lord, this only do I seek"* (Psalm 27:4).

It is safe to say too many of us generalize our time. To be a "Jack of all trades, and a master of none" is not a compliment, but a sad commentary. The secret of growth is a laser-beam focus on the goal. It is a fact that many Christians are involved in too many things, pushing the most important thing to the side. Too many irons in the fire is a sure way to get burnt. The enemy knows if he can break our focus from what is important he can stop our progress. If the devil cannot distract us with an evil ambition, he will try to distract us with a righteous one!

All successful athletes realize they cannot succeed at everything. They only win when they perfect the "one thing." Being double-minded and uncertain about your future is a sure path to failure. Staying focused and concentrating on the goal is the secret to success (see James 1:5-8).

Fixing our eyes on Jesus, the pioneer and perfecter of faith. For the joy set before him he endured the cross, scorning its shame, and sat down at the right hand of the throne of God (Hebrews 12:2).

───────────◦∼◦───────────

Father, when my concentration falters, help me to get back on track. I have decided today to keep the main thing the main thing. Amen!

STAY ON COURSE

*...Forgetting what is behind and straining toward
what is ahead* (Philippians 3:13).

Well-trained athletes would never expect to win the race by constantly look-ing over their shoulder. They know in order to win they must keep focused on the finish line. As believers we cannot run the race always looking to the past. We must focus our attention toward the future. We can learn from the past, while living in the present, and focusing on the future.

When it comes to past experiences there are two basic attitudes:

First, some learn from the past and are helped. When Paul said he was, *"forgetting what is behind,"* he was not suggesting a memory failure. God did not create us with an erase button behind our ears so we can eliminate hurtful memories. That's not what it means at all. It means to no longer be influenced or affected by our past. When God said He would not remember our sins and iniquities (see Hebrews 10:17), He was not saying He will have a memory lapse. That is impossible with God. What He is saying is that our sins will no longer affect our standing with Him.

Second, some people live in the past and are hindered. Sadly, there are many believers who never progress any further in their walk with God because all of their time is spent on painful memories. No doubt there were things in Paul's past that could have been too heavy for him to carry into his future (see 1 Timothy 1:12-17). Instead of allowing his past memories to hurt him, they became inspirations to push him forward! Paul could not change what had hap-pened to him in his past. But he determined to gain a new understanding of what they meant. He is a perfect example of a runner who refused to run the race backward!

Without the power of the Holy Spirit it is impossible to break the shackles of past regret and hurt. No amount of "mind power" can accomplish what only God's power can do. While we cannot change past events, like Paul, we can change how they affect us today.

Father, I know I am easily distracted by hurtful memories. I pray for the power of the Holy Spirit to break their influence. Amen!

STAY DETERMINED

I press on toward the goal to win the prize for which God has called me heavenward in Christ Jesus (Philippians 3:14).

All athletes know in order to win the prize they must have more than hunger, focus, and even dissatisfaction. It takes bulldog determination! The phrase, "I press" in Philippians 3:14 means "intense endeavor." You don't become a winning athlete, or a Heisman Trophy winner by reading books and listening to CDs on how to get it done. It takes more than being an armchair quarterback. It would be an exciting prospect to consider if believers put as much determination into "winning for Christ" as they did in their leisure activities.

The apostle Paul had a goal in mind: *"the goal to win the prize for which God has called me heavenward in Christ Jesus."* He is not suggesting we reach Heaven by our hard work. He is using a common illustration to say as athletes win the prize for their determined performance, so the faithful Christian will be crowned when Jesus Christ returns (see 1 Corinthians 9:24-27).

Determination is required but we must be careful of the extremes. On one hand, there is the "I must do it all by myself" attitude and on the other hand the attitude of "God must do everything for me." The first describes the "pushers," and the second the "passives." The passives are so super spiritual they never actually get in the race. They would rather sit in the grandstand and tell others how to run. The other extreme are those who are so self-sufficient they never take time to get in the Word or ask the Holy Spirit for power. There must be a balance between the two.

God must work in us so He can work through us. Jesus made it clear, *"without Me you can do nothing"* (John 15:5 NKJV). Paul echoed the same truth when he said, *"I can do all this through him who gives me strength"* (Philippians 4:13). The same determination Paul used in persecuting the church (see Philippians 3:6) he now used in serving Christ.

The key is to reach the goal He has set before us. While it is true in the natural only one athlete may receive a prize—all Christians may receive the reward. It does not matter what others think about our success. We cannot be rewarded unless we have an intense determination to *"press on toward the goal to win the prize!"*

Father, keep me in balance. I know without You I can do nothing. You are my Source and my strength. Amen!

STAY DISCIPLINED

All of us, then, who are mature should take such a view of things. And if on some point you think differently, that too God will make clear to you. Only let us live up to what we have already attained (Philippians 3:15-16).

No doubt when Paul referred to the athletic contest, he was referring to the Greek games. They were very common in his day, and by using the analogy, he was pointing to something everyone understood. It was also common knowledge in the Greek games that the judges were very strict about any infringement of the rules. Any athlete who broke the rules was disqualified immediately. He did not lose his citizenship, but he did lose the privilege of competing for the prize.

The emphasis of verses 15 and 16 in Philippians 3 speaks of the importance of remembering the "spiritual rules" laid out in the Word. In order to win the prize, athletes knew they must obey and practice self-discipline and training. This is exactly what Paul was referring to in First Corinthians 9:25: *"Everyone who competes in the games goes into strict training. They do it to get a crown that will not last, but we do it to get a crown that will last forever."* In Paul's culture, breaking training rules would result in disqualification.

Athletes may practice self-control in their training method, and yet still be disqualified if they broke the rules. *"Similarly, anyone who competes as an athlete does not receive the victor's crown except by competing according to the rules"* (2 Timothy 2:5). The question was never what the athlete said or what the spectators thought. All that mattered was what the judges said!

One day each and every believer will stand before Christ at His *"judgment seat"* (see Romans 14:10-12). The judgment seat is not to determine our salvation, but our service to Christ. The same Greek word for "judgment seat" is the same word used to describe the place where the Olympic judges awarded the prizes. We can have full assurance if we have disciplined our lives and obeyed the rules, we shall receive the reward. It is an exciting prospect to consider the future. So therefore we run the race daily with excitement and anticipation: *"And let us run with perseverance the race marked out for us, fixing our eyes on Jesus, the pioneer and perfecter of faith"* (Hebrews 12:1-2).

Father, I discipline my life so that when I stand before You I can hear You say, "Well done good and faithful servant!" Amen.

MONDAY

"STOP…THIEF!"

The thief comes only to steal and kill and destroy; I have come that they may have life, and have it to the full (John 10:10).

———————◆◇◆———————

Who is the thief Jesus is referring to in this verse? No doubt, he is the devil, the archenemy of God and God's people. But this enemy does not always act alone. He has assistance from people and circumstances. There are no shortages when it comes to multiple thieves that would like to keep you and me from enjoying the abundant life promised by Christ. Whether it be hurtful memories from past failures, fear and worry for the future, or the attitude that no one cares. It is heartbreaking to think about going through life and not really living!

The truth of the matter is, we are either allowing our lives to waste away, spending our lives on useless pursuits, or investing our lives into something greater than ourselves. It is really up to us whether we choose to live life abundantly or not. God loves us so much that He gives us the choice.

Jesus promised abundant life for those who want it. Abundant living is not pie-in-the-sky, by-and-by living. It is not some fanciful dream only reserved for the few. Abundant living is meant for every one of us who know Christ in a personal relationship. To live life "to the full" is to answer the central questions, "Who am I, and why am I here on this planet?" Taking the direction of our lives for granted is one of the most dangerous attitudes we can take. As the old saying goes and as mentioned previously, "If you don't know where you're going, you might end up someplace else."

The solution to an identity crisis is not reading the latest book on how to feel better about yourself. Nor is it attending the latest seminar or conference on how to get the most out of life. There's nothing wrong with reading a book or attending a seminar, but the answers lie in a personal, one-on-one relationship with the One who saved you—His name is Jesus!

Jesus tells us who we are and why we are here. He is the vine; we are the branches (see John 15:1-16). Understanding this truth puts us on the path to abundant living.

Father, I pray that You will open my eyes and help me understand the real secret to abundant living. It is not in the abundance of things or others, but in You. Amen!

JUST ABIDE

Remain in me, as I also remain in you. No branch can bear fruit by itself; it must remain in the vine. Neither can you bear fruit unless you remain in me
(John 15:4).

———————————

The Christian life is about bearing fruit, nothing more and nothing less. Jesus made it clear He is the vine and we are the branches: *"I am the vine; you are the branches. If you remain in me and I in you, you will bear much fruit; apart from me you can do nothing"* (John 15:5). At least twelve times in John 15 Jesus uses the word "remain" or "abide." Why? Abiding is the secret to fruit-bearing and abundant living.

What does it mean to abide? The best definition I have come across says this: *"It means to keep in fellowship with Christ so that His life can work in and through us to produce fruit. This certainly involves the Word of God and the confession of sin so that nothing hinders our communion with him."*[7] If that definition is true (and I believe it is) how can we know we are genuinely abiding in Him? Does it come from a special feeling, or a sense of superiority? No, it's not about feeling, it's about fruit.

When we maintain a close, intimate fellowship with Him, the result will be fruit in and through our lives. Many have tried to manufacture fruit in their own strength, but only the Holy Spirit can produce fruit that is lasting and meaningful. A machine can be built to produce results. Even today, people are building robots to replace the work of humans. But one thing a machine or robot can never do is produce fruit. In order to produce fruit, it will take a living organism!

There are two things important to remember: First, as a branch we do not produce fruit for self-enjoyment. Fruit is produced for others to enjoy. Second, when our abiding in Christ produces true spiritual fruit, God gets the glory. Others around us will see the Source of the fruit. They will know it is God at work doing something we could never do for ourselves.

Abiding in Christ can never be passive. To cultivate a deeper relationship (abiding) demands worship, prayer, spending time in the Word, and service.

———————————

Father, help me to always abide in You. I want my life to bear life-giving fruit for others to enjoy. Amen!

I KNOW A SECRET

He cuts off every branch in me that bears no fruit, while every branch that does bear fruit he prunes so that it will be even more fruitful (John 15:2).

If you want to grab someone's attention, just ask them if they want to know a secret. Not many of us can turn away from the juicy details of the latest rumor. In this verse Jesus gives us the "secret" to bearing fruit, much fruit, and more fruit (see John 15:2-5).

So what is the secret? *"While every branch that does bear fruit he prunes so that it will be even more fruitful."* It is the vinedresser who is in charge of pruning the branches so that more fruit is produced. It is interesting that many Christians ask God for a fruitful life, but as soon as He begins the pruning process they run the other way! Let's face it, no one in their right mind looks forward to the pruning process. Why? It is painful, but absolutely necessary!

The pruning process is the Father cutting away things in our lives that hinder us from becoming more fruitful. You can be sure He will cut away anything that keeps the life of the vine from producing the maximum amount of fruit. It may not be just the "bad things" that are pruned. It can also mean cutting away the good and the better so that we might enjoy the best. It is time for Christians to discover that God will always give us His best when we leave the choice up to Him!

In the natural, someone who is employed to prune must know exactly what they are doing or an entire crop could be destroyed. They must know not only where to cut, but how much to cut, and even at what angle to make the cut.

Our Father has many pruning tools at His disposal. He may use the Word to convict us and cleanse us (see John 15:3). He will also use the inner guide of the Holy Spirit to sound the alarm when we get off track (see Colossians 3:15; Psalm 32:8-9). Whatever tools He employs, it is for our good and His glory!

Our heavenly Father loves us so much He does all that He can to help us produce an abundance of fruit. He does not want us to miss the opportunity for glorifying Him in fruit-bearing. To be fruitless is a disgrace and shame to the One who keeps watch over His vineyard!

Father, I know that You love me too much to leave me the way I am. Keep me close, and never let me run from the pruning process. Amen!

LOVE AND OBEDIENCE GO HAND IN HAND

If you love me, keep my commands (John 14:15).

Many Christians obey God as slaves would obey their masters. They live in fear because they are afraid if they don't obey, God will take revenge and hurt them. They view God as a policeman standing on the corner waiting for them to break the law. Fear is a terrible motive for obedience. Jesus said to His disciples, *"I no longer call you servants, because a servant does not know his master's business. Instead, I have called you friends, for everything that I learned from my Father I have made known to you"* (John 15:15). Jesus made it clear His relationship to them was much deeper than an ordinary slave. Fear is a terrible master. It will make us think we obey Him because we have to. Real love obeys because it wants to!

The highest motive for obedience is love. Real love always focuses its attention on the giver not just the gift. We obey God not for what He can do for us. Loving God in order to get something in return is the height of selfishness. The highest goal is to develop and desire a personal relationship with Him no matter what He gives. *"Whoever has my commands and keeps them is the one who loves me. The one who loves me will be loved by my Father, and I too will love them and show myself to them"* (John 14:21).

Real love does not keep score nor does it measure sacrifice. *"Greater love has no one than this: to lay down one's life for one's friends"* (John 15:13). Our obedience is not measured, nor does it weigh the cost involved. I am so thankful that Jesus did not measure His sacrifice when He faced the cross. He gave everything He had to give. He did not stop to count the cost of obedience to His heavenly Father.

Real Christian love is not based on emotion or a certain feeling—it is an act of the will. We prove our love not by our emotional response, but in our actions. Love and obedience go hand in hand. God gives us His commandments because He loves us, and because we love Him in return, we obey Him. We never have to fear obeying God's will because First John 4:18 declares, *"There is no fear in love. But perfect love drives out fear, because fear has to do with punishment. The one who fears is not made perfect in love."*

Father, I know my obedience comes from my heart. More than ever I desire a closer relationship with You so that I may hear Your still, small voice. Amen!

TO KNOW HIM IS TO LOVE HIM

Now this is eternal life: that they know you, the only true God, and Jesus Christ, whom you have sent (John 17:3).

It is a proven fact—the more you know about Jesus Christ, the more you will love Him! Sadly for many believers, their knowledge of Christ only extends to their salvation experience. We need to realize that salvation was just the beginning. We have the joy to *"grow in the grace and knowledge of our Lord and Savior Jesus Christ"* (2 Peter 3:18).

Since salvation is not a static experience but a living relationship, it is impossible to grow as a believer apart from intimate fellowship with Jesus. Many Christians substitute other things that are not bad, just not the best. Going to church, attending conferences, and listening to tapes can be good. But these things can never substitute a one-on-one personal relationship with Jesus. In order to grow in maturity and deepen our love, we must spend time with Him. The apostle Paul expressed the truth when he wrote, *"I want to know Christ—yes, to know the power of his resurrection and participation in his sufferings, becoming like him in his death"* (Philippians 3:10).

It is often said when a husband and wife have been married for many years they begin to sound alike, think alike, and even take on each other's personalities. As you and I grow closer to the Savior, the more we become like Him. His thoughts become our thoughts, and His ways become our ways. Becoming more like Jesus is the ultimate goal. As we know Him better we grow more. And, the end result is we love Him more!

Jesus made it clear, His desire for us was to know Him better. That's why He did not call us *"slaves"* but *"friends."* You give orders and commands to slaves, and you do not share your heart or your innermost thoughts with them. The word *"friends"* literally means *"an intimate at court."* You and I have royal blood flowing through our veins—we are friends of the King!

He is our friend; therefore we can talk with Him. We share with Him our innermost feelings and thoughts and listen to His voice. Then, as we read His Word, we pray and ask the Holy Spirit to guide us. As the Holy Spirit illuminates the truth, we get to know Christ better! If you want to love Him more—get to know Him, you won't be disappointed!

Father, I don't want to know what others say about You. I want to know You in a deeper relationship. I treasure my time with You. Amen!

DELAYS ARE NOT DENIALS

But the angel said to him: "Do not be afraid, Zechariah;
your prayer has been heard. Your wife Elizabeth will bear
you a son, and you are to call him John (Luke 1:13).

Have you ever asked yourself, *"Why doesn't prayer seem to really work some-times?"* How is it possible to sincerely ask God to help meet your need and still your prayers seem to go unanswered? Maybe you have prayed about something for years and still not received an answer. Is it possible you are approaching God with the wrong attitude? If so, you are not alone. Zechariah gave a typical response to the messenger of the Lord when it was announced that his prayer was finally going to be answered. He did not jump for joy, instead he voiced doubt and unbelief.

Why did Zechariah doubt what he was hearing? He doubted because they were "well along" in years, and had given up on ever having a son. *"Zechariah asked the angel, 'How can I be sure of this? I am an old man and my wife is well along in years'"* (Luke 1:18). They knew it would take a miracle for them to have a child! The birth of John the Baptist was about "timing" not "time." God did not need John the Baptist on the scene when they first prayed their prayer. He needed him now, and age was not a factor.

Zechariah and Elizabeth needed to learn the same lesson we need to learn. It is not always in our best interests for God to give us what we want right when we want it! Sometimes He delays answering our prayers for our own good. Just because I want answers right away does not mean it's the best thing for me. You would never dream of giving the keys to your new car to your five-year-old. Why? Besides the fact the child couldn't reach the pedals, a five-year-old is not mature enough to handle the responsibility. Keys are only given to the mature. The same with God. He often delays answering our prayers because we are not mature enough to get what we're asking for.

A sure sign of maturity is the willingness to wait for something you want or need. Not being willing to wait is a sure sign of immaturity. There are times when God waits for the situation to become impossible before He answers. God wanted to do something greater than they had asked for.

A great attitude is a willingness to let God answer in His own time. Don't look at the calendar for your answer—look toward Heaven!

Father, help my attitude when it comes to my prayer life. I know if I allow You to answer my prayers in Your own time, You will give me Your best. Amen!

DON'T GIVE UP

*Then an angel of the Lord appeared to him, standing at
the right side of the altar of incense* (Luke 1:11).

No doubt you, like me, have considered giving up on prayer at some point
in your life. It is easy to get discouraged and quit because we wonder if our
prayers really make any difference. When we stop praying and give up on God
we become useless to Him to do more than we asked for. God found in Zechariah and Elizabeth a couple who would not give up on Him when it seemed that
their prayers were never going to be answered.

When the angel of the Lord appeared to Zachariah he was not at home
brooding. Quite the contrary. Zechariah was in the temple faithfully serving
the Lord. *"Once when Zechariah's division was on duty and he was serving as priest
before God"* (Luke 1:8). He chose to remain faithful in spite of his situation. Here
was a righteous couple faithfully serving God in spite of the disappointment of
not having a child.

Is there ever a time when we should give up, and stop praying about a certain
situation? I suggest we should keep praying until one of three things happens:

First, keep praying until you get the answer. It is the attitude of the persistent
widow in Luke 18 who would not stop asking for justice from an *"unjust judge."*
She knew the judge had the authority and the power to answer her prayer. She
would not give up! (See Luke 11:9-13.)

*Second, keep praying until you get the assurance that you are going to get an
answer.* God will find a way to bring encouragement to your heart. It is the
encouragement that keeps us from giving up. The angel said to Zachariah, "God
has heard your prayer" (see Luke 1:13). The message was clear—His answer is on
the way!

Third, keep praying until God says "No." There are times when God will reveal
to you it is not His will to answer a particular prayer. Even when we receive a
"no" God will give us His peace. When the peace comes we know it's time to
stop praying about the situation (see Colossians 3:15).

*Father, I believe You want what's best for me. I will keep praying until You tell me
to stop. Amen!*

GOD WILL GIVE MORE THAN WE EXPECT!

But the angel said to him: "Do not be afraid, Zechariah; your prayer has been heard. Your wife Elizabeth will bear you a son, and you are to call him John. He will be a joy and delight to you, and many will rejoice because of his birth, for he will be great in the sight of the Lord... (Luke 1:13-15).

A story is told about a clerk in a large candy store who always had people waiting in line, even when the other clerks were standing around with nothing to do. One day the manager finally asked her why she was so popular with customers. "It's easy," she responded. "The other clerks always scoop more than a pound of candy and then start taking away. I always scoop less than a pound and then add to it."

A simple story with an eternal truth. God's ways are not our ways, and His ways are bigger and better! God always scoops more than we expect when He answers our prayers in His time, and in His way, with His own power!

You cannot fault Zechariah and Elizabeth for wanting what everyone else had. They wanted children, so when they realized things were not going their way, they prayed for a miracle. God did not give them what they wanted, the way they wanted it. God wanted to give them someone special—a unique son for a supernatural purpose. God was about to "scoop out" a bigger answer than they ever dreamed. John the Baptist was no ordinary son. He was a prophet whose cousin would be Jesus Christ Himself. John's role was pointing everyone to the *"Lamb of God, who takes away the sin of the world"* (John 1:29).

We should never be content to settle for less than what God wants to give us. We are encouraged in the Word to ask God for His best. Ephesians 3:20 declares, *"Now to him who is able to do immeasurably more than all we ask or imagine, according to his power that is at work within us."*

Don't settle for average when God wants to give you extraordinary. Don't settle for a handful of blessings when God wants to "scoop out" a bountiful supply. Remember, God will always give us His best when we leave the choice up to Him!

Father, I no longer want to settle for less than what You have for me. Today, I have determined to make Ephesians: 3:20 my very own. Amen!

LESSONS FROM THE STORM

That day when evening came, he said to his disciples, "Let us go over to the other side." Leaving the crowd behind, they took him along, just as he was, in the boat. There were also other boats with him. A furious squall came up, and the waves broke over the boat, so that it was nearly swamped (Mark 4:35-37).

———————————————

Not many of us enjoy getting caught in the middle of a storm. The disciples of Jesus were no exception. They had weathered many storms, but this one terrified them. These professional fishermen were caught in a circumstance they were not prepared for.

It is obvious the disciples had trouble behaving correctly in the storm. Keep in mind, the journey to the other side was at the Lord's command. They responded with instant obedience. No doubt this made the storm harder to understand and the Lord's attitude quite confusing.

Sometimes the storms of obedience are greater than normal storms. Why? We have been told for years that the safest place to be is in the center of God's will. I suppose it depends on your definition of "safe." If you were to ask the apostle Paul, he might refer you to his life experience after becoming a Christian (see 2 Corinthians 11:22-23). Obedience is the correct response to the Lord's command, but it does not mean we will not face trials, difficulties, and pressure. Turn the pages of your Bible and you will discover every great man or woman of God faced some of their greatest challenges when they were walking in obedience, not disobedience!

The storms we face may not be physical, but the fact remains, we are not immune from them because we are Christians. I have discovered we are usually in one of three places when it comes to storms. We are either in one now, we just came out of one, or we are about to enter another one!

How should we respond when a sudden storm threatens to overwhelm us? The disciples provide a beautiful object lesson. They turned to Jesus realizing they were at the end of their resources. They abandoned their pride and threw themselves upon Him as their only hope. They also learned that no storm can wreck the plan and purpose of God. They learned that it is safer to be with Jesus in the middle of a storm than without Him safe on the shore! *When the next storm hits, we need to make sure Jesus is in the boat!*

Father, I know I am not excluded from the storms of life. When faced with a storm help me to honor You and give You all the glory. Amen!

YOU ARE IN THE WILL!

Praise be to the God and Father of our Lord Jesus Christ! In his great mercy he has given us new birth into a living hope through the resurrection of Jesus Christ from the dead, and into an inheritance that can never perish, spoil or fade. This inheritance is kept in heaven for you (1 Peter 1:3-4).

I heard about a family that gathered because of one of their rich uncles passed away. The uncle was filthy rich, having made a fortune in the oil fields of Oklahoma. With great anticipation they gathered for the reading of the will. It read something like this: "To George, my cousin, I leave my oil stocks; to Nancy my longtime friend, I leave my bank accounts; to my brother Tom, I leave my condo in Florida. Finally, to Willy, my cousin who always wanted to be remembered in my will, 'Hi, Willy!'" I doubt you and I would ever have an experience like poor Willy.

When it comes to our inheritance in Christ we won't have to worry about such a ridiculous ending. Inheritance is something you leave to someone else. It is something you have that you desire to pass on to future generations. Simon Peter tells us Jesus has been resurrected from the dead and He is leaving us an inheritance. In other words, Peter is saying, "Congratulations, you and I are in the will!"

This is the *"living hope"* to which Peter is referring. For hope to be alive it must have a foundation to stand on. Hope without a foundation is just wishful thinking. For example, I could tell you that I hope to play quarterback for the San Francisco 49ers next year. Friend, that's not hope—that's a fantasy!

The foundation we stand on is incorruptible...*it is death-proof.* It is undefiled...*it is sin-proof.* It will never fade away because...*it is time-proof.* It is kept by the power of God...*it is thief-proof.* You and I can live confidently with hope for the future because there is a future in our hope. It is not based on wishful thinking or fantasy, it is based on the *"resurrection of Jesus Christ from the dead."* To know Him in a personal relationship is to know our future is secure.

> *Through him you believe in God, who raised him from the dead and glorified him, and so your faith and hope are in God* (1 Peter 1:21).

Father, I thank You for my inheritance. I don't have to worry about my future because it is secure in Jesus Christ. Amen!

SECTION II

FEAR AND
FORTITUDE

MONDAY

DON'T SIT IN THE DARK

Do not gloat over me, my enemy! Though I have fallen, I will rise. Though I sit in darkness, the Lord will be my light. Because I have sinned against him, I will bear the Lord's wrath, until he pleads my case and upholds my cause. He will bring me out into the light; I will see his righteousness (Micah 7:8-9).

Total darkness can be very scary. Every sound is magnified. Even when we were young the most comforting thing we could have was a nightlight to scare away the darkness. I do not believe the prophet was referring to "natural" darkness. He was referring to a spiritual darkness that can be just as frightening.

There are times we end up in spiritual darkness and don't know why. We can be driving along life's highway and all of a sudden the gloom of darkness overwhelms us. It may be an unexpected bill, difficult people, or just the circumstances of life in general crashing together.

There are other times we end up in darkness because of our own doing: *"Though I have fallen, I will rise."* There is no one else to blame, as the prophet said, *"Because I have sinned against him* [God]."

Whether it be by the unexpected circumstances of life or by shooting ourselves in the foot, we must understand we have an enemy whose one desire is to keep us in the dark. *"Do not gloat over me, my enemy!"* The enemy is gleeful when he knows his strategy is working. As long as he can keep us in the dark we are no threat to his kingdom. His main desire is to cut us off from our future, create weakness in our present, and impede our progress. Why does he want to keep us in the dark? He knows the Father has an intentional future with a powerful purpose for each one of us (see Jeremiah 29:11; Psalm 139:11-18).

No doubt there are times when we will fail to live up to our own expectations. It's not a sin to fall or to fail. The sin is not getting back up. Remember, just because we fail does not make us a failure! The apostle Paul in his prayer for the Ephesians said, *"I pray also that the eyes of your heart may be enlightened"*

(Ephesians 1:18). The desire of the Holy Spirit is that we walk in light, and not sit in the dark.

It is time for believers to recognize the Source of our success: *"Though I sit in darkness the Lord will be my light."* Jesus Christ is our light and only hope for victory (see John 1:4-13).

Father, show me the way when I slip in the darkness. Light my path by the power of Your Word. Amen!

VICTOR OR VICTOR

*Consider it pure joy, my brothers and sisters, whenever you face
trials of many kinds, because you know that the testing of your faith
produces perseverance. Let perseverance finish its work so that you may
be mature and complete, not lacking anything* (James 1:2-4).

The issue of trials and pressure has been debated for centuries. On one hand there are those who say if you are a Christian you will never face the pressures of everyday life. The popular teaching states if you are right with God you will be prosperous, happy, and will never face trials. They say if someone is facing trials or experiencing sickness, it is due to the work of satan, or because of some sin in his life. The book of Job refutes that teaching.

The truth of God's Word is clear, there will be trials and testing for the believer: *"You know that the testing of your faith produces perseverance"* (James 1:3). It is not a matter of whether or not they are going to come. The real issue is how we are going to respond to them. Some get "bitter" while others get "better." Peter speaks of the trials of your faith (see 1 Peter 1:7). He tells us to arm ourselves to face suffering with the same mind that Jesus had (see 1 Peter 4:1-13).

You will notice James does not say that our love will be tested. Nor does he say our loyalty will be tested. It is our faith, not our church attendance that is put in the fire of testing. The testing of our faith is not for punishment, rather it is intended to mature us. We may not know the root of our trials, but we can see the fruit in them. Our trials are working for us, not against us. The word *"work"* refers to "work done" to finish an article. Trials are used of God to finish us and to make us complete.

The testing of our faith should leave us wanting for nothing. But if we lack wisdom we are encouraged to ask God for it in prayer (James 1:5). If there is ever a time we need God's wisdom, it is when we are faced with trials!

An encouraging thought: *God will always test us to bring out the best, while satan will tempt us to bring out the worst!* God's goal for every believer is to live above adversity not beneath. To live a life of a victor not a victim.

*Father, I know trials are going to come. Give me Your wisdom and Your perspective.
I choose today to be a victor not a victim. Amen!*

STOP JUDGING EACH OTHER

Brothers and sisters, do not slander one another. Anyone who speaks against a brother or sister or judges them speaks against the law and judges it. When you judge the law, you are not keeping it, but sitting in judgment on it. There is only one Lawgiver and Judge, the one who is able to save and destroy. But you—who are you to judge your neighbor? (James 4:11-12)

Have you ever noticed how most people are ready to give and receive something evil, rather than something good about a person? Rarely do we hear stories of good people and good actions making headlines. Not many news specials are made about things that are happening in our world that are good. The fact is, people have an insatiable appetite for the bad.

Please do not misunderstand the clear teaching of the Bible when it comes to judging. The Bible does not teach that discipline is not to be carried out regarding evil. James gives instruction that has to do with motive and truth. We are to allow the Word of God to bring judgment, and not take judgment into our own hands.

To speak evil of another person violates the *principle of love.* He is talking about public gossip that defames the character of someone. It is especially harmful when it is spoken against a fellow believer. How can we convince those who are not Christians that we love them unless we demonstrate love to one another? Jesus said, *"By this everyone will know that you are my disciples, if you love one another"* (John 13:35). Paul, under the inspiration of the Holy Spirit, enlarges upon the commands of Jesus to love one another by saying, *"Therefore, as we have opportunity, let us do good to all people, especially to those who belong to the family of believers"* (Galatians 6:10).

To gossip, backbite, and speak evil of others is to tread into an area where we should never go. To pass evil judgment on someone is to step into the place of God and become judge, jury, and executioner. There is only One who is qualified—and it's not you or me! The Lord alone is the Judge, Lawgiver, and King (see Isaiah 33:22). He has the power to save, and He will do the judging.

Father, set a watch over my words. May they be pure and peaceable, not mean and hateful. May they bring joy and not sorrow. Amen!

TWO EARS, ONE TONGUE— DO THE MATH

My dear brothers and sisters, take note of this: Everyone should be quick to listen, slow to speak and slow to become angry, because human anger does not produce the righteousness that God desires (James 1:19-20).

Just as a mother is quick to hear the cry of her baby, or the servant is quick to hear the master's voice, so we must be quick to hear what God is saying. It seems to me based on God's design of the human body and instruction of the Word of God (see 1 Samuel 3:10), that we are to listen twice as much as we speak. It is no accident we were created with two ears and one tongue!

The meaning of the word "swift" or "quick" in James 1:19 defines runners who run as fast as they can to reach the finish line before the competitors. It is a picture of a runner so engaged in the race that he or she puts everything else out of mind. The runner's main focus is on the finish line, and pressing and straining forward to obtain the prize. The literal translation of what James is saying is: Wherefore, my beloved brethren, set your focus on becoming a good listener— and do it with all of your might, as if you are in a competition to win the race of being the best listener.

Our desire should be to win first place when it comes to listening. In Mark 4:24 Jesus emphasized the importance of listening when He said, *"Consider carefully what you hear,"* he continued. *"With the measure you use, it will be measured to you—and even more."* Jesus emphasized the law of increase. When I listen correctly I can be assured there is more revelation to come. We better understand what others say when we understand what God is saying.

In order to become a good listener, we must learn to slow down our mouth. It is possible to fill the atmosphere with so many words that our ears become dull of hearing His voice, or any other for that matter. The writer of Proverbs puts it this way, *"The one who has knowledge uses words with restraint, and whoever has understanding is even-tempered"* (Proverbs 17:27). Wrong speaking can destroy or take the cutting edge off our testimony and hinder the purpose of God in our lives. A sure evidence of maturity is right speaking as it pertains to faith, concern, and understanding. We need to "hear" from God to find out what He is doing in and through our lives!

Father, thank You for reminding me of the importance of listening to Your voice. I want to hear everything You have for me. Amen!

CONQUER YOUR FEAR

For the Spirit God gave us does not make us timid, but gives us power, love and self-discipline (2 Timothy 1:7).

———————————

The apostle Paul reminded Timothy of something we all need to remember: *it is the Holy Spirit who gives us the power to serve God, and through Him we can conquer fear and weakness.* The word *"timid"* in this verse is translated in the King James as "fear." The meaning is "timidity or cowardice." Paul is not referring to a normal fear God has created within us for protection. But rather an abnormal fear that paralyzes the heart. There is nothing worse than waking up each morning paralyzed by fear. We don't have to live with the attitude of, "I'll just pull the covers over my head and make life go away!" Unfortunately, no matter how long you stay in bed, life with all of its ups and downs will be there to greet you when you get up.

God has given us three tools to combat and conquer the spirit of timidity:

First, He gives us His *power.* This kind of power is not in our physical strength. This is the power given us by the Holy Spirit to do everything He has called us to do. It is senseless to try to serve God without His power working in us and through us. We do not have to face the trials and tribulations of life alone!

Second, He has given us His *love.* If we have love for others, we will be able to endure any trial or difficulty and accomplish the work God has called us to do. Real agape love is energized by the Holy Spirit within us: *"And hope does not put us to shame, because God's love has been poured out into our hearts through the Holy Spirit, who has been given to us"* (Romans 5:5).

Third, He is also the One who gives *self-discipline* or *self-control.* Sometimes the greatest source of our fear is our own mind. The phrase *"sound mind"* that Paul uses describes someone who is well-balanced, who has life under control, is calm and able to meet life's challenges head-on.

Timothy had every reason to be encouraged by Paul's letter, and so do we! We can be assured the Holy Spirit does not leave us no matter how we struggle on a certain day. He does not walk away at the least sign of trouble. As a believer we have all the power needed to accomplish our purpose in life—what more could we ever ask for?

Father, my heart is filled with joy because I know You will never leave me or forsake me. Thank You that I don't have to live in fear. Amen!

MONDAY

PLUG IN!

Meanwhile, the people in Judah said, "The strength of the laborers is giving out, and there is so much rubble that we cannot rebuild the wall" (Nehemiah 4:10).

Nehemiah was a Spirit-filled building contractor. He was not a prophet, priest, or king. He was just an ordinary man on a mission from God to head up a building project that had all the appearances of being harmless, innocent, and rather simple. After all, what could be so hard about building a wall around the city! Yet he faced a very common problem that has affected many. The project started with great excitement, but as you read through the entire chapter 4, you discover the people were ready to quit. Why? One simple word—*discouragement!*

The meaning of the word discouragement is *"to deprive of courage or confidence; to hinder by disfavoring."* To "dis" something means to "take away." Literally it means to "dis connect" from courage. If you unplug an electrical cord from the wall socket, the lights go out. The same is true in following our purpose and calling from God. If we are disconnected from our Power Source, we have no fuel to complete the task. On the other hand, when we connect to the Power Source—the Holy Spirit—He gives us the power to overcome and defeat discouragement.

Nehemiah learned something we all know and can identify with. Things don't always work out the way we think they should. He was facing enemies from without, and enemies from within (see Nehemiah 4:1-10). No matter which way he turned he was getting negative feedback. Any of this sound familiar?

What can we do when we find ourselves ready to throw up our hands and quit? One thing I love about Nehemiah is he did not ignore the problem. Discouragement is something that cannot be ignored. It's like trying to ignore a flat tire. Pray all you want, keep driving, and hope somehow air will miraculously get back into the tire. Unfortunately, it doesn't work that way—you have to stop and fix it!

After Nehemiah lifted up his voice in prayer, he started to infuse new hope and encouragement into the people. He pointed them back toward their original goal of building the wall. He reminded them of the greatness of God (see Nehemiah 4:14). If the rubbish—our problems—become so great they blot out the face of God, it's time to stop what we're doing and seek Him. *Plug in and reconnect to your Power Source—that's a sure way out of the pit of discouragement!*

Father, help me to keep my eyes focused on You and not the rubbish around me. Amen!

BE PREPARED

Whatever happens, conduct yourselves in a manner worthy of the gospel of Christ. Then, whether I come and see you or only hear about you in my absence, I will know that you stand firm in the one Spirit, striving together as one for the faith of the gospel (Philippians 1:27).

The Christian life is no place for weaklings. It is never described in the New Testament as a picnic, but a battle. The believer can be sure that conflict and warfare are a part of who we are. In Paul's writings he couches the life of a Christian in terms of striving, standing, and struggling. We must understand that although we are in a fight, we are not left alone. We have resources for the battle.

First, we must have *consistent conduct.* Christianity is meant to be lived, not just talked about. Paul makes it very simple when he says, *"conduct yourselves in a manner worthy of the gospel of Christ."* It is exciting to be a child of the King, but we must also live like one! I am afraid average believers want to see how close they can live to the world and still be considered a Christian. A great Christian writer wrote, *"Many Christians have been extremely skillful in arranging their lives so as to admit the truth of Christianity without being embarrassed by its implications."*[8]

Second, if we are to be successful against the forces that would knock us off track, we must have *courageous convictions.* Paul pleads with us to *"stand firm in the one Spirit, striving together as one for the faith of the gospel."* I believe we are living in a day when not many are willing to stand for what they believe. The old saying is worth repeating, "If you don't stand for something, you will fall for anything!"

We are living in times of immense conflict. We are being attacked as a culture on every front. As believers we must stand together with unwavering convictions based on the truth of God's Word. God will always honor those who have the courage of their convictions and unashamedly stand for the truth of the gospel. If we are willing to stand for Him, you can be assured He will stand for us! Do not fear or run away from the battle. We have been given all the tools necessary to win!

Father, help me to stand strong in the face of so much going on around me. I choose to live my life according to the truth of the gospel. Amen!

BE CERTAIN

For to me, to live is Christ and to die is gain (Philippians 1:21).

In twelve one-syllable words, Paul gives his philosophy of life. When you strip away all the accolades and accomplishments, it boiled down to one thing for him, *"For to me, to live is Christ."* Paul recognized that Christianity is not a philosophy or a system of teaching. Christianity is a Person, and that Person is Jesus Christ. Every life has its center, and for Paul that center was Jesus Christ. Everything else was rubbish!

Just having a belief about Christ is not sufficient. To know the joy and fullness of the Christian life as a personal commitment is an absolute requirement. To know Jesus is to live the greatest adventure a person can ever know. Having that kind of personal relationship on a daily basis will give us a certainty not only about the present, but also about our future.

Perhaps the simplest definition of a Christian is: a follower of Jesus Christ. To follow Him means to go to many places and experience the joys of life that nothing else can offer. If Paul were alive today I doubt seriously he would live by the philosophy of a recent popular song that exhorts, "Living is what you do while you are waiting to die."[9] Sadly, many have adopted that twisted view of life. Many substitutes are offered, but only One can fill the void—Jesus Christ! No matter what philosophy of life we ascribe to, the ultimate question is, "Where is what I believe leading me?"

When you have time and in a quiet moment, take a blank piece of paper and finish this statement: "To me to live is…." Whatever life is to you, write it down. What things are you certain about in life and in death? Is it money? Sports? Self-gratification? Whatever it is write it down and look at it seriously. If living means anything but Christ, the only thing you can write down is "loss!" Don't get distracted with other things and miss out on the most wonderful relationship you can ever know.

It's very simple, you cannot have Paul's philosophy of death unless you have his philosophy of life! Success in business is marvelous. Taking care of our family is admirable. Having many friends is a treat. But knowing Christ in a personal way is the greatest joy of all!

Father, thank You for giving me the joy of knowing You. You are my Rock and my Salvation and forever I will rejoice. Amen!

STAND FIRM

Therefore, my brothers and sisters, you whom I love and long for, my joy and crown, stand firm in the Lord in this way, dear friends! (Philippians 4:1)

Oh how Paul loved his people! Of course it wasn't always that way. Before he came to Christ, Paul (then known as Saul) was anything but a loving and compassionate person. In his past he could brag about his religion (see Philippians 3 for his religious credentials). It was his religious zeal that led him to persecute the Church. He was so religious if you didn't agree with him he would kill you! What we need today is relationship not religion. Religion will always kill what it cannot control. Paul lived the life of a religious zealot and it almost destroyed him.

In this one verse (Philippians 4:1), Paul uses a term of endearment that was precious to him. He called them *"my brothers and sisters."* He was not using meaningless phraseology. For Paul to call others his brothers and sisters was very real. I think it is very possible he was recalling the first time he ever heard the word "brother." His life changed when he was knocked off of his donkey into the dirt (see Acts 9). His supernatural encounter with Jesus changed everything. After his Damascus Road experience, he was blinded and led into the city of Damascus. The first Christian who ever greeted him said, *"Brother Saul."* I think it must have broken Paul's heart. Therefore, this term became sacred to him, and it ought to be sacred to us!

To these dearly beloved people, Paul gave a word of encouragement to *"stand firm in the Lord,"* which means "to stand one's ground." It is a military term. Paul encouraged them to hold the ground God had given them. When the enemy is coming against you, hold your ground! The temptation is to give way and to give in. When others are running away from the battle the temptation is strong to join them in the stampede.

There is so much despair and discouragement all around us. God's people are not immune to the infection of defeatism. In the darkness that surrounds us I believe God speaks to our hearts and says, *"Don't run, stand firm!"* Paul does not leave us clueless, but gives us the secret of standing firm. He says, *"Stand firm in the Lord."* That is the secret to victory. It is not in our strength, but His. It is not in our wisdom, but His. So be encouraged my brothers and sisters, God will give us the victory!

Father, I know we are living in confusing times. Help me to see that running away is not the answer, but standing firm in Your strength. Amen!

JUST SHINE

Do everything without grumbling or arguing, so that you may become blameless and pure, "children of God without fault in a warped and crooked generation." Then you will shine among them like stars in the sky as you hold firmly to the word of life (Philippians 2:14-16).

———————————

Paul paints a beautiful word picture of the Christian life surrounded by a world darkened by sin. We know God created the stars to give light to the earth, and in like manner, Christ has created us to give light to a darkened world. The word "lights" in this Scripture passage is literally "luminaries or stars." As Christians we are God's "stars."

The genuine Christian life shines in sharp contrast to what we see all around us. When Jesus was here He said, *"I am the light of the world"* (John 8:12). He anticipated His return to Heaven so to His disciples He said, *"You are the light of the world"* (Matthew 5:14). I doubt there would be much disagreement even among nonbelievers that the culture around us is getting darker. Our world is indeed crooked. It is not straight in its thinking, actions, nor its deeds. Its sense of values is twisted. But, I remind you, the darker the place, the more the light is needed. The light shines the brightest in the darkest places!

Once we have been "lit" we have the privilege to *"hold firmly to the word of life."* It is a joy and privilege to show others the positive cure for the maladies of this broken-down world. Remember, there is no shining unless there is burning. All selfish motives and desires must be burned out of our lives if we are to burn for Jesus. We only become a blessing when we burn!

When we read the context of what Paul is saying, we see he is talking about God working within our lives. He does this in the person of the Holy Spirit, which is our fuel to keep the light shining. To shine as a Christian, the light of our lives must be filled to overflowing with the Holy Spirit (see Ephesians 5:18).

You may feel you are in a dark place right now. Consider the possibility you are where you are because God needed someone to hold firmly the word of life! Don't despair or give up—*just shine!*

———————————

Father, thank You for giving me the privilege to shine for You. Give me the courage to be a shining light wherever I go. Amen!

MONDAY

KEEP GROWING

*I am writing to you, dear children, because your sins have
been forgiven on account of his name* (1 John 2:12).

One of the apostle John's favorite terms in his first letter (1 John) is the term
"dear children." It was John's customary way of greeting all of those who are
members of God's family. The phrase is actually one word that means "born
ones." It comes from a verb that means "to birth" or "to bring into existence." It
is a general term of love and endearment to describe everyone who is a member
of God's family.

We may be different ages or at different stages of spiritual development, but
one thing we all have in common is this: *young or old our sins have been forgiven.*
It is an exciting truth to know that God has taken care of the sin problem. The
Bible says that when God forgives our sins, He has put them behind His back
(see Isaiah 38:17). The psalmist declared God has removed our sin as far as the
east is from the west (Psee salm 103:12).

How is it possible to say we have been forgiven? John said our sins are forgiven, *"on account of his name."* The wonderful truth of forgiveness is not because
of something we have done, but because of what Jesus has done! Humankind
has tried every way possible to figure out what to do with sin. All religions are
based on the idea that through good works or good deeds we can handle the
problem without help. Religion is nothing more than humanity trying to figure
out how to reach up to God. Christianity is God reaching down to humanity!

Being part of the family of God brings great privilege and responsibility. Birth is only the beginning of life, and we can certainly expect there to be
growth. What a tragedy it is in the natural world for a little baby to be born and
never to grow. It would be a terrible thing for a man and woman to bring a child
into the world and never nurture and mature and develop the child. The same
is true in the spiritual realm. We have a responsibility to do all that is necessary

to grow and develop spiritually. If we don't, we will end up with stunted growth, and that is the greatest tragedy of all!

It is exciting to know our sins are forgiven, but we must move from childhood to maturity. God wants us to be members of Hhis family, but He also wants us to move out of infancy into adulthood (see 1 John 2:13-14). God wants us to grow up into Him (see Ephesians 4:15). Yes, our sins are forgiven, but that is just the beginning of a wonderful journey of *knowing Him!*

———————————————⟨⟩———————————————

Father, thank You for forgiving my sins. I know that my spiritual growth comes from a personal relationship with You on a daily basis. Teach Me your ways. Amen!

CITIZENS

But our citizenship is in heaven. And we eagerly await a Savior from there, the Lord Jesus Christ (Philippians 3:20).

Our viewpoint has everything to do with the way we approach life. If we approach life from Heaven's viewpoint, we will get Heaven's perspective. The Christian is a citizen of Heaven who lives on this earth. Paul made it clear in an earlier statement that the Christian has dual citizenship. We may be citizens of a particular country, but we are also on the citizenship registry of Heaven.

Remember, Paul is writing his letter to the church in Philippi, a Roman colony. This kind of terminology would be familiar to them because they understood what it meant. When Rome conquered a region they would establish colonies. To maintain order, they would send out citizens, mostly soldiers, to represent the Roman government. Regardless where they were, the citizens maintained the customs and conduct of their citizenship. They were still enrolled on the Roman register, they wore the Roman dress, they spoke the Roman language, and they were governed by Roman laws. In every way they were "Rome away from Rome."

The essence of Paul's statement is we really don't belong down here. In a small Southern city there is a sign that reads: *"If you lived here, you would be at home now."* That sums it up, this world is not our home! We're just strangers and pilgrims passing through. Because we belong in Heaven, we are to demonstrate Heaven upon this earth every day. Our lives are to be governed by heavenly standards, and we are to bring a touch of Heaven wherever we go.

Heavenly citizens may keep their minds on what is in front of them, but their hearts and eyes are looking above *because we are eagerly looking toward Heaven waiting for the Savior.* The greatest event of any Roman colony was a visit from the emperor. The streets were cleaned, the houses were decorated, and the people were prepared for the day he would arrive. We are to live as if Christ would come at any moment, yes even today!

When you are feeling down and hopeless, and the events of the earth are crashing all around you, remember—*one day He will come again and make everything right.*

Father, I pray You will help me to bring a positive atmosphere of Heaven wherever I go. May I always live up to my citizenship, here and there. Amen!

FILLED

And this is my prayer: that your love may abound more and more in knowledge and depth of insight (Philippians 1:9).

———————

The apostle Paul loved to pray. As you read his letters, you will discover he bathed each one of them in prayer. In this particular prayer Paul expresses some things that are needed in the life of every Christian. I do not think it is a stretch to say that God has taken this prayer and made it the expression of His own desires for us.

Paul prays that we might be filled with a *life overflowing with love.* Every life will be filled with something because nature abhors a vacuum, and so does the human heart. If our heart is not filled with love, it will be filled with hatred, animosity, selfishness, etc. But the good news is our hearts can be filled with a love the world cannot offer. Why is that? Because as Christians the seed of love has already been planted in our hearts by the Holy Spirit (see Romans 5:5). God's love has been poured into our hearts, and that love can continue to grow because there are no limits to the love that can flow through our lives. We are living in a love-starved world that needs the love of God more now than ever before!

You will notice that Paul says this kind of love *"must have knowledge."* Where do you find out what love is? I can guarantee you will never find out what love is through the latest magazine or the most popular movie. We learn what love is from God's love letter to us—the Bible! In the Bible we learn that love is selfless, not self-ish; it is spiritual, not sensual; it is a matter of giving, not getting.

Paul also told us in this prayer that this kind of love must be guided by *judgment or depth of insight.* He is talking about discernment. It is the practical application of what we learned. It is the ability to express love with the knowledge we have. We must have a spiritual sensitivity or our expression of love will be tasteless and tactless.

God wants our love to grow. And He wants our knowledge to grow along with spiritual insight. What would our world be like if each Christian was overflowing with this kind of love to the point it impacted everyone around us? A tsunami of love would hit with such impact that entire nations and cultures would be changed!

———————

Father, give me the strength to demonstrate Your love to everyone around me. My greatest desire is to let everyone know how much You love them. Amen!

THE REAL STORY

*For in him all things were created: things in heaven and on earth,
visible and invisible, whether thrones or powers or rulers or authorities;
all things have been created through him and for him. He is before all
things, and in him all things hold together* (Colossians 1:16-17).

The reason many people are confused today is because they are not getting the real story about how everything began. Our entire educational system is teaching young people that everything just "happened." The most popular view is called the Big Bang Theory. But is that the real story? No wonder people are confused, yes, even Christians.

What is the real story? First, God created all things. God created us and everything around us. It is not a fairytale, it is fact. Let's face it, most of us have never spent enough time studying the four most important words that are the key to believing everything about creation: *"In the beginning God"* (Genesis 1:1). The Bible makes it clear that things in Heaven, earth, visible and invisible were all created by God. Once you get past Genesis 1:1 everything falls into place.

Second, God claims all things. All things were created by God, and at the same time all things were created for Him. Why is that important? This fact helps us remove the selfish mind-set we have toward our own "things." He allows us to be stewards and to rule over things, but He reminds us that these things were created for His good pleasure. If it is not for His glory, then it is all empty and useless!

Third, God controls all things. For many Christians that statement is hard to believe. Sure, we have free will, but things created by God are things controlled by Him. He holds all things together. So before we blame everything on the devil and give him more credit than he deserves, we must remember God is ultimately in control. He is never confused or in doubt as to what to do.

The next time you turn on the television and hear about the latest pandemic or the latest scandal, remember you don't have to live in fear—God is in control! The next time some well-meaning person tells you a particular country is about to build a nuclear bomb, remember, God is in control! The greatest cure for worry and fear is the very first statement in the Bible. Read it and get the real story.

Father, please remind me of Your truth every time I feel afraid or in doubt. Amen!

STOP COMPLAINING

Now I want you to know, brothers and sisters, that what has happened to me has actually served to advance the gospel. As a result, it has become clear throughout the whole palace guard and to everyone else that I am in chains for Christ
(Philippians 1:12-13).

The apostle Paul had every reason to complain. When you read his letters you realize things had not gone as he had planned. I guess you could say the breaks had certainly gone against him in every circumstance. Instead of reading a list of criticisms, you discover Paul viewed his adversity as a positive rather than a negative.

Bible scholars agree that the word "happened" was not in the original text. It may have been added for clarity but instead it clouded the issue. Why? Paul did not feel the circumstances that came his way just happened by chance. He called his imprisonment his chains for Christ. Nothing ever just happens to a Christian. We have a heavenly Father who loves us and orders the events of our lives, even when we don't understand how they can all fit together. Nothing gets to us without first being filtered through the throne!

The greatest cure for complaining is to realize Jesus Christ is absolutely first in our lives. Paul looked upon adversity as opportunities to spread the good news of the gospel. He learned how to turn obstacles into opportunities, and disappointments into His appointments. The key to dealing with adverse circumstances is the right attitude of the heart. Looking at things from Heaven's point of view enables us to go through "stuff" with a victorious mind-set.

The next time a complaining spirit rises up, why not ask a central question: "Can anything I am going through right now spread the good news of Jesus Christ?" The apostle Paul would answer unequivocally, "YES!" How do I know? He said so, "As a result, it has become clear throughout the whole palace guard and to everyone else that I am in chains for Christ." The word "advance" means to "cut before." It refers to cutting a trail before the advance of an army. Paul looked upon himself as a spiritual engineer. One of God's pioneers who blazed new trails for the gospel. Because of his positive attitude many were set free!

It is time for Christians to stop complaining and start pioneering. It is time to stop criticizing each other and start facing the world with positive hearts and spread hope that in Christ you don't have to live in gloom and doom.

Father, help me to turn my complaining into joy. I declare You are first. Amen!

MONDAY

A TINY MIRACLE

Remember this: Whoever sows sparingly will also reap sparingly, and whoever sows generously will also reap generously (2 Corinthians 9:6).

The next time you visit a farmers' market or your local hardware store, you will find many varieties of what I call "tiny miracles." What are they? Seeds! Seeds are mysterious and remarkable things. God has created in their DNA the power to multiply, if the laws of the harvest are properly followed. What a seed can do is nothing short of breathtaking and mind-boggling.

In 1968 a scientist discovered a 600-year-old seed necklace in a Native American grave. He planted one of the seeds, and guess what it did? It sprouted and grew! Keep in mind it had been dormant for 600 years, but the potential for life was still there.

Have you ever thought about what motivates a farmer to labor and sacrifice with great patience for weeks and months after the seed was sown in good soil? The farmer knows that if enough seeds are planted to grow 1.4 million plants (about one acre of wheat) the efforts will yield around 77,300,000 kernels!

All of us are seed sowers and life farmers. We have been given an assignment on earth to fulfill. We have access to good and bad seeds with which we can sow and reap a much greater blessing or cursing in our lives. Not only do the seeds affect our lives, but the lives of others around us.

God's view of success is much different from most. Success from Heaven's point of view is not having it all so others will look at us and measure our lives by what we have. He has made us to function within His purpose, and it involves growing to our full potential within His plan. As we sow tiny miracles of good seed from our lives into others, we will see a tremendous harvest. The only biblical way to secure a generational transfer is to take what's in our hands and sow into others. There can be no success without a successor!

Father, help me to be more sensitive to those around me. I realize You have placed in my hands seeds that can produce many miracles. Amen!

LIFE IS IN THE SEED

For you have been born again, not of perishable seed, but of imperishable, through the living and enduring word of God (1 Peter 1:23).

The Bible uses the concept of "seed" in numerous ways. Jesus is referred to as the *"Seed of the woman."* The Word of God is designated as *"seed."* The declaration of the gospel message is likened to a massive scattering of seed. The seed received in good soil will produce a vast harvest.

From the very beginning of creation God built on the principle of seed time and harvest. At the very center of divine order is the simple, yet miraculous seed (see Genesis 1:11-13; Mark 4:3-9). From the vast array of the heavens to the small yet powerful seed, God created certain patterns and principles with order and beauty.

One of His masterful works are plants and trees bearing seed. They are created to reproduce life after their design. Can you imagine a God-created system that only allowed for a seed to reproduce just one seed? That would mean death would have been built into the system. But the life of one seed can produce a bountiful garden, which in turn can reproduce much more! The life of the seed holds the key to reproduction, thereby eliminating the possibility of extinction. It is the principle that governs and regulates all of the created order.

There is a proverb that describes the glory of the seed: "You can count the number of seeds in an apple, but you cannot count the number of apples in a seed." Every life began by the seed principle. Every act of our lives since our beginning has also operated by the seed principle—sowing and reaping. Whether we recognize it or not, we continually sow the seed of God's Word into the soil of our purpose. In order to be successful in life we must learn and function within God's created pattern. Indeed, there is life in the seed!

Father, today I celebrate the life of the seed. My commitment to You is to sow positive life seeds into those around me. Amen!

WHAT GOES AROUND COMES AROUND

*Do not be deceived: God cannot be mocked. A man
reaps what he sows* (Galatians 6:7).

———————————————————

In order to be a successful "life farmer" a clear understanding of the principle of the law of "sowing and reaping" is necessary. In the Word of God, this law is described as the principle of "the Law of Reciprocity." A physics professor would describe it as the law of "cause and effect" or "for every action there is an equal and opposite reaction." A financial consultant would call it the law of "investment and return." Your pastor might refer to it as the law of "giving and receiving." Then again, talk to a farmer and he would call it the law of "planting and harvesting." The ordinary person sitting in a pew might refer to it saying, "What goes around comes around!" By whatever name you call it, the results are the same—you reap what you sow!

Stephen Covey, in his excellent book *The Seven Habits of Highly Effective People*, refers to this principle by using the phrase "emotional bank account." It is his way of describing the principle of reciprocity. According to Covey it is the "credit-withdrawal" process in relationships. The emotional bank account describes the trust that accumulates in a relationship. Like any good financial institution, you must make a deposit before you can make a withdrawal!

I think we have the idea if we share one negative word, there is just one negative result. That is simply untrue. The repercussions are much greater because one negative seed has the power to cause a multitude of negative results. Some have compared sharing negativity and harmful words to emptying a feather pillow on a windy afternoon. It might be easy to empty the pillowcase of its contents, but impossible to gather them all together again.

It is imperative to make deposits of positive words and deeds into the bank account of those around us. If you want a positive withdrawal, continue to make positive deposits!

———————————————————

Father, help me to always think about the words that I say. Guard my lips that I may say pleasing words that honor You. Amen!

SEED TO YOUR FUTURE

Now he who supplies seed to the sower and bread for food will also supply and increase your store of seed and will enlarge the harvest of your righteousness (2 Corinthians 9:10).

———————————⟨∼⟩———————————

When it comes to our future we all have a choice to make. We can choose to continually "seed" the future we "see" with positive ideas, words, visions, or pictures needed that will take us from where we are to where we want to go in God's purpose. If we fail to do this, we will end up consumers and not reproducers; reapers and not sowers; getters and not givers. Before we realize it, the harvest will be exhausted.

A wise farmer knows sowing seed is not an occasional hobby. He realizes in order to reap an abundant harvest it must done consistently with a plan for the future. The only time we can control our future is when we release the seed in our hand. An unwillingness to continue to sow into future generations will leave them (and us) with an empty seed barrel!

Author and leadership expert Mike Murdock says, "If what you have isn't big enough to be your harvest, make it your seed, because that seed is the only influence you have over your future." Another way to put it, "When what you have won't meet your need, use it as seed."

Another aspect of wise farmers is that they do not wait until the day of harvest to decide how big of a harvest is needed. No, that decision is made many months before, and the farmer plans accordingly. It is always unwise to wait until our future is on top of us, and then quickly decide to scatter seed to avoid a bad outcome. A farmer who takes that approach will experience crop failure, and the family will go hungry!

What and where you "see" yourself a few years from now will only become a reality because you are "seeding" the good seed, presently and consistently. The good seed carries the DNA that will produce the harvest you have seen. When I release the seed in my hand, God will release the harvest from His hand.

———————————⟨∼⟩———————————

Father, I praise You today because I know You have a wonderful plan for my life. May I ever be obedient to "seed" to my future.

START TODAY

If clouds are full of water, they pour rain on the earth.
Whether a tree falls to the south or to the north, in the place
where it falls, there it will lie (Ecclesiastes 11:3).

Happy is the person who starts each new day with an attitude of gratitude. Taking a cue from the psalmist it would be wise to say, *"This is the day the Lord has made; we will rejoice and be glad in it"* (Psalm 118:24 NKJV). The truth is we have no promise of tomorrow, and there is nothing I can do about yesterday's harvest. It is gone, good or bad. What I can do is to begin today to sow for the future harvest.

Sad to say there are times, in spite of our best efforts, things do not work out like we want. If we are not careful, we focus on the negative and the "What if" events of life to the detriment of our life's purpose. Solomon warns, *"He who observes the wind will not sow, he who regards the clouds will not reap"* (Ecclesiastes 11:4 NKJV). The Living Bible's paraphrase of this verse says, *"If you wait for perfect conditions, you will never get anything done."* What is the warning? Don't wait for perfect conditions before starting to invest in life and the lives of others.

Oliver Wendell Holmes, former U.S. Supreme Court Justice, said, "Many people die with their music still in them. Why is this so? Too often it is because they are always getting ready to live. Before they know it, time runs out." Determine not to live your life looking in the rearview mirror. Today is the first day of the rest of your life, and whatever you do don't waste it—invest it!

Start with where you are, or as one leadership expert said, "You don't have to be great to get started, but you have to get started to be great." If you wait until you have more time, more money, a bigger house, or until retirement to begin the adventure of your life's purpose, you will never get started. Or as the old Nike commercial used to say, "JUST DO IT!"

Father, help me to learn from my past, rejoice in the present, and focus my eyes on the future. Amen!

MONDAY

YOUR EYES CAN FOOL YOU

Stop judging by mere appearances, but instead judge correctly (John 7:24).

Every day we all make judgments in a variety of ways. It is a fact of life. It is easy to be confused over the issue of judging one another. On one hand we are warned not to judge (see Matthew 7:1-2), and yet we are told to exercise righteous judgment (see John 7:24). A lot of people assume what Jesus meant in Matthew 7:1-2 is we are to see no evil, speak no evil, and hear no evil when it comes to the sin of others. It is the attitude of neutrality, or never make any kind of biblical examination or exercise discernment. The common theme among believers is that Christians are not supposed to judge!

So, are we or are we not to exercise judgment? Yes, and no! We are commended and commanded to judge biblically and we are forbidden to judge unbiblically. Unbiblical judgment is destructive, hypocritical, and presumptuous. When I do so with a self-righteous attitude, I am in effect replacing God's judgment with my own. Passing judgment on someone is strictly forbidden in Scripture.

Too many lives have been destroyed by others assuming things based on appearance alone. Destructive judgment is easy to spot. It oftentimes wraps itself around rumor, innuendo, and half-truths. Our natural tendency is to always judge harshly and put the most negative spin on what we see and hear about others. People who are always judging others are normally guilty of hiding what their favorite judgment is.

What did Jesus mean when He said, *"Stop judging by mere appearances?"* Based on an understanding of the word "judge," Jesus meant that we are not to critique, judge, and examine on the basis of looks or appearance. He goes on to say, *"but instead judge correctly."* The apostle Paul said in Romans 14:1, *"Accept the one whose faith is weak, without quarreling over disputable matters."* I believe the church would do well to exercise more forgiveness and less judgment, wouldn't you?

Father, give me eyes to see what You see in others. Give me the strength to avoid hypocritical judgment of fellow believers. Amen!

DON'T RUSH YOUR HARVEST

Let us not become weary in doing good, for at the proper time we will reap a harvest if we do not give up (Galatians 6:9).

What do you call a farmer who goes out and plants seed in the ground, and then goes out the next morning ready to reap a harvest? Unwise, and very hungry! A wise farmer knows that you don't sow seed on Monday and reap a harvest on Wednesday. He knows there will be a long time of waiting between sowing and reaping. If he did not remember the experience of past harvests, he might get impatient and rush the outcome.

We are living in an age of instant gratification. We are the only generation who will stand in front of a microwave, tapping our foot, looking impatiently at our watch saying, "Hurry up!" We have instant coffee, instant tea, instant potatoes, and instant pain relief. We have become so accustomed to receiving everything instantly that we have great difficulty waiting for anything. Someone put it well, "Overnight success is a two-to-five year plan!" Let's face it, instant success just doesn't exist, not in the marketplace nor in the kingdom of God.

The number-one character trait of a successful farmer is *persistent patience*. The farmer knows if patient in sowing and cultivating the crops, he or she will reap an abundant harvest. The farmer also understands the law of sowing and reaping means you harvest the crop when it is ready, not just when you are ready to start putting crops in the barn.

The United States of America is a land of abundance, and the church has reaped the benefits. However, there is a shortage in the land—a shortage of persistent patience. We all know we need to learn the importance of patience, but unfortunately we are not willing to wait. We don't like to wait for anything, whether in line at the bank or for a parking space at the mall. We want what we want and we want it right now!

Remember, *patience and persistent people are those who never fail because they never quit.* Don't rush your harvest!

Father, slow me down when I act impatiently. I know the harvest is on the way. Amen!

ME, MYSELF, AND I

He thought to himself, "What shall I do? I have no place to store my crops." Then he said, "This is what I'll do. I will tear down my barns and build bigger ones, and there I will store my surplus grain. And I'll say to myself, 'You have plenty of grain laid up for many years. Take life easy; eat, drink and be merry'" (Luke 12:17-19).

One of the first lies ever perpetrated upon man was, *"You will be like God"* (Genesis 3:5). From that day until this, the anthem of many successful people has been, "It's all about me, myself, and I," or as the late Frank Sinatra sang, "I did it my way."

The farmer in our parable felt the same way. He basically took credit for the abundant harvest he received. If you read closely you will discover God is nowhere to be found. The farmer's focus of attention is on himself. The counsel he gives and receives is within himself. If you had the chance to interview him about the abundance of his harvest, no doubt he would say he was the captain of his destiny, the master of his fate.

The great theologian Augustine said, "God being God offends human pride." Why? The answer is simple. If God is running the universe, guess who isn't? You and I! It was a wonderful day for everyone around me when I resigned as CEO of the universe. The longer I live the more I realize there is a God in Heaven, and He's not me! The psalmist said it this way, *"Know that the Lord is God. It is he who made us, and we are his; we are his people, the sheep of his pasture"* (Psalm 100:3). The subtlety of the psalmist is not overlooked. In a kind and gentle way, he said, "God is the Creator, and we are not!"

It's time for us to allow God to do His work His way. He is certainly not against us living in abundance. We just need to be careful who gets the credit. Upon hearing an influential person boast, "I am a self-made man," someone replied, "Such a statement only proves the worthlessness of unskilled labor."

Father, I give up all rights to running the universe. And I will always be careful to give You the credit for all You have done for me. Amen!

I CAN'T, NEVER COULD

What is more, I consider everything a loss because of the surpassing worth of knowing Christ Jesus my Lord, for whose sake I have lost all things. I consider them garbage, that I may gain Christ (Philippians 3:8).

Living with regret over past failure is a total waste of time and energy. Regret only leads to the quicksand of self-pity. It only takes one to have a pity party, but of course it's always more fun to drag people along with you. The most popular song titles at that party are, "If only" and "I can't."

Life can sometimes be understood looking back, but it must always be lived looking forward. If you study the lives of successful people you will find in most, if not all, cases they experienced failure at some point in their journey. Just remember, many fail because they take the path of least resistance while laboring with the least persistence. It is a fact of life that every person falls and fails frequently, but the only time failure is final is when you let it be!

If you allow, "If only" and "I can't" to continually be sown in the soil of your mind, you will ensure a life of failure. W. A. Ward said, "Failure should be our teacher, not our undertaker. Failure is delay, not defeat. It is a temporary detour, not a dead-end street."

Babe Ruth was known as the "Sultan of Swat." He is still remembered today for hitting 714 home runs during his career. Did you know he also struck out 1,330 times? That is a statistic nobody talks about. He struck out almost twice as many times as he hit home runs. His philosophy was simple: "Never let the fear of striking out keep you from taking a swing at the ball." There are times we are so afraid of failure that we never take a swing to be successful. As a matter of fact, we just don't try, or we try something and then give up.

Why not ask the God who made you and loves you to help you eliminate seeds of unhealthy shame and the seeds of undeserving blame. Start today and sow the seeds that have the pattern to produce the future God has for you!

Father, I choose to no longer allow negative seeds of self-pity to influence my life. Direct me toward Your purpose. Amen!

GIVING THANKS…ALWAYS

*Give thanks in all circumstances; for this is God's will
for you in Christ Jesus* (1 Thessalonians 5:18).

Christians are not exempt from life's difficulties and perplexities. There are experiences that come to us we simply don't understand or comprehend. Let's face it, there are times when it's very difficult to *"Give thanks in all circumstances."*

There are some who say there is a difference between giving thanks "in" everything and giving thanks "for" everything. I would not argue with that at all. An understanding of Scripture teaches me the Lord wants us to do both. The apostle Paul wrote, *"always giving thanks to God the Father for everything, in the name of our Lord Jesus Christ"* (Ephesians 5:20). It is clear that God expects us to give thanks no matter what circumstances come our way.

Do you think God is commanding the impossible? God will never command us to do something He will not give us the power to obey. If He didn't give us the enablement He would be denying His own Word. So when God commands us to be thankful *"for all things"* and *"in all things,"* He knows we will be more complete Christians because of it.

If you reflect on the ministry of Jesus, His commandments were the enabling for people to do what they could not otherwise do. Jesus commanded a paralytic to take up his bed and walk, and he did it! Jesus commanded a dead man to come out of the grave, and he did it! The list is endless.

Through the power of the Holy Spirit and the encouragement of the Word, God infuses us with His unequaled power to obey. In times of difficulty it is helpful to remember God is still on the throne, and He has not abdicated His position of ruling and reigning!

The next time you are faced with adversity or painful circumstances, remember that your Father loves you and knows your circumstances. You can trust Him and declare with Job, *"Though He slay me, yet will I trust Him"* (Job 13:15 NKJV).

Father, I know difficulties and adversity will come my way. I choose today to give You thanks always for and in all things. Amen!

MONDAY

FASTER THAN A SPEEDING BULLET

*My days are swifter than a weaver's shuttle, and they
come to an end without hope* (Job 7:6).

———————————————

Some of us are old enough to remember the old television series Superman. He was able to "leap tall buildings in a single bound," and fly "faster than a speeding bullet." He was definitely a guy you wanted on your side if you ever got into trouble. Have you ever felt like Superman has invaded the hands on your clock because time seems to go by faster than a speeding bullet?

The Bible has much to say about the swiftness of time. Job compared his days to a weaver's shuttle. Today the speed of the shuttle is nothing compared to what it was in Job's day. Weaving cloth today is definitely faster than Superman could fly!

What are we to do with the swiftness of time? One is to constantly live in the past and ignore the world around us. That attitude is difficult because the world we live in is instantly connected through technology. For example, if a tragedy happens in Israel or Russia, we know about it immediately. We are constantly bombarded with "instant" news, good and bad. Christians cannot bury their heads in the sand and let the world go by. Another approach is to fight change and try to slow down time. You might as well try to leap a tall building in a single bound as to slow down the forces of time in today's world! That approach is useless.

As Christians we have to live in the real world and trust the power of the Holy Spirit to give us peace and strength day by day. I remind you that Jesus Christ is the same yesterday, today, and forever. God's Word is forever settled in Heaven, and His Word will never pass away.

So, if you feel the sands of time are pouring all over your head, relax and surrender to Christ and let time work for you, not against you. After all, none of us are Superman, but we serve a super God!

Father, keep my mind and my heart focused on You. Help me to never allow the swiftness of time to stop me from Your purpose. Amen!

HELP, PLEASE

*Blessed are those whose help is the God of Jacob, whose
hope is in the Lord their God* (Psalm 146:5).

"Blessed are those whose help is the God of Jacob...." Let's face it, there are times in our lives when we all need help. No matter how capable or qualified we may be, there comes a point when outside help is necessary. It does not matter if it is the world of business, sports, or church, we often get off track; and when we do, we must depend on the help of the experts.

When it comes to offering help there is One whose help is far above all—the *"God of Jacob."* I have often wondered why the psalmist framed this wonderful statement that God is *"the God of Jacob?"* I believe it's a word of encouragement, because Jacob was one person in the Old Testament who always seemed to need some help (Genesis 25–50). You know his story. He tricked his brother and father, moved to a hostile land, yet God protected him and met his every need. No matter the circumstances, God fulfilled His divine purpose in Jacob and made him the father of the tribes of Israel. If God can help such a man as Jacob, He certainly can help us!

David says in Psalm 46:1, *"God is our refuge and strength, an ever-present help in trouble."* Many times we turn to others when we need help, and sad to say they fail to come through. But when we place our trust in God, He gives us the kind of help that never lets us down.

Hebrews 13:6 reads, *"So we say with confidence, 'The Lord is my helper; I will not be afraid. What can mere mortals do to me?'"* What a confident statement, and a source of encouragement for all of us. Everything we could ever need or hope for is bound up in these words. Reading them is a sure prescription for a life of joy and abundance. We don't have to live in fear of others, nor fear anything that may hinder us from our purpose. Why? The God of Jacob is on the scene!

Father, I praise You for always being available no matter my circumstances. I know I do not have to live in fear any longer. Amen!

MEET YOUR ENCOURAGER

And I will ask the Father, and he will give you another advocate [encourager, comforter] *to help you and be with you forever* (John 14:16).

───────────⟪∿⟫───────────

There are many reasons today for believers to be discouraged. Some are discouraged because of adverse circumstances, broken relationships, or just simply life in general. In today's culture you don't have to look far to find a reason to be discouraged.

As a Christian, we have been given the awesome gift of the indwelling Holy Spirit, who is our encourager. While it is true He offers words of conviction and discouragement when we sin, He will never offer discouraging words just to make us feel badly.

Jesus was addressing a group of people who felt as though their world had crashed and burned around them. The disciples were in the upper room, and Jesus just told them one of their number would betray Him to the enemy, and Peter (of all people) would turn his back on Him. Needless to say there was discouragement in the air. Something had to be done to change the atmosphere.

Jesus used the word "comforter," which means "someone who sympathizes and feels pain with us." Literally it means, "one who is called to one's side." The best translation of the word would be "the encourager." God's gift of the Holy Spirit is our eternal Encourager, and He is always by our side to help us live victorious lives. The word "comfort" comes from two Latin words: *com,* which means "with" and *fort,* which means "strength." God's eternal Comforter does not look at us and say, "Just pull yourself up by your bootstraps," which is physically impossible to do. No, He gives us the strength we need when we need it!

Jesus said He would send them *"another advocate* [comforter]*,"* which literally means another of the same kind. He is equal to the Son and able to encourage us just as Jesus encouraged His disciples. So if you are feeling discouraged, it may be you are not depending on your eternal Encourager!

───────────⟪∿⟫───────────

Father, I know there are times when I am discouraged. Thank You for the indwelling Holy Spirit who knows exactly how to strengthen me when I am down. Amen!

BIGGER IS NOT ALWAYS BETTER

Who dares despise the day of small things, since the seven eyes of the Lord that range throughout the earth will rejoice when they see the chosen capstone in the hand of Zerubbabel? (Zechariah 4:10)

———————

Zechariah asked an interesting question one day, *"Who dares despise the day of small things?"* No doubt he was trying to encourage the nation as they were rebuilding the temple. Things had not been going so well. Difficulties abounded, and the lack of money led to low morale. Low morale was evidenced by the fact they felt the job would never be completed. The people were discouraged because the whole project seemed so small—it just wasn't the same temple they were used to.

It would be wise for us to never despise the day of small beginnings! Remember when God wanted to deliver His people from slavery, He chose a baby (Moses) who years later led his people out of bondage. When God wanted to break the chains of sin off of humankind, He sent another baby whose name was Jesus Christ. He started out as a baby only to grow up so that He would one day sacrifice Himself on the cross.

Throughout the pages of history God used small things to accomplish great and eternal purposes. Thumb through the pages of the Bible and read for yourself how many times what started out insignificant and small turned out to be mighty miracles!

It is important to realize that if we cannot be trusted with small things, we can never be trusted with the big things. Jesus said that if we are faithful with the least, we will also be faithful with the greatest! No work done for the kingdom is ever considered insignificant and small. It may be to those casual observers around you, but I guarantee you it is not overlooked in Heaven! The key is to not measure yourself with others. Let God do the measuring because He measures for eternity, and that is all that counts.

———————

Father, if I feel insignificant and small, please remind me not to despise the day of small beginnings. Amen!

JOY—IT IS YOUR BIRTHRIGHT

I have told you this so that my joy may be in you and
that your joy may be complete (John 15:11).

———⟨∽⟩———

Joy is the birthright of every child of God. There is a big difference between happiness and real Christian joy. Happiness is based on outward circumstances and can change as often as the weather. Joy is not based on circumstances, but an inward relationship with Jesus Christ. Have you ever been around people who exuded joy in spite of going through a mountain of trouble? You come away from those type of Christians wondering how they do it. The answer is simple. They have developed an inner relationship that provides a source of joy even when their world is falling apart.

As believers we have much to be joyful about. Our sins are forgiven, and we have a heavenly Father who cares for us. In addition to all of the wonderful benefits here on earth, we have a home in Heaven waiting for us when this life is over. While it's true we cannot always rejoice over our circumstances, we can certainly rejoice in our circumstances. The apostle Paul wrote in Philippians 4:4, *"Rejoice in the Lord always. I will say it again: Rejoice!"* Keep in mind when Paul wrote those words he was not sitting in a luxury suite at the Hilton—he was in jail!

In John 15:11 Jesus told His disciples, and us, to have joy. If the disciples had never witnessed Jesus smiling or laughing, they might have wondered, "What kind of joy is He talking about?" It is true He was described as a *"Man of sorrows and acquainted with grief"* (Isaiah 53:3 NKJV), but He was also a Man of joy. Some have argued that to be a real Christian is to be solemn and sad. God wants us to be serious-minded, but I don't know any place in the Bible where we are commanded to have a long face and a miserable attitude. The Christian life is not a funeral, but a celebration!

———⟨∽⟩———

Father, thank You for reminding me today that I can live with abundant joy in spite of my circumstances. Amen!

MONDAY

THE FORGOTTEN HERO

Now give me this hill country that the Lord promised me that day. You yourself heard then that the Anakites were there and their cities were large and fortified, but, the Lord helping me, I will drive them out just as he said (Joshua 14:12).

When you think of heroes in the Bible, Caleb is rarely mentioned. Time and space will not permit retelling the entire story of how Joshua and Caleb were the only two out of twelve spies who gave a positive report of the Promised Land. The sad story records how the majority overruled, and the nation turned back to wander in the wilderness for forty years until the unbelieving generation died, except Moses, Joshua, and Caleb (see Numbers 14).

Joshua 14 details the account of this eighty-five-year-old warrior who came and staked out his inheritance. Without hesitation this forgotten hero said, *"Now therefore give me this mountain!"* Caleb did not ask for something easy. The mountainous territory was inhabited by a race of giants. I'm sure they did not take it kindly for someone to come and drive them off their land.

Caleb was a mountain claimer! He shows us an important lesson, that the unbelief of others need not make us losers as well. Even though Caleb had to experience the same hardships for forty years as the others, it did not deter him from keeping his eye on the prize. Caleb refused to give up just because the majority were wrong. He trusted God that one day he would walk up the side of the mountain shouting, "You better run because I am taking what God has given me!"

Another lesson we can learn from this mountain claimer is age is no road-block to fulfilling your purpose. Eighty-five years is a good age to settle in a warm cabin in the valley. But Caleb asked for a mountain instead. Caleb's attitude was simple—my most fruitful years are not over, because the best is yet to come! How could he say that? Because he trusted in God who gave him the strength to overcome his enemies. No matter the age, we can trust God for the future and become a mountain claimer like our forgotten hero.

Father, thank You for reminding me about the exploits of Caleb. May I demonstrate the same trust in my future that Caleb demonstrated in his. Amen!

WHATEVER

I am not saying this because I am in need, for I have learned to be content whatever the circumstances (Philippians 4:11).

———————◆———◇———◆———————

The *"whatever"* Paul is referring to is not some slang word used to brush off someone you don't want to engage in an intelligent conversation. No, he is giving insight on how to live with the whatevers of life. He sums up his philosophy in one statement: *"For I have learned to be content whatever the circumstances."*

True contentment and inner peace cannot be built on external things or circumstances. We must have something deeper and more satisfying. The trap that many fall into is building their lives on circumstances that have a way of changing and losing their value. The kind of contentment Paul speaks of is not based on the world we see. It is based on our relationship within. There is an old saying: "What life does to us depends on what life finds in us."

The word "content" does not mean to be lazy or complacent. The word Paul used means "contained." It is the thought of being self-sufficient. What he was really saying is, "I don't have to depend on outside things to give me inner peace. I carry my own sufficiency inside of me." Paul said, *"For I have learned."* The meaning of the word is "learn by experience." Learning to be self-sufficient is not a gift given at birth, nor does it come automatically with salvation. We learn by experience. I have discovered the learning process is best taught through troubles, trials, and difficulties. Growth will never come without challenge, and there is no challenge without change. Real change never comes without pain, at least for most of us.

Avoiding difficult circumstances will never lead to contentment. The evidence of real contentment is shown when we do not fall apart when things don't go our way. The inner sufficiency is the power of the Holy Spirit inside us that allows us to say with Paul, *"I can do all things through Christ who strengthens me"* (Philippians 4:13 NKJV). This secret is not just for the super spiritual, but for any believer who wants to learn it!

———————◆———◇———◆———————

Father, I want to learn the secret of real contentment, no matter the cost. Amen!

LEARN TO SOAR

But those who hope in the Lord will renew their strength.
They will soar on wings like eagles; they will run and not grow
weary, they will walk and not be faint (Isaiah 40:31).

Isaiah lived in difficult times. Jerusalem was about to be destroyed by the invading Babylonian army and the days were getting dark and perilous. In the middle of all the confusion and discouragement, he received a life-changing message from God. It was a promise straight from the throne to a nation of people who were ready to give up and quit.

You may be ready to throw up your hands and quit. Maybe life's pressures are so great you feel like you're going to faint, and you want turn in your resignation from life. I have good news—it's time to soar!

Isaiah's promise contains three distinct words of encouragement. *First, God promised to help us soar.* God wants to make eagles out of us who soar above, not chickens confined to the barnyard! Soaring above circumstances does not mean you bury your head in the clouds and ignore them. When you are soaring you can see from Heaven's perspective. Just like an eagle can spot prey from a mile above, so can we. When that happens, things look much smaller and manageable.

Second, God promised to help us to run. No one is exempt from the feeling of weariness. There are times when we have to keep running, whether we want to or not. The boiling pot of pressure keeps our glands working, and puts power into the bloodstream. And we are able to accomplish amazing things physically. That infusion of power is also available to us spiritually. God promises to enable us to run toward our purpose, no matter the pressure.

Third, God promised to help us walk. It is one thing to soar like an eagle or run with exceptional spiritual fuel, but what about walking! Walking is the daily grind. It is strength to walk day by day and not be complacent or bored!

How should we respond to this magnificent promise? The word "renew" means exchange. We exchange our limited ability for His strength. Or, we hand our AA batteries and plug into His nuclear power plant!

Father, I am ready to exchange my feeble strength and soar like an eagle. Amen!

FOLLOW THE LEADER

Lord, I know that people's lives are not their own; it is not for them to direct their steps (Jeremiah 10:23).

When you were little did you ever play the game Follow the Leader? You remember the game don't you? Everyone had a turn. The group would line up behind the chosen leader and follow the person wherever he or she went. You had to match the leader's movement footsteps, or you're out of the game. As we grew older we put away childish games, didn't we? But I have discovered something. The longer we live the more we need to follow the Leader, and it is not a game!

The prophet Jeremiah put it very bluntly: *"It is not for them to direct their steps."* Who can argue with his assessment? Left to ourselves we have a tendency to get lost; but if we allow the Lord to direct us, we will never get off the path toward our divine destiny. I heard it said the reason Moses wandered in the wilderness for forty years is he refused to ask for directions. I'm not so sure about that, but the truth is we don't like to ask God for guidance when we feel we are perfectly capable of guiding ourselves. It is only when we end up in a ditch on the side of the road that we realize how inefficient we are.

Recognizing our own limitations is an important first step in allowing God's guidance. It takes trust to allow guidance. Proverbs 3:5-6 says: *"Trust in the Lord with all your heart and lean not on your own understanding; in all your ways submit to him, and he will make your paths straight."* Asking for guidance is not something new. When we need legal advice we go to a lawyer. If we need medical advice, we go to a doctor. And if we need financial advice, we go to a banker.

God communicates His guidance through His Word and the indwelling Holy Spirit. As we study the Word with a prayerful attitude, we discover the Holy Spirit will enable us to "hear" God's leadership. If you find you're on the wrong road, don't be afraid to pull over and ask for directions!

Father, thank You for Your guidance. I don't want to end up in a ditch. Amen!

PAIN HAS PURPOSE

I consider that our present sufferings are not worth comparing with the glory that will be revealed in us (Romans 8:18).

———————————◆◆◆———————————

I have not met one person who deliberately looks for pain. My experience is we will do anything and everything to avoid it. If you are not sure about that, just watch a child when told it's time for the six-month checkup at the dentist. Once the screaming and crying stops, the little angel will tell you he or she is not going. The underlying refusal is simple—this could be a painful experience.

Thomas Jefferson was a brilliant thinker and a founding father of the country. He once wrote a letter to his friend, Mrs. Cosway, and in it he wrote, "The art of life is the avoiding of pain." On first reading it appears to be a true statement. But when you investigate his life, Thomas Jefferson paid a huge, painful price to help set free the struggling colonies from England. Every patriot experienced loss and pain. Personal experience teaches the impossibility of Jefferson's statement. If we ran from pain, we would never mature. Pain has a royal purpose if allowed to do its work. The greatest life lessons I have learned have come through the cauldron of pain.

God does not promise to remove us from pain, or even painful situations. What He does promise is to transform it and use it for eternal purposes. I do not believe God deliberately makes us suffer for His amusement. There are many who turn against God when they go through suffering, but this need not be so. Instead of allowing pain to widen the gap in our fellowship with God, we need to allow pain to draw us closer (see Philippians 3:10).

The apostle Paul knew the ministry of pain. He confessed a thorn in the flesh and did what any Christian would do—he prayed for the pain to be removed (see 2 Corinthians 12:7-10). God did answer Paul's prayer, but not the way he expected. God gave him the grace to transform his weakness into strength, and suffering into glory. He will do no less for you and me!

———————————◆◆◆———————————

Father, glorify Your name through my pain. Help me to learn the lessons You want me to learn. Amen!

TRUTH AND TIME

MONDAY

ONE THING MONEY CAN'T BUY

For it is by grace you have been saved, through faith—
and this is not from yourselves, it is the gift of God—not by
works, so that no one can boast (Ephesians 2:8-9).

Money can buy many things. In today's culture almost anything and everything is in reach, so long as you have the cash or credit to pay for it. But the apostle Paul made it clear there is one thing money cannot buy. It is something that everyone needs, but does not deserve. And no amount of negotiation will give it to you. What am I talking about? One simple word—*grace!*

One definition of grace that fits so beautifully is, "Grace is something that we need but do not deserve." Jesus demonstrated grace throughout His ministry. If you examine His teachings, you will find that almost every parable He told centered on the grace of God. One reason why the religious crowd was so adamantly against Him was His teaching on grace.

In the parable of the prodigal son, the word "grace" does not appear, but the word "worthy" does. *"I am no longer worthy to be called your son; make me like one of your hired servants"* (Luke 15:19). I wonder what would have happened if the young son's father had agreed to his request? I venture to say Jesus would have never told the story. It would not have been worth the time. There is no doubt the most wonderful word the young prodigal heard from his father's lips was the word "son." His father gave him what he needed, not what he deserved!

Of course the best demonstration of grace is seen at the cross. Jesus willingly gave Himself for the sins of the entire world. The cross was the culmination of grace. When Jesus prayed, *"Father, forgive them, for they know not what they do."* He verbalized the essence of grace. He could have prayed, "Father, don't give them what they deserve, but what they need!"

What would it mean for us if we used grace as the guiding principle for all that we do? Divorce courts would be empty, health problems would disappear, and broken relationships would be repaired. *Don't try to buy it, you can't—just enjoy it!*

Father, thank You for giving me something I did not deserve. I rejoice in Your grace today. Amen!

HALF-BAKED OR FULLY COOKED

Ephraim mixes with the nations; Ephraim is a
flat loaf not turned over (Hosea 7:8).

It appears God had a hard time with the tribe Ephraim. The prophet Hosea compared the tribe of Ephraim to a cake of bread that was placed on the hot coals, but was never turned over. It was edible, but it wasn't very good. Uncooked dough is never pleasant!

Ephraim is a perfect example of being "half-baked." They were more interested in their idols than following after God. On more than one occasion they promised obedience, but only made it halfway. It is a sad commentary to read how much they were corrupted. They failed miserably. They stopped short and never realized that partial obedience is still disobedience!

There are many who have given their lives to Christ, but sadly have squandered their talents and gifting by only making it halfway to their purpose in God. To know why you are put on planet Earth is the most wonderful discovery a person can make. But knowing your purpose and actually walking in your purpose are two different things. Giving "lip service" to God has become a popular indoor sport. It is easy to go to church and sing, "Oh how I love Jesus," but quite another thing when Monday morning rolls around. A half-baked attitude will lead to the attitude of the "rich young ruler" who turned away in sadness because the love of things was more important than obedience to God. In his heart he knew what he wanted, but was not willing to go all the way.

God is not looking for the tribe of Ephraim today. He is looking for people who choose to live their lives "on purpose" with a plan to succeed. It is important to remember when dough goes into the oven it does not become a delicious loaf of bread until it is fully cooked at the right temperature. Staying in the heat may sound painful, but it is the only way for the process to work!

Make a choice to come out of the oven satisfying and delicious. Whatever you do, don't become a half-baked believer.

Father, I thank You for caring enough about me to keep the temperature just right. Help me never to become half-baked. Amen!

JUST RELAX ALREADY!

And give relief to you who are troubled, and to us as well (2 Thessalonians 1:7).

———————————◦◦———————————

No one is immune from stress and anxiety. The believers to whom Paul was writing had been under stress and pressure for a long period of time. Bible scholars tell us the assaults and persecution leveled against them was unrelenting. They were flat-out tired and exhausted from the constant negative bombardment. Paul used an interesting word to describe their circumstances. The word *"troubled"* is a strong word to signify the intensity of the conflict. It is a word used to describe "crushing" with great intense pressure. Have you ever seen grapes being crushed in a winepress? If so, you get the idea.

When Paul wrote his words of encouragement they may have thought he lost his mind. After all, who can rest and relax with so much going on? You may feel like the believers in Thessalonica. It could be hardship due to a sick family member, your business coming apart at the seams, or a teenager in rebellion. Whatever the pressure may be, it is encouraging to know that God offers rest and relief to all of us.

The definition of the word "rest" comes from a Greek word that means to "let up, relax, to stop being stressed, or find relief." One Greek scholar described the word as used in the Greek culture to denote the release of a bowstring that has been under great pressure. The issue is not if trouble and pressure will come, but simply *when.* When dealing with the pressures of life, the last thing we want to hear is someone say, "Why don't you take a few days away from the stress and clear your mind?" Instead of thinking it's irresponsible to relax, why not take Paul's counsel and just chill for a while. The whole world will not fall apart when you take a break. After all, the problems and the stress will still be right where you left them!

Paul recognized the importance of stepping away to get a clear view of the difficulties and was giving them permission to relax. Why would he do that? Sometimes it's helpful for someone outside of our immediate circumstances to look at us and say, *"Just relax already!"*

———————————◦◦———————————

Father, help me never to allow the pressures of life to rob me of learning how to rest in You. Amen!

WHAT TIME IS IT?

*But I trust in you, Lord; I say, "You are my God." My times
are in your hands; deliver me from the hands of my enemies,
from those who pursue me* (Psalm 31:14-15).

"I DON'T HAVE TIME!" How many times have we heard that, or even
said it ourselves? In our fast-paced society time has become a major issue. There
are many things you can do with time—you can kill it, waste it, or just misuse
it. One thing you can't do is get it back. I suggest the best thing we can do with
our time is to surrender it—not to other people, work or bad habits, but to the
lordship of Christ.

What would happen if we surrendered our time to God instead of asking
Him to be satisfied with the leftovers? It is important to realize that we are just
stewards and not owners. Being stewards is a realization God owns our time
just like everything else. All of us—no exceptions—need help with time management. Not allowing God to give us direction in the important area of time
creates a life of confusion. No one wakes up every day and declares, "I think
today I will waste as much time as possible!"

When it comes to time management, think about two instruments we are
familiar with: a compass and a clock. Both are important, and both have very
different purposes. When we surrender our time management to the lordship of
Christ, we are living by a compass rather than being controlled by a clock.

If you want to know the direction you're going, look to the compass. If you
want to know the duration of a task, look to the clock. The first gives vision
and perspective, while the other measures duration. One determines effectiveness, while the other determines efficiency. Each has an important place, but the
compass must always come before the clock—*effectiveness before efficiency*. The
compass will always take priority over a clock!

What's the secret? Give your first minutes to God every day, and then commit the remainder of the day to His lordship. An amazing thing will happen.
The day will become more effective *and* efficient.

*Father, I surrender my time to Your lordship. Help me focus on the compass not the
clock. Amen!*

SET FREE!

Who gave himself for us to redeem us from all wickedness and to purify for himself a people that are his very own, eager to do what is good (Titus 2:14).

———————————

The word "redeem" is without a doubt one of the most important words used in the entire Bible. Why? It sums up in one word everything Christ has accomplished for believers. None of the benefits or privileges of a Christian would be possible without the word "redeem."

The imagery is astounding. Paul often used images from his culture to describe the believer. We may not want to entertain even the thought of a slave being auctioned in a slave market, but the cost of our redemption is beautifully described in the word "redeem."

"Redeem" describes the purchase of a slave from the slave market. Throughout the Roman Empire purchasing slaves was a lively business. Before a potential buyer would negotiate a purchase price, he would inspect and carefully examine his future property. This would include checking the slave to see if he was physically fit and in proper condition to handle a heavy workload. After careful inspection it was time to negotiate the purchase price with the slave auctioneer. Once the price was settled the slave was sent away with his new owner who then could treat his "property" as he wished.

A little-known fact is that some compassionate individuals would go into the slave market to purchase slaves for the purpose of liberation and freedom. The payment was nothing more than a ransom in order to obtain freedom for slaves.

What has all this to do with Christians? Our freedom from the power of sin and satan was expensive! Jesus came into the world—the devil's marketplace—looking for us. Jesus did not negotiate to get a lower price for our redemption. No, a thousand times no! He willingly paid the most expensive price ever paid for a slave. His own blood!

Jesus shed His own blood, guaranteeing our freedom and deliverance. *"He did not enter by means of the blood of goats and calves; but he entered the Most Holy Place once for all by his own blood, thus obtaining eternal redemption"* (Hebrews 9:12).

———————————

Father, thank You for loving me so much that You sent Your Son to go into the devil's slave market to pay the price for my redemption. Amen!

MONDAY

THAT'S THE TRUTH!

*"You are a king, then!" said Pilate. Jesus answered, "You say that
I am a king. In fact, the reason I was born and came into the
world is to testify to the truth. Everyone on the side of truth listens
to me." "What is truth?" retorted Pilate* (John 18:37-38).

Pilate did not ask a new question when he asked Jesus, *"What is truth?"* He simply echoed the same questions that have been haunting humankind since the beginning of time. Why am I here? What is my purpose on planet Earth? How do I make an impact in life, and what does it matter if I fail? Some never find the answer to those questions and end up living lives of quiet desperation. Once Jesus is declared Lord of a person's life, truth incarnate takes up residence.

Pilate wanted to know the truth. I wonder if he looked at Jesus standing before him and thought, "What truth could Jesus possibly testify to that would hold any meaning for me?" Jesus stood before him as a common criminal. He was betrayed by His friends, nearly beaten to death, and about to be nailed to a cross. By outward appearance Jesus would be the last one to give this powerful man the truth.

Jesus knew His purpose in life as He marched toward it with a laser focus. His death testified to the tragic *truth* of humankind's rebellion against God. As He hung on the cross He testified to the *truth* of God's eternal love for all people. His resurrection testified to the truth that satan and sin could no longer hold humankind in bondage—*that's the truth!*

You and I have the awesome privilege to give evidence to the power of the truth every day. Because He set us free we can now live lives on purpose guided by the truth of God's Word. We do not have to struggle or wander aimlessly wondering if we have been created with a purpose. To know Jesus is to know purpose. To know Jesus is to know joy and freedom. To know Jesus is to know the *Truth!*

Father, I acknowledge that You are the Source of truth. I praise You that my life is guided by the light of Your Word and the indwelling Holy Spirit. Amen!

A BALANCED LIFE

And Jesus grew in wisdom and stature, and in favor with God and man (Luke 2:52).

Jesus was a perfect model when it came to living a balanced life. As you consider His life and ministry, you discover that Jesus was under constant scrutiny and pressure. He was pursued by friend and foe alike. Yet, through it all He never seemed to be in a hurry. He never threw up His hands in disbelief. And, He was never surprised by circumstances. He lived a well-rounded life in every area—physically, spiritually, intellectually, and socially. If you are looking for a role model of a well-balanced life, look no further, consider Jesus!

A balanced life should exhibit some of the same characteristics as demonstrated by Jesus. All areas of life are where they should be, and as they ought to be. A life of peace, wholeness, and order are common traits of a well-balanced, well-thought-out life. In our hurry, worry, and bury culture, one of the most difficult challenges is to allow the proper time management to each area. Living in chaos and confusion seem to be the rule and not the exception.

Three important questions:

1. How much time have you spent over the past twelve months on intellectual growth? When was the last time you engaged in something that stimulated your mind, or does that seem boring to you?

2. Is prayer and Bible study a burden or a joy? Making time to balance our intimacy with God is one of life's greatest obstacles to living a well-rounded life. There is an old saying, "If you're too busy to make time with God, you have more to do than He ever intended you to do!"

3. How about physical and personal maintenance? I'm not talking about just losing weight, I'm talking about taking care of the "temple" (your body), the residence of the Holy Spirit. Personal maintenance also includes time for family, friends, and relationship building.

The psalmist said it best in Psalm 46:10, *"He says, 'Be still, and know that I am God; I will be exalted among the nations, I will be exalted in the earth.'"*

Father, help me to take the necessary steps to bring balance, peace, and harmony to my life. Amen!

DEAL WITH DISTRACTIONS

The Pharisees came and began to question Jesus. To test him, they asked him for a sign from heaven. He sighed deeply and said, "Why does this generation ask for a sign? Truly I tell you, no sign will be given to it" (Mark 8:11-12).

If you find yourself spending most of your time going from one crisis to another, you are not alone. Putting out little "fires" will eventually add up to one giant blaze that will distract us from accomplishing our major goals and purposes. If we don't get a handle on distractions, we will come to the end of the day realizing we haven't made any progress at all.

Jesus was constantly interrupted. It would be fair to say He was familiar with distractions, but He knew how to handle them. On one occasion the disciples even interrupted His prayer time. On another, the multitudes hunted them down and begged Him for food. Much of His ministry centered on helping people, and no doubt He wanted to provide healing and forgiveness for all. Jesus was not afraid of distractions because there were times when He used them as an integral part of His ministry.

Still, there were times when He refused to be distracted. When the religious crowd (Pharisees) demanded signs, Jesus simply said *NO!* He could have allowed the distraction and provided a miraculous sign, but He learned to set boundaries for His ministry. He did not come to put on a dazzling show for the unbeliever, but for those who were sick and bound up in sin. He came to set the prisoner free, not to be the centerpiece of a sideshow!

Having the courage to say *NO* to distractions that prove fruitless is something we all need to learn. Of course we should stay sensitive to God's plan and allow the Holy Spirit to show us what is important and what is necessary. Yes, little distractions can move us forward in our purpose, but we must be careful not to allow them to rob us of our time. Learn from Jesus! We must keep our eyes on the big picture. Ask the Lord for wisdom. Why? Because He will teach us how to balance even the distractions of life (see James 1:5-8).

Father, give me the wisdom to know what to do when I am distracted from Your purpose. Amen!

NO FAKES ALLOWED

For the mouth speaks what the heart is full of (Luke 6:45).

Nobody likes a fake. Entire industries have sprung up with the sole purpose of fooling an unsuspecting public. Sadly, thousands of dollars have been and will be spent on fake items.

Recently an article appeared in a popular magazine that highlighted the point:

> For centuries genuine pearls commanded a high price because of their scarcity. Great quantities of oysters had to be examined before a few could be found that contained the coveted treasures. Then suddenly the market became flooded with them. After some investigation, the mystery of the abundant supply was revealed. Enterprising individuals had discovered that if a foreign object is lodged in an oyster's tender flesh, the oyster would form a glistening pearl around the source of discomfort. Deciding to help nature along, these people artificially induced the process by inserting irritants such as tiny beads and buckshot into the shells. When the pearls had formed, they were carefully harvested. Wealthy patrons became suspicious, however, and insisted that the lustrous jewels be subjected to special tests. Although outwardly they seemed perfect, the x-ray showed their impurity. They had "false hearts" of lead or glass![10]

Like fake pearls, people have the ability to be one thing on the outside while being something completely different on the inside. Just like when the fakes were put under the all-knowing eye of the x-ray, the legitimate will eventually be revealed. For us, the x-ray examination may come in the form of a crisis, an unkind word, or just some careless driver cutting us off in traffic.

Jesus said, *"The mouth speaks what the heart is full of."* Sooner or later our outward behavior will flood out any claims we make about our genuineness. Whatever is on the inside, when squeezed, will come out of our mouth. One of the fastest ways to convince unbelievers that Christianity is "fake" is when our words and our actions don't match! Let's ask the Holy Spirit to help our words and our actions say the same thing.

Father, help me to know when my actions and attitudes do not line up with Your Word. I choose to be real and not a fake. Amen!

FINISH WHAT YOU START

I have fought the good fight, I have finished the race,
I have kept the faith (2 Timothy 4:7).

Every long-distance runner knows what it is like to get their "second wind." When they hit the wall, everything inside of them is screaming, "QUIT before you drop dead!" Seasoned runners know there is a critical time in the race when something inside of them keeps pushing them toward the finish line.

In 1968 the Olympics were held in Mexico City. The marathon is normally the final event of an exhausting two weeks. On this particular day the Olympic stadium was packed and the first runner, an Ethiopian, entered the stadium. He crossed the finish line to a standing ovation from the crowd. Way back in the field is another runner from Tanzania. His name is John Stephen Akwhari. He was dead last. During the race he experienced serious leg injuries and even though race officials wanted him to retire he refused. With his knee bandaged, he picked himself up and hobbled the remaining 12 km to the finish line. An hour after the winner had been declared this young man from Tanzania entered the stadium. All but a few thousand of the crowd had gone home. Crossing the finish line, he collapsed. It was one of the most heroic efforts of Olympic history. Afterward, when asked by a reporter why he had not dropped out he stated, "My country did not send me 10,000 miles just to start the race; they sent me to finish the race!"[11]

In the closing days of his earthly life and ministry the apostle Paul declared to young Timothy, *"I have accomplished every goal God has given me."* Translated into our language Paul was saying, *"I finished what I started!"* Christianity is filled with many who start the race, but somewhere along the way have fallen off track. No statues or prizes are ever handed out to those who quit, only to those who finish. The Christian life is a long-distance marathon, not a 110-meter sprint. Each of us have a race to run. Let's make up our mind to finish strong!

Father, thank You for the many examples in life and the Bible of those who would not quit. Give me the courage to finish strong. Amen!

A Confident Leader

Jesus answered, "Even if I testify on my own behalf, my testimony is valid, for I know where I came from and where I am going. But you have no idea where I come from or where I am going (John 8:14).

Without a doubt Jesus was a confident leader. All you have to do is listen to His words and watch His actions, which tell you here is a leader who functioned in His purpose. Being a confident leader is much more than having a "title." It is learning how to get the job done, even if the title is not given.

What made Jesus a confident leader? A few observations:

1. *Jesus' words and actions matched up.* "I know who I am, I know where I am going, and I know how to get there" are statements that exude vision and clarity. The central issue for confident leaders is credibility. Credibility is not related to how loudly we talk, but do our actions and attitude match. Jesus fed the multitudes, healed the sick, taught to scholars, and forgave sinners. But the Pharisees continued to challenge His credibility. Jesus did not back up. He simply stated where He came from and why He was here. He never apologized for who He was!

2. *Jesus gave the people a clear choice.* Jesus spent very little time (if any at all) trying to convince the doubters to follow Him. He did not focus His attention on those who rejected His call to redemption. He turned His attention to those who believed and encouraged them, *"To the Jews who had believed him, Jesus said, 'If you hold to my teaching, you are really my disciples. Then you will know the truth, and the truth will set you free'"* (John 8:31-32).

3. *Jesus used confidence and credibility to carry out leadership functions.* It is true the majority of the religious crowd rejected Jesus. But He was successful in leading some to freedom from the

condemnation of the law. He never allowed the negative to take away from His overall purpose—to call sinners to salvation.

There is nothing more attractive than a confident and credible leader. People are hungry for leaders who not only exude confidence, but demonstrate credibility. It is time to let our "walk" and our "talk" line up!

Father, help me to be a confident and credible leader who others want to follow. Amen!

GET A GRIP

*Like a city whose walls are broken through is a person
who lacks self-control* (Proverbs 25:28).

───────────────

A very wise man once said, "The first victory that successful people achieve or win is the victory over themselves." He was talking about self-control. Self-control is like the banks of a river that keep the powerful water running in the right direction—toward your purpose.

In Old Testament days, cities were only safe because of their walls. What the writer of Proverbs is saying is the moment we lose self-control we are like a city without any kind of protection. Broken-down walls left the city open to every kind of enemy—natural as well as human.

The Greek word for self-control means "to get a hold of" or "to get a grip on." It literally means to get your hands on something until you are in control of it. Maybe it's time for us to tighten our grip on areas that have slowly slipped away.

Three keys to self-control:

1. *Look in the mirror.* The issue of self-control is not looking at some-one else. No doubt we can think of someone who needs to work on self-control, and we would probably be right. It is always easier to point out someone else's lack of discipline than to stare at the person in the mirror.

2. *Start early.* Self-control is the first lesson that ought to be learned, but sad to say it is usually the last. It is imperative we teach our children the great character essential of self-control. It is essential to begin the development of self-control in a small way today in order to be disciplined in a big way tomorrow!

3. *Start today.* When is the best time to get control of our lives? Today, not tomorrow, is always the best time to start. Procrastination is a vision stealer, dream robber, and a destiny killer. The late, great television host Jack Parr said it best, "Looking back, my life seems to be one long obstacle course...with me as the chief obstacle!" Don't delay—get a grip!

───────────────

Father, help me to not lose my grip on the things that are most important. Amen!

WHO'S TO BLAME?

The man said, "The woman you put here with me—she gave me some fruit from the tree, and I ate it." Then the Lord God said to the woman, "What is this you have done?" The woman said, "The serpent deceived me, and I ate" (Genesis 3:12-13).

We all know the story of Adam and Eve. No doubt, they invented the blame game. Blaming someone else for your failure is nothing new. If you're not sure, all you have to do is go back to the Garden of Eden and read how Adam and Eve started the whole thing. Instead of taking personal responsibility, what did they do? They started blaming each other. Eve blamed the snake. Adam blamed Eve. And the snake slithered away saying, "Don't blame me, all I did was make a few suggestions!"

We are living in a culture of *"Don't blame me, I'm not responsible for this."* The trap of avoiding personal responsibility can be fatal to the success of our family, friends, and finances. As one leadership expert said: "The man who can smile when things go wrong has thought of someone else he can blame it on!" Playing the blame game will always come full circle back to the one who started it.

A sure way to stop the madness is to learn how to take responsibility for our own actions. Responsibility always embraces self-reliance, effectiveness, faithfulness, and capability. In essence, responsibility is simply the ability to respond. If we are constantly blaming someone else for past failures, we are going backward not forward. The past will always highlight your failures, while the future tends to be filled with big dreams and powerful vision.

You cannot move toward tomorrow's success while looking in the rearview mirror! When tomorrow arrives it is renamed today. If you have not prepared for your future, your today will look much like your yesterday. A good measure of success is not how many people we can blame, but how many times we get back up after being knocked down!

Father, help me to never play the blame game. My desire is to take responsibility for my actions. Amen!

A FISH OUT OF WATER

*I have considered my ways and have turned my
steps to your statutes* (Psalm 119:59).

———————————

Do you sometimes feel like a fish out of water? No matter how beautiful you make it, fish were not created to live on your living room floor. Why? It is a foreign environment that will lead to death! Today there are millions of people walking around like fish out of water. They make it through the day barely surviving and breathing, and they just don't know why they're still hanging around on planet Earth.

Your prolonged dissatisfaction, God-given gifts, passions, and the voices of others could be telling you that you were created for a different environment. And like fish trying to live on your living room floor, you feel your current environment is poison. God created a perfect atmosphere for you. So if you're having trouble breathing, maybe it's time to jump back in the water and breathe again with purpose. For fish, water is indispensable for life; and for you, so is your divine purpose.

If you are having trouble breathing in your current environment, *listen up:*

Listen to that still, small voice. It may be the Holy Spirit telling you to wake up and consider swimming in a better environment so your gifts and talents can shine. Contrary to popular belief, dissatisfaction with current circumstances is not always a bad thing.

Listen to what others are saying to you and about you. Just as an inner dissatisfaction can be a road sign to show your purpose, listening to what others say about your gifts can do the same. It is quite possible other people are noticing things that you are missing. Pay attention, sometimes they may be right!

Listen to your gifts and passion. All of us—yes, even you—have the seed of purpose planted inside. For the seed to grow it must be fertilized with patience and harvested for use. When passion and talent get together you are well on your way to the proper environment that will explode into a lifetime of fulfillment.

———————————

Father, give me Your wisdom to consider my ways. My greatest desire is to know the seeds of purpose are being fulfilled in my life. Amen!

GOD'S EQUATION FOR SUCCESS

As the body without the spirit is dead, so faith without deeds is dead (James 2:26).

There is a popular opinion that has been going around for decades, and it goes like this: "If you work hard you must not have faith." The Bible makes it perfectly clear believers need to be people who put faith into action. James 2:17 says, *"In the same way, faith by itself, if it is not accompanied by action, is dead."* A person who says they have faith but no action to back it up is like a bird with wings but no feet, or a baseball player with no arms!

To rise above the level of mediocrity—where most people live—never happens accidentally. It is always a result of faith combined with hard work. Real faith is more than just talking about something expecting results. Bible faith is an "action" word. The meaning of the word "faith" as used in the Bible is both a noun and a verb. It is actually talking about putting feet under our words. It's one thing to have fantastic dreams and goals while taking a shower in the morning, but successful people are the ones who dry off, put on their clothes, and go to work!

Work is not a curse! It is not some abstract concept. The word "work" appears in the Bible 564 times. Over the years hard work has taken a bad rap, especially among believers. God was the prime source of creation and became the first worker. As a matter of fact, He worked so hard He rested on the seventh day! I am of the opinion God is looking for busy people who are willing to work toward their dreams. Combining real faith and hard work is God's equation for success.

William Booth, the founder of the Salvation Army, had this to say about faith and works: "Faith and works should travel side-by-side, step answering to step, like the legs of men walking. First faith, and then works; and then faith again, and then works again—until they can scarcely distinguish which is the one and which is the other."

Father, I know that my faith and works have to go hand in hand. Help me to be an example to others. Amen!

MONDAY

IT'S BETWEEN YOUR EARS

For he is the kind of person who is always thinking about the cost. "Eat and drink," he says to you, but his heart is not with you (Proverbs 23:7).

It is a proven fact that whatever we think, we will eventually become. James teaches in his epistle if we need wisdom we can ask for it, but he gives a solemn warning about being double-minded: *"But when you ask, you must believe and not doubt, because the one who doubts is like a wave of the sea, blown and tossed by the wind. That person should not expect to receive anything from the Lord. Such a person is double-minded and unstable in all they do"* (James 1:6-8).

Successful leaders know how to unlock the power of their minds. They also know the head has more use than a place to hang their hat! Spending time on negative thoughts and emotions will never generate the mind power to create an atmosphere of success. As the old saying goes, *"Garbage in, garbage out."* If David thought defeat instead of victory, Goliath would have stomped him into proverbial dust!

God has given us a marvelous creation called the human brain. Scientists tell us we have barely understood or scratched the surface when it comes to tapping into this God-given miracle of creation. To live a life of purpose in today's culture means we must be a "cut above" when it comes to using all available resources. When God saved us, He did not expect us to unscrew our heads and throw away our brains! Our brains are the command center that controls everything we do. It determines how we think, act, and feel. When our brains are working at peak performance, it allows us to be our best because it controls the rest!

I believe Martin Luther King Jr. had it right when he said, "Rarely do we find men who willingly engage in hard, solid thinking. There is almost universal quest for easy answers and half-baked solutions. Nothing pains some people more than having to think."

It is all right between our ears. *Think about it!*

Father, thank You for giving me this wonderful gift. May I never take for granted the power of thought. Amen!

COOL IT

The one who has knowledge uses words with restraint, and whoever has understanding is even-tempered (Proverbs 17:27).

———❦———

No one is immune from the emotion of anger. It would be a fair statement to say that most of us get "hot under the collar" from time to time. Unresolved anger has the ability to destroy personal happiness, blow up relationships, and cause undue hardships for a moment or a lifetime.

Marriage expert Dr. Gary Smalley said, "Anger is the number one cause of divorce and the destruction of personal relationships of all kinds." Or as author and humorist Mark Twain said, "Anger is an acid that can do more harm to the vessel in which it is stored than to anything on which it is poured."

Solomon, the wisest man who ever lived, had much to say about the destructive influence of explosive anger (see Proverbs 14:29; 15:1; 16:32; 19:19). He summed up his thoughts on anger and said, *"The wise turn away anger"* (Proverbs 29:8). The sad truth, even among those of us who are believers, is turning away from anger can be very difficult. God desires us to be *"wise"* when it comes to dealing with this powerful emotion.

A recurring theme found in Proverbs is encouragement for us to slow down: *"Whoever is patient has great understanding, but one who is quick-tempered displays folly"* (Proverbs 14:29). Dealing with anger is always a matter of choice. Whether it is suppressed anger or the constant outburst of anger, you can choose to be a victim or victorious. Sometimes the best way to stop the nuclear explosion of rage is to simply stop talking and remove yourself physically from the detonator, the source of your anger.

Allowing anger to live in our hearts is like wearing a stick of dynamite around our necks. It doesn't take much for someone to strike a match of wrong words or actions to set off an explosion. Solomon's advice is simple—run as fast as you can to get away from it, don't wear it around your neck, and whatever you do when confronted with it, remember to handle with care, it could blow up in your face!

———❦———

Father, thank You for giving me wisdom from Your Word. Help me to be wise, not a wise guy. Amen!

BORN TO CHOOSE

You did not choose me, but I chose you and appointed you so that you might go and bear fruit—fruit that will last—and so that whatever you ask in my name the Father will give you (John 15:16).

———————————————————

The late, great Ray Charles had a popular hit song in the 1960s that summed up the feeling of an entire generation. The song was entitled *Born to Lose.* The first line summed it up: "Born to lose, I have lived my life in vain, every dream has only brought me pain." The song, although talking about lost love, could well describe the attitude of many. If you were alive in those days you could not escape it—from T-shirts to tattoos it was everywhere.

The fact is: you were not born a loser or for that matter a winner—but a chooser! God chose you and pursued you or you would not be a believer today. God set you up to find Him. And now that you are His, you need to know that He has a purpose and a plan for you. The Bible says, *"For I know the plans I have for you," declares the Lord, "plans to prosper you and not to harm you, plans to give you hope and a future"* (Jeremiah 29:11).

What does the Lord require? Simply this, *choose* to respond to His grace. Set your sails each day and God will send the wind of His grace to fill those sails and give you the direction you need. Seeking first the kingdom of God is in reality choosing to please Him in all that you do.

Making bad choices is all too common, even among believers. Choosing to live outside of God's plan creates untold and unnecessary hardships. Make a choice to submit to the wise counsel of God's Word and to those whom God has placed in your life to give counsel and wisdom. The result? One day at a time, one choice at a time, one decision at a time, choose what aligns with His choice for you. The result? Everything starts working together for the good of His purpose and calling for your life. Even the places where you have missed it!

Remember, God has the power to work it all out for His divine purpose and for your blessing!

Father, my greatest desire is to make the right choices every single day. Thank You for giving me a choice—and I choose YOU. Amen!

WORRY—AN INSIDE JOB

Do not be anxious about anything, but in every situation, by prayer and petition, with thanksgiving, present your requests to God (Philippians 4:6).

We are in a war! It is a war of the mind. It is a war against stress and tension brought on by worry. Worry is one of the main reasons we never reach the next level of our purpose. Worry is a killer, both spiritually and physically. Dr. Charles Mayo of the Mayo Clinic said, "Worry affects the circulation, the heart, the glands and the whole nervous system. I have never known a man who died from overwork, but many who died from stress."

The Greek word translated "anxious" in Philippians 4:6 means to be "pulled in different directions." The old English root from which we get the word "worry" means to "strangle." In other words, our hopes and dreams (vision) pull us in one direction, and our worries pull us in the opposite direction. If you have ever found yourself in that state of mind, you know it can almost strangle you! Worry is an inside job, and it takes more than someone saying, "Don't worry about it" to keep us from worrying.

In Matthew 6 Jesus said seven times in ten verses, *"Don't worry."* I think He is trying to tell us something, don't you? Why? After careful study of the Word of God I have concluded worry is a sin. It is a sin because it *distrusts* God's Word. It is *detrimental* to God's temple (your body), and it *destroys* peace of mind and heart.

Worry and peace cannot coexist. Real peace is not the absence of conflict. Go to a graveyard, it is very peaceful, but that is not the kind of peace the Holy Spirit gives. The biblical concept of peace is "all things are as they should be."

His greatest desire is to guard our hearts and minds from the things that rob us of our joy, security, and most of all peace of mind: *"And the peace of God, which transcends all understanding, will guard your hearts and your minds in Christ Jesus"* (Philippians 4:7). We have the peace of God to *guard* us, and the God of peace to *guide* us. What more could we ask for?

Father, guard my mind from worry and guide me with Your peace. Protect my heart from being strangled with worry. Amen!

THE CURE FOR SPIRITUAL BOREDOM

*Do not merely listen to the word, and so deceive
yourselves. Do what it says* (James 1:22).

———————— ⌇ ————————

Have you ever been spiritually bored—with church, or with your spiritual life? If the answer is "Yes, I do get bored with my spiritual life from time to time, but I hate to admit it," you are not alone. James points to the one primary reason why people get bored. It is a simple explanation: Gaining biblical knowledge without application will always lead to spiritual boredom—every single time!

You go to church and listen to sermons week after week without ever taking any action to apply what you've heard. Does this scenario sound vaguely familiar? If so, I can guarantee you there will come a point when you have heard so much you become sick of hearing it. Instead of being excited about what you might receive from the Lord, you think, "Oh no, please not another sermon!"

God's Word is meant to be acted upon, not just listened to. The center of the problem is not church, your pastor, or the kind of preaching you hear. The root of the problem is not with any of those things, no, the problem is you! It is not enough to attend church every time the door is opened. Reading books, listening to tapes and watching Christian television are good things, but will never replace the application of the Word of God.

The answer is simple. Applying the Word you already know will motivate you to have a serious prayer life, which will require great discipline. Walking in the kind of obedience expected by God will take every ounce of focus and energy you can muster. In other words, you will be so busy trying to obey what you've already heard you will never have time to be bored!

Make a decision today not to allow spiritual boredom to overtake you. Determine to put into practice things you already know to be true from the Word of God.

———————— ⌇ ————————

Father, help me to become a doer of the Word and not a hearer only. Forgive me for the times I have heard Your Word and failed to walk out the truth. Amen!

FACING FAILURE

Now I want you to know, brothers and sisters, that what has happened to me has actually served to advance the gospel. As a result, it has become clear throughout the whole palace guard and to everyone else that I am in chains for Christ (Philippians 1:12-13).

God has put a craving in us for adventure. To get out of the boat and try different things has been put in our heart by the One who created us. God is not looking for ability, but availability. God not only sees where we are, but what we can be by His power working through us. Of course, the possibility of failure has stopped many from moving to the next level. But it is important to remember failure is not fatal, nor final. Failure, properly viewed, can be a stepping stone to greatness.

The apostle Paul is a classic example of someone who learned how to deal with the possibility of failure. Everything about his experience spelled failure, but he turned them into success. How did he do it? He was realistic about his situation. *"That what has happened to me has actually served to advance the gospel."* He knew there was going to be opposition and yet refused to be intimidated. He faced the possibility of failure head-on and turned it around. He focused on his desire to share the gospel and not on his potential for failure!

If you spend all of your time and energy worrying about not failing, you will increase your chances of doing the very thing you don't want to do. Stop worrying about things that are out of your control. Paul knew his situation was hard and filled with danger, but all he cared about were others. He kept his eyes off himself and realized that many in the palace were being saved. Paul rejoiced in the fact that Christ's message was being preached!

Paul viewed his circumstance as a fresh opportunity, not a final defeat. By our standard of success Paul was in line to receive the failure of the year award, but in each case he faced failure as an opportunity to keep moving forward.

Father, help me to understand when things are hard it is not time to throw in the towel. Give me the strength and courage to keep moving forward. Amen!

TUESDAY

THE POWER OF ONE

He replied, "Whether he is a sinner or not, I don't know. One thing I do know. I was blind but now I see!" (John 9:25)

What can one person do? Not much alone, but when coupled with the power of Christ entire nations can be influenced to see the glorious light of the gospel. When Paul stated in Philippians 4:13 (NKJV), *"I can do all things through Christ who strengthens me,"* he was not talking about an abstract concept or a slogan to pin on the wall. No, it was a living dynamic truth he learned by experience!

Consider one person who shook nations by the name of D. L. Moody:

> Dwight Lyman Moody lived toward the end of the 19th century. He was an American evangelist and publisher who founded the Moody Church, Northfield School and Mount Hermon School in Massachusetts (now the Northfield Mount Hermon School), the Moody Bible Institute and Moody Publishers, all of which are still in operation today. He was a major player in the early development of the YMCA, and he preached to hundreds of thousands of people on both sides of the Atlantic Ocean. He also gave us the four-colored version of what we know as "The Wordless Book" today.[12]

Henry Varley, a very intimate friend of Dwight L. Moody in the earlier days of his work, loved to tell how he once said to him: "It remains to be seen what God will do with a man who gives himself up wholly to Him." When Mr. Varley said that, Mr. Moody said to himself, "Well, I will be that man." When we look at the life and ministry of Mr. Moody there is no doubt about what God will do with a man or woman who gives himself or herself wholly to Him.

That kind of a walk of faith is rare, but it really shouldn't be. If a person really invests the time and energy to get to know Jesus and becomes familiar with His voice, walking with Him—no matter where it is or what the conditions—will be the most natural thing in the world.

Father, help me to be the one You can depend on. I do not want to go it alone, please give me your strength to do what you have called me to do. Amen!

TWO WINNERS—TEN LOSERS

But the men who had gone up with him said, "We can't attack those people; they are stronger than we are" (Numbers 13:31).

———————◦———————

When Israel arrived at the borders of the Promised Land, we would expect a stampede to get in and possess it. Instead, they did the safe thing. They sent spies to check it out and see if it was true—as if God would lie to them! When the spies returned, instead of praise and joy, we hear unbelief and doubt. When you read the account you are struck by the difference between the ten who said, *"We are not able to go up against the people, for they are stronger than we,"* and Caleb and Joshua who said, *"Let us go up at once and take possession, for we are well able to overcome it"* (Numbers 13:30 NKJV).

In those two contrasting attitudes, we see the differences between winners and losers. Let's look more closely at the distinguishing characteristics between the two:

- Losers are always looking at the obstacles, but winners look at obstacles as opportunities to accomplish something great for God.

- Losers are always asking "Why?" Winners take a different approach and ask "Why not?"

- Losers are stopped by fear of the unknown, while winners are energized by results.

- Losers are famous for making excuses, but the real winners never need them!

- Losers are easily discouraged, and it doesn't take much to stop them. Winners on the other hand never stop because they possess the spirit of a bulldog!

Who are you spending time with? Listening to? Proverbs 4:23 (NKJV) says, *"Keep your heart with all diligence, for out of it spring* [flow] *the issues of life."* It is our job to be careful about what we are taking in and who we are spending time with. If you spend your time with negative people, you will become negative. Spend your time with winners. When you hang around other winners, suddenly you seem to be more interested in what can be accomplished rather than what obstacles are keeping you from winning!

Caleb and Joshua were winners. Why? They refused to be influenced by negative attitudes. They knew with God's strength the Promised Land could be taken for the glory of God.

Father, keep me from the negative and the things that would stop me from accomplishing great things for the kingdom of God. Amen!

TIME TO LEAVE THE NEST

Like an eagle that stirs up its nest and hovers over its young, that spreads its wings to catch them and carries them aloft (Deuteronomy 32:11).

———— ❧ ————

Moses, speaking for the Lord, told us how young eagles were introduced to the practice of soaring in the heavens: *"Like an eagle that stirs up its nest,"* the time has come for the young eagle to leave the comfort of the nest and launch out on its own. Looking down from the dizzying heights of the mountain peak, everything within it says *now is not the time* for such a dangerous endeavor.

Isn't it true that we get very uncomfortable with things we haven't experienced before? At the core of our nature, we do not like change. However, Jesus came for that very purpose—to change our inner selves and transform our hearts.

The mother eagle begins making things uncomfortable for the eaglet in the nest. Room service is no longer delivered, and strange things begin to happen in the nest. From the baby's point of view, Momma has lost her mind! The normal life is coming to end. The nest has been safe and comfortable, and until something changes the eaglet will remain there forever.

Maybe you can identify with the process just described. It may seem like God is taking away your comfort zone. What seemed so comfortable is now uncomfortable. Why is this happening? We will never soar as long as our nest is lined with feathers, leaves, and the soft fur of other animals. God knows we were created for so much more, and our full potential will never be realized as long as we are living the status quo.

You are an eagle believer. An eagle believer is born to soar, not to play around with baby toys in a comfortable nest your whole life. When we are first born of the Spirit we enjoy a season of feeding on the milk of the Word. That is fine for a season, but it is time to grow up into a mature believer. It is time to spread our wings like an eagle and learn to soar above the storms.

———— ❧ ————

Father, I know change is part of the believer's life. Please help me to stand strong and embrace Your changes. I know You have my best interests at heart. Amen!

TIME FOR SOMETHING NEW

Therefore, if anyone is in Christ, the new creation has come:
The old has gone, the new is here! (2 Corinthians 5:17)

———————————————

One of the most difficult things to do is unlearn old habits. Habits are something we learn and not something that is implanted in our DNA. Habits are not instincts, they are acquired reactions. They don't just happen, they are caused. We first form habits, and then our habits form us! I love the old saying, "Sow a thought reap an act; sow an act reap a habit; sow a habit, reap a character; sow a character and reap a destiny!" The contradiction is this: We make our habits, and then they turn around and make us. Some habits are good and some are not so good. Some are innocent, unnoticeable, and of little consequence. However, some habits are deadly obvious and of major consequence to our lives. I doubt anyone would think drug use is productive, healthy, and a good habit to have!

It is possible to go through life with the same old tried and true habits and never give much thought to the fact that God will require us to change. God wants each one of us to experience new life in Him with a complete break from our old way of living, thinking, and acting. One of the first lessons we learn as Christians is growth is not automatic. Unproductive habits don't just suddenly fade away the day we become new creations in Christ. And just by hanging around other Christians does not mean we will automatically progress in the things of God.

When confronting habits that are not productive, it is always helpful to go to the Source of your strength. I am not just referring to friends or family, but the One living inside you—the Holy Spirit. Of course there are many resources available, such as counselors, books, and plenty of Internet advice. But remember, you have access to the greatest resource in the universe. The power of God is available to you right now twenty-four hours a day, three hundred and sixty-five days a year!

———————————————

Father, thank You for being available to me. I know there are times I lose sight of the fact that I have the greatest Counselor in the universe ready to help me. Amen!

MONDAY

OUR SECRET WEAPON

And will give our attention to prayer and the ministry of the word (Acts 6:4).

For thousands of years people have been trying to connect to something beyond their reach, something spiritual or supernatural. A place to run to, to feel, however slightly, that there is someone out there who will take notice of our predicament.

Christians have found the answer. We have a secret weapon! It is not found in some "top secret" underground bunker buried under the Pentagon. It is not found in the missile silos in Russia. This weapon is more powerful than any imagined in the mind of humankind. What is it? The power of a praying Christian! In spite of the current religious environment in the modern church, prayer is not some mundane exercise. Prayer means I never have to say, "There's nothing I can do." Why? Believers are connected to the power Source, and that gives us all the advantage we need.

Prayer is like a missile that can be fired toward any spot on earth, travel undetected at the speed of thought, and hit its target every time. Prayer is an absolute necessity, and satan will fight it tooth and nail. He knows he has no defense against this weapon. He does not have an anti-prayer missile!

There are times when we think our problems and difficulties are too insignificant to bring before God in prayer. We must remember prayer is a two-way conversation between friends. God invites us to talk to Him about everything. He will never get mad or be upset when we bring even the smallest issues before Him. It is a sad commentary when the average believer neglects the most important conversation we can have.

God expects His children to talk to Him. We must never take the attitude, "Do I have to pray every day?" The answer is simple. We don't have to pray as a requirement—we get to as a privilege!

I believe the psalmist said it best, *"Cast your cares on the Lord and he will sustain you; he will never let the righteous be shaken"* (Psalm 55:22).

———————————⚬———————————

Father, may I never take the privilege of prayer lightly. I look forward to our daily conversations. Amen!

You Hold the Key

*Guard the good deposit that was entrusted to you—guard it with
the help of the Holy Spirit who lives in us* (2 Timothy 1:14).

———

Access is the key to your success! The apostle Paul encouraged his young son in the ministry, Timothy, to *"Guard the good deposit that was entrusted to you."* It sounds like an easy thing to do, but it is far from it. Access into your life, like purpose and passion, must be protected. I am not suggesting you lock the door of your heart and throw away the key. Nor am I suggesting to never seek wisdom and counsel from those who have walked ahead of you.

Giving someone access into your life is equivalent to giving the greatest treasure you can give. It is giving others the right to encounter or exchange with you, and quite frankly you hold the *key to that access.* Contrary to popular opinion, you don't have to allow everybody to influence you. Giving access to negative people on a regular basis will have a far-reaching impact. What is spoken into your life affects how you think, feel, and eventually how you act. Of course you are commanded to love everybody, but you don't have to allow everybody in the door of your heart!

It is important to remember when granting others access that you need to make sure they make additions and not subtractions to your divine purpose. God did not design us to fly solo. The right people will always bring out the best in us. A very wise man once said, "I can predict your future by looking at your friends. Where they are, is where you are headed!"

Each day has twenty-four hours. Your success is determined by those whom you allow access to those hours. What do successful people know that unsuccessful people don't? They control who enjoys access to their time. People who do not respect your time will never respect your wisdom. Why would you give your time (access) to anyone who is simply going to waste the opportunity? Never allow anyone access to your time who does not promote your success and is willing to pass that on to others (see 2 Timothy 2:2).

———

Father, thank You for reminding me of the importance of access. Please show me when it is time to keep the door locked. Amen!

ORDER IN THE HOUSE

Where there is no revelation, people cast off restraint; but blessed is the one who heeds wisdom's instruction (Proverbs 29:18).

If you desire to create an atmosphere of chaos in your home or in your business, just live your life without a clear vision. Lack of vision will always take you down the road of disorder. To eliminate chaos your vision must be clear. Everything you are doing right now will either increase order or disorder in your life. Make no mistake about it, God is a God of order. The only thing that seems out of order is humankind and our use of the resources God has given us.

Living in proper order will always increase peace and a sense of well-being. If you find things are out of order, several factors may be the cause:

1. *Allowing disorderly **people** to invade your life is a recipe for disaster.* If you want to see what disaster looks like, all you have to do is allow disorderly and chaotic people around you. Before you know it they will use you as a garbage can to dump all of their past problems. Remember, if God has not assigned someone into your life, you're not responsible to work out all of their problems!

2. *Allowing an **environment** of disorder is also a recipe for chaos.* Disorderly people seem to attract and create disorderly places. It doesn't take a brain surgeon or a rocket scientist to figure out when something is out of order. It may seem trivial, but look around your home, your yard, your finances, and even the way you present yourself. These are great indicators of order or disorder in your life.

3. *Allowing disorderly **practices** will also create an atmosphere of disorder.* Proverbs 16:25 says, *"There is a way that seems to be right, but in the end it leads to death."* It all comes down to making a choice. You can choose to continue to live in disorder or choose to respond and change it before it changes you. Remember, as the old saying goes, "Time waits for no one." So when is a good time to make necessary changes? How about today. Little changes today can make a big impact in your tomorrow!

Father, give me the courage to eliminate any sources of disorder in my life. I choose order, not chaos. Amen!

AN EXCELLENT SPIRIT

Lord, our Lord, how majestic [excellent] *is your name in all the earth! You have set your glory in the heavens* (Psalm 8:1).

———◦—————〜—————◦———

If you want to know what an excellent Spirit looks like all you have to do is go to the Source. *The Lord's name is excellent!* When the psalmist declared God's name is excellent, it means He is excellent in His character, personality, and all of His attributes.

When God created the heavens and the earth, it was excellent. When God provided humanity with salvation, it was excellent. As His children we are commanded to be imitators of God (see Ephesians 5:1). What does that mean? We are to be people of excellence in everything we say and everything we do. Our walk and our talk must match, or those around us will know we are no different from the chaotic culture we live in.

By definition, "excellence" means greatness—the very best. Excellence is a quality that people really appreciate because it's so hard to find. Excellence is the quality of excelling, of being truly the best at something.

The systems of this world are opposed to excellence and will more often than not compromise and take the path of least resistance. Let's face it, many of today's leaders, including politicians and preachers, would rather compromise than stand for principles. Sad to say, that philosophy has had a trickle-down effect all the way from the White House to the church house! It is never easy to raise the standard of excellence. If excellence is worth having, it is worth fighting for!

Vince Lombardi was one of the most successful coaches in the history of the NFL. His overnight success took years to develop. It didn't just happen by accident. In one of his most famous quotes he described the importance of excellence: "The quality of a person's life is in direct proportion to their commitment to excellence, regardless of their chosen field of endeavor."

I am convinced there is no greater legacy you can leave behind as rich as a life of excellence. To develop an excellent spirit is a choice to be made and it does not happen through osmosis. Choose a life of self-discipline, refusing to take shortcuts and always recognizing God as your Source.

———◦—————〜—————◦———

Father, I am determined to live a life of excellence. Give me the grace to never compromise. Amen!

A RUDDER, NOT AN ANCHOR

Here is a trustworthy saying that deserves full acceptance: Christ Jesus came into the world to save sinners—of whom I am the worst (1 Timothy 1:15).

The apostle Paul refused to be controlled by his past. Sadly, many people today are controlled by past sins, regrets, and failures. We certainly cannot change the past, but we can be *changed by the past.* The past should be a *rudder to guide us* to our future and not an *anchor to drag us back.*

Paul learned the secret of moving forward—he was willing to accept God's forgiveness. He said, *"Christ Jesus came into the world to save sinners—of whom I am the worst."* He was a blasphemer and a persecutor of the early church. He was proud and belligerent. He was full of religious pride to the point if you didn't agree with him he would have you thrown in prison. One Bible scholar referred to Paul as a "bully."

In spite of all of Paul's failures, he obtained mercy: *"Even though I was once a blasphemer and a persecutor and a violent man, I was shown mercy because I acted in ignorance and unbelief. The grace of our Lord was poured out on me abundantly, along with the faith and love that are in Christ Jesus"* (1 Timothy 1:13-14).

If you are a child of God, I have good news for you. God has completely dealt with all of your sins and past failures. *Not just part, but all!* How wonderful to know we can look at our past and know it is buried in the sea of God's mercy and grace. We can look at our present and know God is standing beside us. We can look toward the future and know that God has gone before us.

Please do not allow the fact that what you *used to be* is the way you are today. As a Christian you are a new person in Jesus Christ who has experienced the grace and mercy of God. Paul's experience with Christ freed him from the *anchors* of regret. He allowed the Holy Spirit within him to be his *rudder* to navigate his future.

Father, help me to know that my past is buried in a sea of Your mercy. Guide me toward my destiny. Amen!

MONDAY

A GREAT EXCHANGE

It is for freedom that Christ has set us free. Stand firm, then, and do not let yourselves be burdened again by a yoke of slavery (Galatians 5:1).

What does Paul mean when he says, *"We are free from the law?"* Does that mean as Christians we are allowed to be lawless? No, it means our relationship to God is not based on Law, but on grace.

The law is compared to a *yoke*. Yolks were used to control animals, and the law was given to control people. We are told people are basically good on the inside, and any lawless issues were something out of their control. It is either a bad environment, a faulty economy, or lack of education at the root. No, the Bible says we are basically sinners in need of a Savior. Paul made it clear God revealed His righteous judgments in the law; and in spite of that, human-kind still rebelled against God. The law could never change anyone from the inside out!

When we come to Christ we exchange the external *yoke of legalism*—certain rules and regulations—for the *internal yoke of love*. We exchanged the hopeless endeavor of trying to please God by what we do with a new internal loving and living relationship with the Lord Jesus Christ. Jesus said His yoke was easy and His burden is light (see Matthew 11:28-30). His yoke is easy because it is custom fitted to each of us. How remarkable is that!

The yoke of the law puts us under bondage, but the yoke of Christ sets us free. The yoke of the law eventually brings agony and restlessness, but the yoke of Christ will always bring peace and rest to our souls. We no longer need rules and regulations on the outside, because we have His life inside: *"Because you are his sons, God sent the Spirit of his Son into our hearts, the Spirit who calls out, "Abba, Father." So you are no longer a slave, but God's child; and since you are his child, God has made you also an heir"* (Galatians 4:6-7).

Father, I gladly receive and wear the yoke of Christ. I know His yoke is given for my benefit and peace of mind. Amen!

YOU ARE WHAT YOU EAT—REALLY

Finally, brothers and sisters, whatever is true, whatever is noble, whatever is right, whatever is pure, whatever is lovely, whatever is admirable—if anything is excellent or praiseworthy—think about such things (Philippians 4:8).

I am sure we have all heard the statement, "You are what you eat." Okay, so does that mean if I eat a hamburger I will turn into a cow? Of course not. But there's truth to the fact that what you eat becomes part of your physical body. Too much of the wrong stuff will definitely have an impact on how we feel, act, and think. You don't have to be a nutritionist to figure that out! It would also be naïve to think that what we feed our spirit does not affect us.

Consider the eagle again. This majestic bird is considered a connoisseur of the bird world. While other birds are satisfied with worms, berries, and dead animals, eagles much prefer fresh meat. Ninety percent of an eagle's diet is fish. They know what makes them strong and healthy.

You will never find an eagle diving into a garbage dump looking for food! Why? An eagle knows if it doesn't eat the right things it will affect reproductive capabilities. Likewise, if we are going to live a healthy and strong life as an eagle Christian, we must feed our spirit with the right kind of spiritual food. Why? For the same reason as the eagle. Eagle saints will not be able to reproduce other Christians when they feed on garbage.

The apostle Paul is telling us that we really are what we eat—spiritually. Eagle Christians won't be sitting on a tree limb waiting for an animal to stop moving, like the vultures. An eagle saint will not dull its beak by pecking the ground like a chicken. Eagles decide beforehand what they want to eat and then go get it, fresh like God intended.

Don't become an overweight Christian feeding on the fast-food junk of this world. Soar like a strong, healthy eagle feeding your inner self with the things of God!

Father, my desire is to soar like an eagle. Help me to choose the right spiritual food to keep me strong and healthy for the kingdom of God. Amen!

WATCH OUT!

The thief comes only to steal and kill and destroy; I have come that they may have life, and have it to the full (John 10:10).

———————————————

I once read the story of a very cunning trapper. His desire was to trap an eagle alive, but he knew it would have to be in a non-invasive way. Each morning, at the eagle's favorite fishing hole, the trapper made very subtle changes. The story continues:

> Most of the changes please the eagle, because each change brought fresh fish. That was less work for the beautiful bird. It was not a stupid bird, because each time it took a fish it would always carefully look around. The subtle changes, a rock, fish in the grass and, finally a net, didn't seem to alarm the eagle. The wise trapper began to lay the fish closer to the trap until he had the fish on the rock and under the hoop of the net. The last day the trapper snapped the net over the eagle. Caught! The eagle was caught because it had become unaware of danger. Caught, because it quit hunting for itself. Caught, even though it could have been avoided!

Most of the traps set for believers are subtle. Most of us would never knowingly get burned. It may be a trap so beautiful, like Bathsheba to David. Or, based on greed, like Judas. The downward spiral toward sin is a process much like setting a trap for the unsuspecting eagle, or baiting a hook for an unsuspecting fish.

Traps start in the mind, through the eye gate, and then into our souls. God has always promised a way of escape; we must have the wisdom to take that route. We must be aware of the subtle and oftentimes bold tricks of the enemy. We never have to be afraid of what satan may do because God has given us all the weapons we need to win the battle (see 2 Corinthians 10:3-6).

———————————————

Father, keep me ever vigilant to the tricks and traps set by satan. Let me not become complacent and lazy when it comes to Your plans and purposes for me. Amen!

THURSDAY

JUMP

*For he will command his angels concerning you to guard you and
all your ways; they will lift you up in their hands, so that you
will not strike your foot against a stone* (Psalm 91:11-12).

———————————————

I remember sitting by the pool one day watching the playful banter between a father and his two-year-old son. The father, wanting his young son to jump in the pool, found himself trying to coax the young hero with everything imaginable. He tried every bribe known to modern man. When staying up late to watch his favorite movie, and all the candy he could eat didn't work, the exasperated father looked at his son and said, "Son, jump. I promise I will catch you!" Something must've clicked because the next thing I knew, he jumped. The dad, in total shock, barely having time to react, caught the child and they both let out a cheer. A new milestone had been achieved. What a great day for father and son!

As mentioned previously, when an eaglet reaches a point when it's time to learn to fly, the mommy eagle will do everything to disrupt the comfort zone. She has removed all the comforts of home (the nest) and it's now time for flight school. She puts the baby on her wings and carries it to great heights, then suddenly drops it. The eaglet flails and falls, all the while wondering what this is all about. After a few tries, eventually it learns to fly. What they did not realize is while in flight training, daddy is above watching everything take place. He knows if there is a need for rescue, he can fly faster than the eaglet can fall!

We must never forget that our heavenly Father can fly faster than we can fall. Burning and crashing is never God's intended purpose for our lives. He always has our best interests at heart (see Jeremiah 29:11-12). Tragically, sometimes we fall. Whether it is imposed by outside sources or self-inflicted, our heavenly Father has prepared a landing filled with His purpose for which we were created.

———————————————

Father, help me to learn to trust You again. Remind me that You can and will catch me when I fall. Amen!

THINGS

*And God saw everything that he had made, and,
behold, it was very good* (Genesis 1:31 KJV).

One of the most popular questions in the modern church: "Is it wrong to own things." I believe the Lord made it clear that it is not wrong to own things, as long as things do not own us!

We must understand at the outset, God made every *thing* in the universe. In the creation there is God, there are people, and there are things. As one old-time preacher said, "God is to be worshiped, people are to be loved and served, and things are to be used." Let's be clear, God did not make anything that is wrong. Yes, things can be used in the wrong way, but they are not sinful in themselves. Why? Simple, God made them! Your heavenly Father knows we need things to live: *"Your heavenly father knows that you need them"* (Matthew 6:32).

God wants us to enjoy things. Our lives should never be measured by how many *things* we accumulate. When someone dies we may be tempted to ask, "How much did he leave?" Well, he left everything! God wants us to have a proper perspective and enjoy everything He has created (see1 Timothy 6:17).

The issue that destroys lives is when *things* own us. Why? Jesus said things can control your heart. *"For where your treasure is, there your heart will be also"* (Matthew 6:21). A divided heart will destroy a life.

What is the secret? We must recognize God as the Master of everything in our lives! When we seek first the kingdom of God and His righteousness, all the things necessary for a happy and well-rounded life will be added to us (see Matthew 6:33). In other words, we take things out of the center of our lives and let God put things there that really belong. Failure to do so will cheapen the things that we have, our hearts will be divided, and our lives will be defeated. But when Jesus Christ is the Master of everything, then everything in our lives finds proper perspective and order.

Father, thank You for giving me things to enjoy. May I always keep a proper perspective and use things for Your glory. Amen!

MONDAY

READY

For I am already being poured out like a drink offering, and the time for my departure is near (2 Timothy 4:6).

———————————◇———————————

I have always been intrigued by the last words of important people. It was said that John Wilkes Booth, who assassinated President Abraham Lincoln, had two final words before he died: *"Useless…useless."* It was also recorded that British naval hero Lord Nelson said, *"Thank God I have done my duty."* One of the greatest last words of all time was written by the apostle Paul from a Roman prison when he said to his young son in the faith, Timothy, *"For I am now ready to be offered, and the time of my departure is at hand."*

When you read his entire statement to young Timothy, you get the idea Paul faced death without fear or apprehension. He knows that death is just around the corner and yet he speaks with a quiet confidence, totally unafraid.

Paul demonstrated an amazing view of death. He did not consider himself a prisoner in chains waiting to be executed, but a fellow soldier of the gospel ready to be offered as a sacrifice to the glory of the Lord. Paul's expression of faith and trust are no doubt bound up in the idea: "If Jesus can lay down his life for me, I can certainly lay down my life for Him!"

Isn't it interesting that Paul does not use the word "death"? I don't think it is because he is afraid of the word, or even afraid of going through the experience. He recognized that for the Christian there is no such thing as death being the final expression of life. It is simply a transfer from this life on earth to a much greater experience in Heaven. Our bodies are temporary, and when the day comes to be called home we have the assurance of a permanent home for all eternity (see 2 Corinthians 5:1). Therefore, there is nothing to fear!

Are you ready? If you have given your life to Christ, you can face death with confident assurance.

Father, thank You for putting a calm assurance inside my heart when it comes to my departure from this earth. Help me never to live in fear of death. Amen!

WHO'S KNOCKING

Yet to all who did receive him, to those who believed in his name,
he gave the right to become children of God (John 1:12).

The key phrase in John 1:12 is *"all who did receive him."* All of God's part in the marvelous plan of redemption has been completed. Jesus said on the cross, *"It is finished,"* signifying the plan of salvation has been set in motion. Our part is to *receive* it. You can never earn your way, or do enough works to gain access into Heaven.

It has been said the saddest words in all of the Bible are found in the first chapter of John: *"He came to that which was his own, but his own did not receive him"* (John 1:11). The same could be said today. Jesus comes to people knocking on the door of their hearts and they choose not to open the door and receive Him. Why is that? It could be the fear of inconsistency. Some people have enough honesty to say they don't want to live one way on Sunday morning and another way Monday through Saturday. People who know they are God's children will never be easy targets for satan's devices.

Christ will never force His way in. He patiently and gently stands knocking on the door waiting for an answer. He is too much of a gentleman to be pushy. The "knocking" may come through circumstances beyond our control, forcing us to seek guidance and wisdom only He can provide. It may come through a strong word of rebuke from a loved one. He has some unusual ways to get our attention, but one thing is certain, He will never do anything to force us to make a commitment to Him against our will. He loves us too much to do that!

To open the door of our hearts is to allow Him access to every room. He doesn't do well with locked doors with signs hanging on the doorknob that shout, *"NO ADMITTANCE ALLOWED!"* If you hear a gentle knock on the door of your heart, it might be wise to open it. I can guarantee you will never regret it. It will be the greatest day of your life!

Father, I rejoice in the day I heard You knock, and opened the door. It was truly the greatest day of my life. Amen!

WATCH YOUR WORDS

But I tell you that everyone will have to give account on the day of judgment for every empty [idle] *word they have spoken* (Matthew 12:36).

———————————⌁———————————

No one spoke with more authority than Jesus. He meant what He said, and said what He meant. He did not have time for foolish talking or idle words. He said every empty or idle word spoken must be accounted for in the day of judgment. The definition of the word "idle" means noneffective or non-working words.

Do you realize sometimes we speak words that are actually working against us and not for us? It is a scary proposition to think the words that come out of our mouths actually carry weight in the atmosphere. This may shock you, but your spouse, friends, or coworkers are not the only ones listening to you talk!

Fearful words activate the evil one to work in our lives, whereas speaking faith brings God into our situation. You may say, "That sounds like positive confession to me," to which I would reply, *"ABSOLUTELY!"* Would you agree that a positive confession is much better than a negative one? A negative confession is one contrary to the Word of God. A positive confession stands squarely on the Word of God and it is all we need to live lives of victory over the devil (see 1 John 4:4).

The only power the devil has over any believer is the ability to deceive you. And the only way he can deceive you is to get you to believe his lies. When you do, you are falling into his trap. You don't have to back up or shut up, just open your mouth and speak the words of Scripture when the devil comes calling. The next time something goes wrong in your life and you're tempted to agree with the devil, stop and think, "Are these words I'm about to speak working for me or against me?"

We are on the winning team, and if you don't believe me read the back of the Book: *"They triumphed over him by the blood of the Lamb and by the **word of their testimony**"* (Revelation 12:11).

———————————⌁———————————

Father, I know the importance of words and the impact they make. Help me to keep a watch over what comes out of my mouth. Amen!

175

AFTER THE FIGHT

*So, if you think you are standing firm, be careful
that you don't fall!* (1 Corinthians 10:12)

———⌘———

Whether we like to admit it or not, Christians are not immune from battles. There are times when the Christian life is more like a battleground than a playground. Paul warns us to *"Be careful that you don't fall."* Why? The most dangerous time, the time that requires the most vigilance is when we have won a victory. For some reason, after a victory we have a tendency to let our guard down and get overconfident. There's nothing the enemy likes more than a chance to get even after a struggle.

The Bible makes it clear we fight against three enemies: satan and his craftiness; the world system that has turned its back on God; and our own sinful nature that wants to lead us down the path of disobedience. Simon Peter warns, *"Be alert and of sober mind. Your enemy the devil prowls around like a roaring lion looking for someone to devour"* (1 Peter 5:8). Sometimes satan does not come as a roaring lion; he comes like a snake, and we must be able to detect his traps and expose him.

Joshua and the armies of Israel are perfect examples of what happens when overconfidence is the rule of the day. After the tremendous victory at Jericho, they turned their attention to a little city called Ai. What should've been a tremendous victory turned out to be a horrible defeat. Why? Overconfidence. They decided it was such a little city in contrast to the great city of Jericho. They reasoned they ought to be able to take Ai with very little effort. They did not ask God for wisdom; and because there was sin in the camp, men died, and the army ran away in disgrace!

Beware of overconfidence when the next battle is about to be fought. Overconfidence opens the door for the enemy to rob us of future victories. Always keep your eye on the prize, and never let your guard down. If we would be honest with ourselves, most of our defeats don't take place during the fight; they take place after the victory has been secured!

———⌘———

Father, I will put no confidence in my flesh, no matter how good I may feel. I will keep my eyes open and watch out for the enemy. Amen!

KEEP GOING

However, I consider my life worth nothing to me; my only aim is to finish the race and complete the task the Lord Jesus has given me— the task of testifying to the good news of God's grace (Acts 20:24).

It seemed trouble followed Paul wherever he went. When he would land in a new city, one of two things would happen—*a revival or a riot.* And most of the time, both! What kept Paul moving forward? In Acts 20:24, when his friends tried to stop him from going to Jerusalem to a certain death, he responded, *"I consider my life worth nothing to me."* He believed his life was a gift from God, and he would not keep this gift for himself. Because he felt this way, retreat from his mission was not an option. No, he had to keep moving toward his mission.

I hope you realize that your life is a gift from God. *"For in him we live and move and have our being"* (Acts 17:28). Even before you were born, God knew you. He designed you with all of your talents and abilities, your interests, your strengths and weaknesses with purpose for His divine plan. He gave you natural life, but when you came to faith in Christ He gave you spiritual life. So the life you have, both physically and spiritually, is a marvelous gift from your heavenly Father.

Paul would not keep this wonderful gift for himself. He knew the principle: Whatever you try to hold onto, you lose; whatever you give away, you possess for eternity. Paul did not consider this gift of physical life the most precious thing to him. No, it was doing the will of God that pushed him forward. As a very wise man once said, "Your life is not a treasure to guard; it is a treasure to invest by yielding to the will of God."

Never become jealous of somebody else because of their ministry. You and I have a mission to fulfill. It is unique to each of us, and only we can accomplish it. It has been specifically designed to match our uniqueness. *No one can be you, except you.* One size fits all does not apply!,

---

Father, thank You for this wonderful gift of life, both physically and spiritually. May I never take it for granted. Amen!

COMMITMENT AND CHOICES

MONDAY

STAND YOUR GROUND

But Shammah took his stand in the middle of the field. He defended it and struck the Philistines down, and the Lord brought about a great victory (2 Samuel 23:12).

❦

I love this story in Second Samuel! Here was a man who worked hard to till his field and plant his seed for an abundant harvest. But every year something happened. The Philistines decided they wanted it. They would wait until harvest time and simply come and take it.

This harvest season something was different. Shammah decided to stand his ground. As he was preparing to harvest his crop he saw the Philistines coming up the road. Something rose up within him and he stood in the middle of his bean patch and shouted, "If you want this harvest you're going to have to take it from me!"

The Philistines made the fatal mistake of assuming because he was by himself ,they could take whatever they wanted. This mighty warrior learned a valuable lesson that day. One plus one with God is always a majority. No doubt they knew all about the God of the Israelites, but soon discovered it only takes one man clothed in the power of God to stand his ground and defeat the enemy.

We have all had times when we have prayed, planted, and planned for our future destiny. It would seem that the closer we got to the fulfillment of God's promise, the enemy would show up and try to steal what did not belong to him. The enemy knows many Christians give up the fight before the fight ever begins. We need to realize God is with us when we stand our ground against satan and all of his devices.

Never proceed alone. God is with us, and He never leaves nor forsakes us (see Hebrews 13:5). One of the tactics of the enemy is to isolate us from other believers because he knows there is power in agreement (see Matthew 18:19).

God has given us our own "bean patch" to watch over and protect. Whether it's called destiny, purpose, or the will of God, it is ours and no one else's. Never give in, and never give up. Why? He is with us every step of the way!

Father, stand with me when I face the enemy. I pray You will be ever present to my every circumstance. I will stand my ground. Amen!

HEAT IN THE KITCHEN

"Martha, Martha," the Lord answered, "You are worried and upset about many things, but few things are needed—or indeed only one. Mary has chosen what is better, and it will not be taken away from her" (Luke 10:41-42).

Jesus loved to visit the home of Mary, Martha, and Lazarus. It was a home where the Lord could feel comfortable. It was one of those rare places where the Lord could go and feel perfectly at home (see John 11:5). We all need to have a place like that in our lives.

Martha had a unique way of expressing her love for Jesus. Her attitude was, "I will show my love by what I do for Him." As the story unfolds we find Martha running all around, tending to the various details of the kitchen. That was her personality.

But something happened that almost shipwrecked the happy occasion. Martha was fretting because Mary was not helping, *"But Martha was distracted by all the preparations that had to be made. She came to him and asked, "Lord, don't you care that my sister has left me to do the work by myself? Tell her to help me!"* (Luke 10:40). Martha was "feeling the heat" because she was not handling the work, but the work was handling her! She was so busy working for Jesus that she found herself in a position of being distracted; an offended spirit was just around the corner.

What was the attitude of Jesus? He calmed her anxiety by simply speaking a word. If you find yourself fretful and worried, stop what you're doing, and allow the Lord's word to calm you. Jesus said, *"Come to me, all you who are weary and burdened, and I will give you rest"* (Matthew 11:28).

Jesus encouraged Martha to consider her sister who *"has chosen what is better."* Mary discovered the secret of priority and how to put worship and work in the proper perspective. The answer to Martha's problem was not to stop working but to allow her work to flow out of her worship. Our busy activity is only a ministry as it flows from our relationship with Jesus Christ. Failure to do so will always lead to *heat in the kitchen!*

Father, keep reminding me that it is important that my work for You always follows my worship. Amen!

HONEY FOR THE HARD TIMES

*But you would be fed with the finest of wheat; with honey
from the rock I would satisfy you* (Psalm 81:16).

———————————◆———◆———————————

Honey is one of the sweetest substances nature can produce. A rock is one of
the hardest. God has given a promise to His people that He will satisfy us with
honey from the rock. I do not believe God is speaking in literal terms. Why?
Honey comes from a honeycomb, or a jar. You can easily purchase the finest
honey at the local supermarket.

I believe the Lord is saying something much greater, such as, "When you run
up against a hard place, there are going to be rocks. But, be encouraged I am
going to give you honey out of the rock!" In other words, you're going to experience sweetness out of the most difficult experiences of life. Wow, what a promise!

Let's be honest, none of us enjoy going through the hard places and running
our head into a rock. How many times have I heard someone say, "If God really
loves me, I wouldn't be going through this." It never seems to occur to us that
God sees the big picture and knows exactly what He is doing. I have learned
from personal experience some of the "sweetest" experiences of life have come
because of huge boulders.

A very wise man once said, "One of the tests of maturity is how a person gets
his or her enjoyment out of life." Some find enjoyment in doing things contrary
to the will of God, and that is the lowest possible way to live. While others get
their pleasure by dodging difficult circumstances. Neither one of those ways will
make a person strong and mature.

Mature believers never look for difficulties, but neither do they run nor hide
from them. Rather they accept them because they know God has their best interests at heart. A mature Christian knows on the other side of the difficulty there
will be *"honey from the rock"*!

If you find yourself going through a hard and difficult place don't try to ignore
and pretend the problems don't exist. Just turn everything over to the Lord.
Allow Him to make something wonderfully sweet. He promised He would!

———————————◆———◆———————————

*Father, Your promises are wonderful. I know You have my best interests at heart.
Amen!*

PROTECTED

Whoever dwells in the shelter of the Most High will rest
in the shadow of the Almighty (Psalm 91:1).

———————⌒———————

I love to read the life experiences of the great warriors of the faith. We tend to think these men and women never faced difficulties. Nothing could be further from the truth. One of my all-time favorites is an evangelist named D. L. Moody. He was considered one of the greatest preachers and innovators for Christ in the nineteenth century.

The following is one of the many stories that have been written about this great man. It reminds us again of the awesome promises of God.

> In 1892, after a year of intensive work in Great Britain, Moody sailed for home. About three days out in the ocean, the ship ground to a halt with a broken shaft; and before long, it began to take on water. Needless to say, the crew and passengers were desperate, because nobody was sure whether the vessel would sink or not. Mr. Moody asked for permission to hold a meeting, and to his surprise, nearly every passenger attended. He opened his Bible to Psalm 91 and, holding to a pillar to steady himself, he read: *Whoever dwells in the shelter of the Most High will rest in the shadow of the Almighty.*
>
> Moody wrote later, "It was the darkest hour of my life...relief came in prayer. God heard my cry, and enabled me to say, from the depths of my soul, 'Thy will be done.' I went to bed and fell asleep almost immediately."
>
> God answered his prayer and saved the ship. Another vessel was dispatched to tow the crippled ship into port. Psalm 91 became alive to D. L. Moody, and he discovered what you and I need to know... *The safest place in the world is living in the shadow of the Almighty, "under His wings"!*[13]

Psalm 91 was not given just for the D. L. Moodys of the world, but for every child of God. The promise of divine protection does not mean we will never experience accidents or sickness. He does not promise to keep us from trials or difficulties, but to protect us as we go *through them. READ IT AND CLAIM IT—IT IS YOURS!*

Father, I praise You for the promise of protection. As I go through trials I claim Your promise of protection. Amen!

YOU ARE NOT FORGOTTEN

I was young and now I am old, yet I have never seen the righteous forsaken or their children begging bread (Psalm 37:25).

Many of the psalms written by David were based on his own experiences in life. These words in Psalm 37 were written when David was an old man. He looked back and remembered how faithfully God had cared for him. There are some things we can't do anything about, and getting older is one of them. Each day we live on planet Earth the body gets older, but the good news is the spirit becomes more like Christ. With each passing day we move closer to seeing Him face to face. Paul summed it up this way, *"Therefore we do not lose heart. Though outwardly we are wasting away, yet inwardly we are being renewed day by day"* (2 Corinthians 4:16).

Instead of complaining about growing old, David looked back at all the experiences of his life and came to a marvelous conclusion: *God had never forsaken him!* Even in times of disobedience, and yes there were times when David did not walk in perfect obedience, God did not forsake him. David's failure has been on display for the whole world to see for centuries, so there is no need to recount it here. So before we start throwing the proverbial stones, we need to remember that none of us have always perfectly obeyed. David was not perfect, and neither are we.

The promise of this psalm is also a guarantee and assurance of God's *provision.* We will never have to become beggars. David is saying that God will always provide whatever we need so that we do not have to turn to anyone else except Him. If God watches the birds when they fall, surely God sees and knows our every need.

If you are feeling forsaken because of some area of disobedience, I have good news. You can claim the promise of Psalm 37:25. The promise is not just for David. It is for all of God's children. God never forsakes His own. Jesus said, *"And surely I am with you always, to the very end of the age"* (Matthew 28:20).

Father, keep my memory sharp when it comes to remembering Your faithfulness. I know Your promise to take care of me—I trust You completely. Amen!

MONDAY

DON'T STOP ROWING

This, then, is how you ought to regard us: as servants [ministers] of Christ and as those entrusted with the mysteries God has revealed (1 Corinthians 4:1).

Paul used a very interesting term to describe himself and others who are part of the family of God. He said we are "servants" or ministers of Christ. What do you think of when you hear the term "minister" being used? Do you picture a godly looking man dressed in his Sunday best standing behind an ornate pulpit? The options are unlimited. The definition of the word Paul used is far different than our modern thinking would imply.

The Greek word used to depict a servant or minister is not very classy at all. The word describes "the very lowest class of criminals." Not very flattering is it? I'm sure Paul must've had a reason for using this terminology.

In Paul's day criminals were assigned a life sentence in the bottom galley of huge ships. If you were to open the hatch and look below you would see the "engine" that propelled the ship forward. The engine was not machine powered, but man powered—by criminals. These men were seated and chained to a bench along with other criminals. They shared a common chain, held a common oar, and worked together as a group. The huge ships could not be powered by one man rowing alone. It was a total team effort!

The next time you are tempted to complain about the largeness of the task before you, remember this—God will give you all the resources needed to complete it. Part of the resources He provides are other people placed around you to help fulfill your destiny. Fulfilling God's vision for your life requires working together with other "under-rowers" who are committed just as much as you are.

The easy part is to start rowing. The difficult part is to continue rowing when times get tough and you're tempted to jump ship. If the rowers stop rowing, the ship grounds to a halt. If you stop rowing, it could possibly hinder the destiny God has called you to fulfill. Whatever you do—*don't stop rowing!*

Father, help me to maintain a right perspective on my vision. My desire is to continue rowing to produce eternal results for the kingdom. Amen!

TUESDAY

BITE YOUR TONGUE

But no human being can tame the tongue. It is a restless evil, full of deadly poison (James 3:8).

James was not one to beat around the bush. He compared the human tongue to a poisonous snake. There are all kinds of snakes, but the ones you have to watch out for are the ones that can strike with deadly accuracy and unload poisonous venom. Poisonous snakes by nature are not only vicious, they are nervous and easily agitated. James pictures the human tongue as a poisonous and unruly snake. He said an uncontrolled tongue is nervous, easily agitated, and ready to inject deadly poison into its next victim. Not very complementary is it?

"But no human being can tame the tongue." The literal meaning of the word "tame" is to "domesticate, subdue, or to bring under control." James uses a strong word to point out the human tongue can never be domesticated or brought under control by human methods. The tongue, like a snake, may appear to be docile when in fact it is waiting for its next victim to come along. If you were to try to stroke and pet a rattlesnake, as you might a python or boa constrictor, you can be sure the rattlesnake will find a way to bite you!

James continued his description of the unruly tongue by saying it is *"full of deadly poison."* If we are not careful our tongue can inject destructive and harmful words (venom) that can cause as much destruction and death as the most poisonous snake on the planet. The writer of Proverbs said the power of life and death are in the tongue (see Proverbs 18:21).

How exciting would it be if we could live in such a way as to never have to ever go back and undo the damage our words have done? It is possible when we allow the Holy Spirit to control what we say. Living with regret over destructive words can be a thing of the past when we submit to the lordship of Christ. Yes, the poisonous tongue can be transformed. Allow Him to put a tight rein on your mouth!

Father, I am submitting my mouth to the lordship of Christ. I realize I cannot control my tongue by myself. I ask You for Your power to control my words. Amen!

A TIME FOR EVERYTHING

*There is a time for everything, and a season for every
activity under the heavens* (Ecclesiastes 3:1).

Solomon's use of the word "season" in this verse is different from other uses of the word "time." There are three uses of the word "time" in the Bible: *aeon, chronos,* and *kairos.* The first, *aeon,* has to do with different ages and generations. *Chronos* is the succession of time; for example, 2 o'clock. *Kairos* has to do with seasons. According to Strong's Concordance the meaning of kairos is "A period of time and seasons at which a certain order of events or accomplishments take place."

Seasons are times of processing, not finishing. Every farmer knows there is a season for planting, one for waiting, and one for harvesting. It is impossible to expect the seed to produce a harvest outside of its proper season. The mistake many believers make is they try to harvest before they plant, or wait when it's time to harvest.

A pastor friend of mine said this about seasons of preparation, "Your season of preparation is that period of time when you are still watering your dreams and visions with the tears of prayer." The psalmist said, *"Those who sow with tears will reap with songs of joy"* (Psalm 126:5).

By nature humans are impatient. We want what we want, and we want it now. We don't like to wait for anything. Whether it's waiting in line at the bank, the grocery store, or the fulfillment of our destiny. Many times we fail to remember there is a season for planting, cultivating, and harvesting. Discerning the seasons of our lives may be the most important component of God's destiny and purpose.

I have seen many people try to launch a vision before its proper season. Their vision was not necessarily wrong—more than likely it was a timing issue that missed the mark. The greater the vision, the greater the time of preparation. A mistake in timing could lead us to make many other mistakes that could abort God's calling and purpose. Unripe fruit always leaves a bitter taste; so does failure to discern the seasons!

Father, when I am impatient and anxious about my destiny calm my spirit. I do not want to run ahead of Your plans for my life. Amen!

THURSDAY

WHO'S WHO OR WHO'S NOT?

*Jesus looked at him and loved him. "One thing you lack," he said.
"Go, sell everything you have and give to the poor, and you will have
treasure in heaven. Then come, follow me" (Mark 10:21).*

To be successful in life it is vitally important to focus on what matters the most. It is painfully obvious the *"rich young ruler"* was focused on the wrong things. As far as I know this is the only time a person who encountered Jesus walked away sad, and not glad: *"At this the man's face fell. He went away sad, because he had great wealth"* (Mark 10:22).

What a contrast between two men. Here they were standing face to face. One had great possessions, and the other, the Lord Jesus, had left the possessions of Heaven's glory and made Himself poor to become our Savior! The rich young ruler could have been in salvation's *"Who's Who,"* but instead he turned out to be in the Bible's *"Who's Not."*

This young man made the mistake of choosing material things rather than the eternal. He asked all the right questions, received the right answers, and yet turned and walked away because he was not ready to change his lifestyle. There is nothing wrong with having possessions, as long as possessions don't have you! He chose gold over God, and riches over redemption—how sad.

We are not told what happened to this young man. We don't know the details of his future. It could be that he went home and the sorrow he felt worked into a godly sorrow that led him to later receive Christ as his Savior. Or it may have been that he shrugged off the temporary emotion and said to himself, "I can't believe I made such an idiot of myself in front of everybody, I will never do that again!"

We just don't know how it ended for him, but what about you? Jesus Christ is the answer and the primary need of every individual life. As one old-time preacher used to say, "That one thing you lack is the main thing. It's the only thing."

Father, I am so thankful one day I made the right choice. Help me to focus my attention on others who are still struggling. Amen!

A GUARANTEED VICTORY

If someone dies, will they live again? All the days of my hard service I will wait for my renewal to come (Job 14:14).

———————————

Guaranteeing a victory does not always work. Of course, there are exceptions. For example, Super Bowl III between the upstart AFL and the powerful NFL. Most sports writers and fans believed the New York Jets stood absolutely no chance of defeating the powerful Baltimore Colts. Undeterred, Jets quarterback Joe Namath made an appearance three days before the Super Bowl at the Miami touchdown club and guaranteed a victory. His team backed up his words, and the Jets won 16-7. It is regarded as one of the greatest upsets in American sports history.

Consider Job. Here he was sitting in the rubble of his once palatial house when he suddenly found everything destroyed. He knew in his heart he had done nothing wrong. It is true sometimes bad things happen to good people.

Job responded to his adversity by declaring he would wait on God until his situation changed. Against the advice of friends and family he chose to trust God. Job is an Old Testament example of a New Testament truth: *"No, in all these things we are more than conquerors through him who loved us"* (Romans 8:37).

You might find yourself sitting in the rubble of an unfulfilled vision. To turn the situation around requires change. God desires for you to experience new power and a new level of trust. Change is necessary because we are often tempted to be content to celebrate our past victories instead of our future potential.

It does not matter how the battle began; what matters is how it ends. The Christian army is the only army in the world guaranteed to win. How do I know? Because the Word of God says so: *"You, dear children, are from God and have overcome them, because the one who is in you is greater than the one who is in the world"* (1 John 4:4). If you want a new level of success, be prepared to change. Don't settle for second best when God is guaranteeing victory.

———————————

Father, I know I need to change from the inside and out. I refuse to listen to the lies of the enemy when it comes to my future. I trust You. Amen!

MONDAY

GOD MISSES NOTHING

For the eyes of the Lord are on the righteous and his ears are attentive to their prayer, but the face of the Lord is against those who do evil (1 Peter 3:12).

"Life just isn't fair!" Sound familiar? How many times has that statement been said by Christians and non-Christians alike. There is something inside each of us that hungers for circumstances to be fair. I think that is the reason the old Western movies were so popular. The good guys wore white hats, and they always came to the rescue at the end of the movie. Unfortunately, life is not a Western movie or a fairytale!

As Christians we know that in the end righteousness and goodness will prevail over evil. The problem persists when we realize the end is not yet, and injustice and unfairness is prevalent in our world. How is it possible to keep on keeping on when life isn't fair?

The way I see it, we only have two choices:

The first choice is to *look around* and conclude the best way to handle unfairness is to look out for number one. Grabbing for all you can while there is something to grab is the attitude of most living in this generation. If you are unfair to me, I will be twice as unfair to you. As the old saying goes, "I don't get mad, I just get even." Sadly, that kind of attitude does not bring peace and contentment. More than likely it will only bring bitterness and anger.

The second choice is to look up and realize God misses nothing. Peter states, *"For the eyes of the Lord are on the righteous."* Do you see what Peter is saying? God is looking out for us and listening to our prayers. He does not turn a blind eye to evil or unfairness. God sees the end from the beginning. We must remember it may take an infinite amount of time, but justice will be served.

Yes, it's true. Life is not a Western movie or a fairytale. But the good news we can read the end of the book...the good guys and gals win in the end!

Father, I am so thankful You are with me right now. When I face unfairness, give me Your perspective. Give me grace to face any situation. Amen!

WE ALL HAVE TO DO IT

Therefore let us move beyond the elementary teachings about Christ and be taken forward to maturity, not laying again the foundation of repentance from acts that lead to death, and of faith in God (Hebrews 6:1).

The road to maturity can sometimes be a painful process. I love what one old-time preacher said, "En route to maturity, we all spill our milk, say things we shouldn't, and at times, don't act our age. Every now and then we skin an elbow, bruise a knee, or bloody a nose from falling on our faces!"

Immaturity is not just reserved for a three-year-old. Throwing a temper tantrum and pouting with massive mood swings is not just a characteristic of awkward teenagers. The process we all go through is called "growing up." And I must admit it can sometimes be a painful struggle characterized by more mistakes and missteps than "acting our age." Sooner or later, whether we like it or not, we all have to do it!

After reading what the writer of Hebrews had to say, the obvious conclusion is that he was facing a lack of maturity on the part of his readers. They may have grown old in the Lord, but they had yet to grow up. Instead of feasting on the meat of God's Word they were crawling around playing with building blocks. They became babies sucking their bottles instead of steak-eaters sharpening their knives. There is nothing sadder than a Christian who has known the Lord for many years, and yet is still unable to appreciate the wonderful truth of God's Word. The baby believer (like all babies) still has to rely on someone else to spoon-feed and change his or her spiritual diaper.

Moving from childhood to adulthood should be the stated goal of all believers. None of us will ever arrive at perfection. That is not a realistic goal. What we can do is determine to put away our childish toys and allow the indwelling Holy Spirit to constantly guide us into maturity. Without the searchlight of God's Word to lead us, we will continue to recite our ABCs instead of pressing on to maturity.

Father, show me any area of my life that is childish. I desire to be a mature and productive Christian. I want to feast on the meat of Your Word. Amen!

IT ONLY TAKES A SPARK

*I know your deeds, that you are neither cold nor hot. I wish
you were either one or the other!* (Revelation 3:15)

———————————

One of the most popular songs at youth camp back in the day was called, "It Only Takes a Spark." It was a catchy little song. The first line is, "It only takes a spark to get a fire going, and soon all those around you can warm up to its glowing." It is easy to look back on those simplistic words and think how naïve we were. But in all honesty it is the simple things that can make the biggest impact.

Fulfilling your purpose and walking in your destiny requires passion. Passion by definition is "a strong liking for or devotion to some activity, object, or concept." Passion is the internal fire that motivates and energizes us to fulfill our calling. It is one thing to intellectually know your purpose, but quite another to have the fire to complete it. No worthwhile cause has ever been accomplished without a certain amount of passion. It is the deciding difference between success and failure.

Passion is not something that is static or stays the same. Much like a fire, it will either spread or burn out. The tendency of a fire, if left alone, is to burn itself out. Nothing will quench your passion and fire faster than living without clear direction. It seems ridiculous to give time and energy to any activity without a clear understanding of why you're doing it in the first place.

Paul told his young protégé Timothy to *"fan into flame the gift of God, which is in you through the laying on of my hands"* (2 Timothy 1:6). He did not want his son in the faith to forget the importance of the internal fire. It was his fuel that got him out of bed every morning and moved him into action.

God put inside you a divine purpose for which nothing else can compensate. If you are not sure of your purpose, the best place to start is asking the One who created you. I guarantee you He will give you an answer.

———————————

Father, thank You for reminding me of the importance of direction and purpose. I do not want to ever allow the passion of my heart to grow dim. Amen!

WHAT TO DO WITH A GIANT PROBLEM

So David triumphed over the Philistine with a sling and a stone; without a sword in his hand he struck down the Philistine and killed him (1 Samuel 17:50).

One of the most familiar stories in the Bible is the classic battle between David and Goliath. Everybody knows the story of how the Israelites were on the verge of being defeated by the Philistine army. Every morning Goliath would hurl insults at the Israelites and challenge them to send him one man to fight. Saul's army huddled in fear.

Enter David. He was only a visitor, a shepherd boy too young to join the army. Something happened inside David that moved him from casual observer to active participant. He was faced with a giant problem and decided to take action. No need to recount the details here, it's all so familiar. But suffice it to say he took his sling and five smooth stones and took care of business (see 1 Samuel 17:48-51). Goliath was not too big to hit, he was too big to miss!

Does David's experience with Goliath teach us anything about facing giant problems? I believe it does. We can face any challenge as long as we have conviction and strength of resolve on our side. Problems will always be part of our experience. Wishing and hoping will not make problems disappear.

David viewed Goliath as a doorway into his next level of success. The giant problem David faced was nothing more than a new opportunity for growth. He did not bury his face in the sand. On the contrary, he saw beyond Goliath and moved to eliminate the obstacle.

If you take the time to read about the great leaders and innovators of history, you will discover most would say that working through difficulties and problems made them better. You and I were created to be problem solvers. It is time to stop running from problems and embrace them as doorways to a new level of opportunity and promotion.

Are you facing a giant problem today? Read James 1:5. Ask God for wisdom. He will give you a battle plan to overcome your giant!

Father, faced with a giant problem give me the wisdom to overcome it. Without Your strength I will surely fail. Amen!

ARE YOU A ROCK?

Therefore, my dear brothers and sisters, stand firm. Let nothing move you.
Always give yourselves fully to the work of the Lord, because you know
that your labor in the Lord is not in vain (1 Corinthians 15:58).

What makes a person a rock? In Paul's statement he uses the phrase *"stand firm,"* or in the original text *"be steadfast."* The definition of the phrase perfectly describes a person who is "stationary, such as something that sits in one place for a long time, or something that is firm and steady." So when Paul uses that phrase he is challenging us to be totally reliable like a rock. This type of person will faithfully stand in his or her place. This person will hold things together and not be easily shaken or moved.

Another way to describe this phrase is like "a huge stone pillar in a building." What is the purpose of a stone pillar? It supports the roof structure or another load-bearing wall in a building. If you were to suddenly take the pillar out of its place, the entire building would collapse, would it not? Our churches, businesses, and homes need more *rocks* for steady and reliable foundations. We don't need to throw rocks, we need to build with them!

Are you a rock? Someone who can be depended on? God challenges His people to be rocks in the foundation of His house. Are you faithfully standing in place and helping to hold things together? Even when circumstances are crumbling, a rock will be there for others to lean on.

You may not consider yourself a rock. You may think your role is so unimportant that it is up to others to provide the steadfastness needed to hold things together. If that is your thinking, it is time to change. There is no such thing as an insignificant part of the body of Christ. We all have our place to fit in. A surefire way to be considered a rock is to eliminate roller-coaster emotions, unpredictable behavior, and ever-changing attitudes.

Father, help me to realize that I am important in the body of Christ. I want to be the kind of person who others consider a rock—a person who is dependable and steadfast. Amen!

MONDAY

TALK IS CHEAP

So we cared for you. Because we loved you so much, we were delighted to share with you not only the gospel of God but our lives as well (1 Thessalonians 2:8).

No one would doubt Paul's ability to teach the Word. Some have suggested he was probably one of the best teachers of the New Testament era. His goal was not to dispense information but revelation knowledge that would change the lives of those who heard him.

Paul did not just preach the gospel, he gave his very life as a demonstration of the Word in action. His life was an open book. Because of his willingness to be open before the church at Thessalonica, he modeled the very message he was preaching.

A common failure among Christians today is to say one thing and do the opposite. If we desire to be true mentors to young believers, we must give them examples to follow. Sadly, we find in the modern church more talking and less demonstrating the truth of the gospel. Gaining Bible knowledge is useless until it becomes a living Word that produces change.

In his second letter to the Thessalonians Paul wrote, *"For you yourselves know how you ought to follow our example. We were not idle when we were with you"* (2 Thessalonians 3:7). When he encourages the believers to *"follow our example,"* he isn't referring to a casual approach to discipleship; rather, the implication is an intentional study of the life, deeds, actions, and thoughts of another person. It is an attempt to fully understand that person and then to replicate the person's attributes in our own lives.

There is a common misconception that if we give our very lives to those who are following us they will somehow lose respect. Nothing is further from the truth. Paul did not feel he would lose their respect, on the contrary he wanted them to observe him so closely they would be able to duplicate his life themselves.

There's nothing wrong with getting close to those you teach. Opening up will allow them to see our action matches our message. Talk is cheap. What people need is an example to follow!

Father, I want to be a good example to those around me. Help me demonstrate the truth of my message. Amen!

NO DOUBT ABOUT IT

Being confident of this, that he who began a good work in you will carry it on to completion until the day of Christ Jesus
(Philippians 1:6).

Is it wrong to have doubts? There is no sin in having doubts pop into your mind. Doubts are very human. They become sin when you allow them to remain; after all, it is impossible to stop a bird from flying over your head, but you do not have to let it build a nest there! Doubts often find a place in our thinking because we have lost sight of who God really is. I am afraid there are times when we doubt our beliefs, and believe our doubts.

Paul said God has the cure for the burden of doubt: *"Being confident of this, that he who began a good work in you will carry it on to completion until the day of Christ Jesus."* Who is "he"? He is the supreme King of kings, the omniscient and omnipresent God who promised to finish what He started! The greatest cure for doubt is to remember who God is and what He can do. If you want doubts to melt away, just remember Numbers 23:19: *"God is not human, that he should lie, not a human being, that he should change his mind. Does he speak and then not act? Does he promise and not fulfill?"*

God takes the responsibility in whatever He commands. If you are experiencing doubt. it may be you have missed the fact that He uses many steps to bring everything to completion. Doubts creep in when we do not see all of the steps line up in logical order. Human nature wants everything to make sense, and quite frankly it doesn't always work out that way. Impatience will always lead to doubt.

You can have supreme confidence in Him. He did not begin a *"good work"* in you and then decide to move on to the next project. Nor will he lose interest in you and decide you are a lost cause. When a little boy complained that the lantern his father was carrying did not give light far ahead, the father replied, *"It shines far enough for the next step. That's enough!"*

Father, I know You have a wonderful plan for my life. When I doubt, stabilize my mind with positive thoughts that You will complete what you started in me. Amen!

A LOVELY CHRISTIAN

But I think it is necessary to send back to you Epaphroditus, my brother, co-worker and fellow soldier, who is also your messenger, whom you sent to take care of my needs (Philippians 2:25).

When you read Paul's letters you will notice he constantly talks about other people who helped him in spreading the gospel of Christ. There was not a selfish bone in his body! He was a living example of the attitude he urged in Philippians 2:3-4, when he said, *"Do nothing out of selfish ambition or vain conceit. Rather, in humility value others above yourselves, not looking to your own interests but each of you to the interests of the others."* The man who received the greatest honor in the book of Philippians is Epaphroditus. I would not suggest you name your son that, but I am sure we would all desire to live our lives like his. His name means "lovely" or "handsome."

Why did Paul choose to honor him? He displayed unselfish service in the cause of the gospel. This "lovely Christian" was grateful to be a team member. He did not have to be the quarterback or a big fish in a little pond.

We know very little about him, but he seems to have been a worker in the church at Philippi. Later on we learn he was the one chosen to send a gift to the apostle Paul. He substituted for an entire church and brought a love offering to help the man of God. In the process we are told he almost died. He did not regard his own safety or comfort in order to spread the good news.

Think about this. This man has been gone more than 2,000 years now, and yet we're still being blessed by his unselfish service. He is an example for us to follow. Only eternity will reveal the influence of men and women who have given all to serve as trailblazers to open doors for the gospel. You may not know their names today, but I guarantee you one day when Heaven calls the roll, everyone will know who they are!

Father, thank You for giving me the example of this "lovely Christian." I want to live my life to serve You like this man. I do not desire the applause of others, but only the applause of Heaven. Amen!

HOLD ON!

*Let us hold unswervingly to the hope we profess, for he
who promised is faithful* (Hebrews 10:23).

———————————◆———————————

God-given dreams are very powerful. At first they seem impossible, but it is usually those who accept the challenge of the impossible who see their dreams come to pass. The Bible, as well as history, is filled with men and women who saw impossible dreams become realities. Think about Thomas Edison. If he had given up on his dream of the lightbulb every time he failed, he would not have had the great honor of being part of an invention that literally changed the world. He pushed through discouragement and negative comments until the lights finally came on!

The writer of Hebrews encourages us to *"hold unswervingly to the hope we profess."* It literally means "to embrace something tightly." It is the picture of a person who finds the object of his or her dreams and grabs on, and holds tight. He is simply giving us encouragement to have the attitude of personal possession. If you want to see the fulfillment of God's dream in your life, you have to grab on, wrap your arms around the imparted Word, and never stop believing until the dream comes to pass.

The next time you are tempted to give up on your dream, think about the attitude of Abraham and Sarah. The fulfillment of their dream did not come immediately. In spite of the obstacles, not the least of which was old age, they refused to let go (see Genesis 11–21). They did not give up, they simply held on to the dream. There came a day when they looked into the face of Isaac and realized the dream was real.

When the enemy tries to steal your dream, place *all of your weight on top and hold on.* Declare to all who will listen that nothing will rob you of your God-given dream. It may seem it's never going to happen, but with patient perseverance it will come to pass. God is not bound by your watch or your calendar. Remember, with Him it's about *timing, not time.*

———————————◆———————————

Father, fill me with strength and courage to refuse to let go of my dream. I confess Your faithfulness to bring to pass everything You have promised. Amen!

SONGS IN THE NIGHT

About midnight Paul and Silas were praying and singing hymns to God, and the other prisoners were listening to them (Acts 16:25).

The next time you think you are having a bad day, take a moment and read the entire sixteenth chapter of Acts. Paul and Silas are having the mother of all bad days! They were arrested for doing a good thing. They cast an evil spirit out of a young slave girl, and instead of receiving the applause of the locals they were put on trial. It seems that the local merchants were more interested in making money than seeing this young person set free. After a mock trial, Paul and Silas were beaten with rods and put in prison in the innermost dungeon with their feet in stocks.

They had a choice. They could complain and grumble about their circumstances. They could sink into the black hole of despair and depression, or they could choose to encourage themselves by praising God. They chose to sing praise at the darkest hour of their lives. Wow!

Dr. Luke the apostle tells us that while Paul and Silas sang, the other prisoners were listening. No doubt they were. I cannot imagine the shock when they heard the sweet melodies of a gospel concert! How did God respond to their remarkable faith? He delivered them from the dungeon by sending an earthquake: *"Suddenly there was such a violent earthquake that the foundations of the prison were shaken"* (Acts 16:26).

Recovering from the worst day of your life starts by releasing praise and joy. The devil knows if he can steal your joy he can defeat you. He also knows grief and depression will sap your strength. So he will do everything to keep you from being aware of the spiritual truth revealed to Nehemiah: *"Do not grieve, for the joy of the Lord is your strength"* (Nehemiah 8:10).

Paul and Silas did not fall for the trick of the enemy. The moment they released praise from their mouth, joy was recovered and their entire situation turned around! So the next time you find yourself at a "midnight hour," try praise—who knows God may send an earthquake to change your situation!

Father, today I will choose praise over complaining about my circumstances. I believe when I release praise from my mouth, You will release new strength and joy into my life. Amen!

MONDAY

AN UNLIKELY CANDIDATE

By faith Abraham, when called to go to a place he would later receive as his inheritance, obeyed and went, even though he did not know where he was going (Hebrews 11:8).

If you were looking for someone to start a new nation, I wonder if this man named Abraham would be your first choice? Today just the mention of his name inspires faith, hope, and trust in the promises of God. If you page through the Bible you will discover his name is referred to or talked about 308 times in the Old and New Testaments.

This hero of the faith was not perfect. Heroes never are. Abraham did not come from a godly home. Quite the contrary. Abraham came from a place called the Ur of the Chaldees. Abraham's hometown was the center of idol worship. His parents were idol worshipers, and no doubt he was too.

When Abraham first met God he was seventy-five years old, married to Sarah, and they had no children. It would be a safe bet to say that Abraham was not on his knees crying out to God. As far as I can tell, he is not searching for God at all. But I can tell you this, God was looking for him!

God told Abraham to leave his country and his people. He had to leave it all behind in order to follow God's call on his life. God called him and he went. He may have had his doubts, but he went. He may have wondered if he was doing to the right thing, but he went. You see the only real response God is looking for when He calls is obedience to get up and get moving. He will fill in the details along the way!

The central truth about the life of faith is it rarely sees the big picture in advance. When God calls, He doesn't have to always explain Himself and give us the fine print. He will always give us enough "light" to get moving. What made Abraham so great? When God called he simply obeyed and went! What would you do?

Father, I know You do not have to give me all the details. I have determined to walk in the light I have. Amen!

COME BEFORE WINTER

Do your best to get here before winter (2 Timothy 4:21).

You recognize these words of the apostle Paul were written to his young protégé, Timothy. He urges Timothy to come before winter. Why the urgency? Paul was in a Roman prison and he seems to have a premonition that his days are numbered. He has already said, *"The time for my departure is at hand."*

But I think there was another reason for his sense of urgency. Timothy was located in another city, and in wintertime travel on the Mediterranean was difficult at best. Harbors were generally closed down. Timothy, if you're going to come, now is the time. Winter may overtake you and death may overtake me—don't delay!

I have no idea if Timothy reached Paul before his death. I would like to think that he received Paul's letter and immediately set sail. One thing I do know, if Timothy delayed for any reason he would have missed his opportunity. Did he get to spend time with his mentor? I have no idea. The Bible gives us no indication.

What does that have to do with us? Wintertime is a picture of the uncertainty and brevity of life. It is a natural truth with a spiritual meaning. James 4:13-14 states, *"Now listen, you who say, 'Today or tomorrow we will go to this or that city, spend a year there, carry on business and make money.' Why, you do not even know what will happen tomorrow. What is your life? You are a mist that appears for a little while and then vanishes."*

Yesterday is gone, and we have no promise of tomorrow. It is no use to grieve over decisions we should have made yesterday. And what we're planning to do tomorrow may never come. The devil's word is always "tomorrow." God's word is *"today."*

If you need to change the direction you're heading, do it today. If you need to repair a broken relationship, don't wait till wintertime, *do it today.* If you need to make a decision about your relationship with Christ, *do it today!*

Time is passing. Winter is coming. Don't delay.

Father, may I never take for granted the precious gift of time. I know whatever I am going to do, I need to do it before it is too late. Amen!

YOU'RE IN GOOD HANDS

Yet you, Lord, are our Father. We are the clay, you are the potter; we are all the work of your hand (Isaiah 64:8).

One of the most popular television commercials in recent years has to do with car insurance. After showing all the terrible things that can happen when someone has a car crash, the announcer says for us not to worry because, "You're in good hands." When someone tells you that, what is really being said? The obvious inference is to convey a sense of security and protection. The prophet Isaiah is conveying a wonderful truth. When faced with the challenges and opportunities of life, we can rest assured we are in good hands. He tells us that our Father has everything under control.

A skilled Potter can transform a lump of clay into a beautiful and useful vessel. He is our Creator, and He doesn't just let us sit around like a useless clump of clay. Each time His hands works the clay—our lives—there is intention and purpose. Day by day He fashions the clay with patience and persistence until the tapestry of our purpose is formed.

What happens to a piece of clay if you forget and leave it out for a long time? It can dry up and become very hard. If we are not careful, we can stray from the purposes of God and our hearts become hard and difficult to mold. But the good news is if we turn back to the Master Potter, He will continue to shape us according to His good pleasure and perfect will (see Philippians 2:13).

Our heavenly Father is a patient and perfect Potter, and we can rest assured we are in good hands as He molds each of us into the person He intended. Never be discouraged by the pressure of His hands as He works with you. There are no mistakes or throwaways with your heavenly Father. The secret is to remain pliable and moldable, trusting in His loving plan. We need to relax and chill out. After all...He is still the Potter and we are still the clay!

Father, forgive me when I allow my heart to become hard to Your purpose. Shape me into what You want for me today. Amen!

WHO'S LEADING WHO?

For those who are led by the Spirit of God are the children of God (Romans 8:14).

I have noticed a trend. Almost everyone I talk to wants to be a leader. Walk into your local bookstore and ask for books on leadership. Trust me, there is no shortage. Don't get me wrong, I love the subject. But if everyone is leading who's doing the following? One characteristic of great leaders is before they were great leaders they were superb followers. You might say it's the "number-one, all-time, gold standard of leadership"!

The Holy Spirit is the Leader, and we are the followers. In Romans 8, the word Paul uses for "led" is very interesting to me. It has two distinct meanings that give an indication of how important it is to "follow our Leader."

First it simply means "to lead" and is often used to describe farm animals who were led around by a rope. The rope would usually be tied around the neck, and the animals would willingly submit to follow the owner wherever he led it. Second, the word "agony" is also found in the root meaning. This describes an intense conflict such as the struggle in a wrestling match or a struggle of the human will. Once we determine to allow the Holy Spirit to lead us, an immediate struggle and intense fight to determine who is going to be in control happens.

Our old nature does not like to be told what to do. It does not matter if it is our spouse or our family doctor. We like to be in charge, and the captain of our own ship. If we are ever going to learn how to be *Spirit-led*, we must learn how to defeat our own flesh and allow the Holy Spirit to have His way. Learning to be sensitive to His voice is the key.

There are many translations of Romans 8:14, but the best I have found states, "Following the leadership of the Holy Spirit is one of the privileges of being a son (or daughter) of God, although it may be agonizing to learn how to defer to Him and to really let Him be your leader."

Father, my desire is to learn how to follow the leading of the Holy Spirit. Help me to learn to recognize and listen to Your still, small voice. Amen!

CAUGHT!

When they kept on questioning him, he straightened up and said to them, "Let any one of you who is without sin be the first to throw a stone at her" (John 8:7).

What a dramatic encounter. Once again the scribes and Pharisees were trying to test and embarrass the Lord Jesus. These "spiritual turf shepherds" caught a woman in the very act of adultery. The Pharisees smugly said, "The Law of Moses said stone her, and we want to know what you say Jesus?" They thought they had it all figured out—they just didn't realize who they were dealing with! Needless to say the answer they received was not what they were expecting, *"Let any one of you who is without sin be the first to throw a stone at her."*

The Pharisees wanted harsh justice for this woman. Instead, Jesus gave her grace. He said to the woman, "Don't sin like this again." He wasn't excusing sin. He gave her a new identity and a new purpose.

A question rarely asked whenever this story is read is "Who is this woman?" She is a picture of all of us. Why? We have all been caught red-handed in our sins. Before you get righteously indignant, consider that James 2:10 says, *"For whoever keeps the whole law and yet stumbles at just one point is guilty of breaking all of it."* That simple statement places all of us on the same moral equivalent as this poor woman. Whether it's adultery, rage, jealousy, lying, or gossip (you pick it) whatever form it takes, sin is sin. No one is exempt.

I find it interesting John chapter 8 opens with a group of men wanting to stone a woman, and it ends with a group of men wanting to stone Jesus. Why? When their hypocrisy was exposed, their first instinct was to kill the messenger. A self-righteous religious spirit exposed an adulterous woman, but Jesus exposed them for what they were. According to Jesus only those without sin had the right to carry out the sentence demanded by the law. He didn't overturn the law, He simply reestablished righteousness on the basis of grace. Hallelujah!

Father, the next time I start to judge someone, help me to remember this woman. I need Your grace just like she did. Amen!

MONDAY

GIVE AND GET

Great peace have they that love Thy law: and nothing shall offend them (Psalms 119:165).

———————

Knowing how to respond when someone offends us is one of the hardest things to do. It happens more often than we think. I have discovered most people who offend me don't do it on purpose. By the same token, I am sure I have offended others by a certain action or attitude, and I didn't even know it until much later. Yes, we have all been misunderstood. All of us have the capacity to offend. Wouldn't it be wonderful if everyone thought the best about us and did not rush to judgment?

Here are the real questions: If someone offends you, do you rush to judgment or are you willing to assume the offending person never intended to be offensive? Are you willing to give the same mercy and grace to others that you want to receive yourself? The law of "sowing and reaping" not only is in operation in the natural world, but it also operates in the atmosphere. If you and I give mercy to others, we are guaranteed to reap in mercy ourselves. A good rule of thumb: You are never wrong when you do the right thing!

The apostle Paul said in Romans 15:7, *"Accept one another, then, just as Christ accepted you."* The word "accept" literally means "to receive closely, or with a welcoming attitude." What he is telling us is to receive one another with open arms, just as Jesus accepted us when we first came to Him. It is always helpful to remember the times when we have been forgiven and freely accepted in spite of offensive actions and attitudes.

The next time someone is offensive, try a different response. Instead of rising up with a condemning spirit, offer grace and mercy and watch the situation turn around. As a wise man once said, "Always take the route of mercy, and you will never be sorry. Believe it or not there are times when it's better to close your eyes to what you see other people do and just let it go!" I would say that is pretty good counsel wouldn't you?

Father, forgive me when I give out judgment instead of mercy and grace. Never let me forget how You extended mercy to me when I needed it the most. Amen!

DON'T GO BY THE SCOREBOARD

As it is written: "For your sake we face death all day long; we are considered as sheep to be slaughtered." No, in all these things we are more than conquerors through him who loved us (Romans 8:36-37).

———————————————

Most of our teaching and preaching today is about winning. America loves a winner; and let's face it, everyone wants to be winners in everything we do. No one likes to lose. Unfortunately, life does not always work that way, even for Christians. There will be times when you look up at the scoreboard and it says you are losing.

The apostle Paul knew the secret of winning *"in all these things."* The next time you think you're having a bad day consider what this man had to endure in order to spread the gospel of Jesus Christ (see 2 Corinthians 11:22-33). He faced every challenge by prioritizing God's call on his life. He did not allow the set-backs to set him back. He did not pay attention to the scoreboard because he knew his calling was more important than anything the devil could throw against him.

You may find yourself in a difficult season, so how is it possible to become *"more than a conqueror"* and learn how to win while losing? Worldly wisdom might tell you to "tough it out, and quit complaining." Church wisdom might tell you to "fake it till you make it." I suggest a different approach. If you feel you have lost your sense of calling and commitment, go back to that moment when you gave your life away to Christ. Get a vice grip on your calling once again. You may find yourself in a losing season, but I guarantee you it is possible to win while losing. Joseph sat for years in a dark dungeon but held on to his calling of greatness. Job lost his wealth and health but held on to his call to be a righteous man.

You have a calling and purpose, so never settle for the fact that, because circumstances have knocked you down, you are not knocked out. Yes, we may lose a battle here and there, but we will win the war!

———————————————

Father, when I fall give me the strength to get up. When I feel discouraged remind me of the day You called me to serve You. Amen!

HANG ON

But as for me, my feet had almost slipped; I had nearly lost my foothold. For I envied the arrogant when I saw the prosperity of the wicked (Psalm 73:2-3).

The psalmist had a problem. He was bothered by the apparent contradiction between what he had been taught in the Scripture and what he was actually seeing all around him. On one hand, he had been taught that if he was righteous and pure in heart God would provide for him and take care of him. On the other hand, he was watching the arrogant and unrighteous prosper. His attitude was, "Why are my own circumstances so difficult, while the unrighteous are doing so well?"

By his own admission he declared, *"my feet had almost slipped; I had nearly lost my foothold."* Do you get the picture? He was envious and disturbed. Why? How could God be righteous and allow the unrighteous to prosper? He came to the place where he was almost ready to walk away and turn his back on his faith. He was living in the middle of a contradiction, and it caused him to stumble.

One of the things I love about the Psalms is they speak to our own experience. He is only echoing what many believers feel. Let's be honest. When you became a new Christian did you have the idea that challenges and problems were a thing of the past? Did life suddenly become fair the day you said yes to Christ? Do the good guys always win, and the bad guys always lose?

The psalmist was honest and not afraid to ask God the hard questions. He was not afraid to admit things were not working out as he had hoped. I have learned God is not upset when we ask hard questions. On the contrary, He invites us to be honest about our struggles. He is not "put off" when we confess that we don't understand why life is not fair. Be encouraged that your heavenly Father knows and cares about your every circumstance. The secret to peace and contentment is to allow the power of God to work in and through you. Take care of your own situation, and believe me, God can handle the rest!

Father, help me to trust You despite what I often see around me. I will stop worrying about the prosperity of the unrighteous. Amen!

SHUT EVERY DOOR

And do not give the devil a foothold (Ephesians 4:27).

I have good news. You do not have to allow the devil access to any part of your life! You can shut every window, close every door, and seal up any cracks through which the enemy can operate. The enemy is always looking for places to penetrate and gain footholds where he can cause confusion and chaos. Contrary to what you may have been told, you can walk in victory over his tactics.

The word "foothold" literally means "a marked off geographical location, or a specific region or zone." It is from this word we get the word for a topographical map. By using this word Paul lets us know the devil will attack any region or zone in our lives. It may be our marriage, finances, business, our children, and even our ministry.

One of the first entry points he will try to use is through our relationships. Allowing conflict and unresolved issues with a loved one or friend will often become the very crack he is looking for. He loves nothing more than to build a stronghold of offense in our minds that will eventually lead to a wall. And we all know that walls are for separation, not inclusion. If we refuse to deal with hurt, old wounds, and unresolved grievances, we are headed for trouble. It is like holding up a sign to the devil that reads: "I have marked off a place for you to enter."

Paul makes it clear that allowing entry points for the devil is a choice we make. We can also choose to walk in the Spirit and never give one inch of territory. We can choose to be offended, upset, and mad, or we can choose to lovingly forgive. We can choose to hold grudges, or we can choose to put it under the blood of Christ. We can choose to put a guard on our tongue, or say things that we will later regret.

The next time the accuser of the brethren starts to nibble around the edges looking for a place to attack, stand up and boldly declare, *"No, not here, not now, not ever!"*

Father, help me to stay free of any unforgiveness and bitterness. I refuse to allow any entry points in my heart. Amen!

WHEN GOD SAYS NOTHING

*He inquired of the Lord, but the Lord did not answer him
by dreams or Urim or prophets* (1 Samuel 28:6).

Running ahead of God can be risky business. If you are not sure about that, consider King Saul. You remember him don't you? He was selected the first king of Israel. He is the "poster boy" of what can happen when you run ahead of God and take matters into your own hands.

Saul was getting ready to go to battle, and he went to God and asked, "What do You want me to do about this situation?" He had not been right with God for a long time, and yet he still expected God to give him a quick battle plan. The Bible says God did not answer by a dream, a sign, or a prophet. Saul got desperate. He turned to demons and the occult to find the strategy. I can't help but believe that he knew it was wrong, but he did it anyway. He could not figure out any other way to make it happen. He lost everything. He lost the war, his reputation, and even his own life. The consequences were devastating.

So what are we to do when God is silent and says nothing?

First, remember God is always in control. Job 34:29 says, *"But if he remains silent, who can condemn him? If he hides his face, who can see him? Yet he is over individual and nation alike."* Just because God is silent about a plan or a direction does not mean He doesn't have one. Never equate God's silence with loss of control. He loves you and will take care of you if you are patient and willing to wait.

Second, you can trust Him. Proverbs 3:5 says, *"Trust in the Lord with all your heart and lean not on your own understanding."* The issue is always about trust. Trusting God with every issue of our lives, especially when He is silent, can be frustrating. Trusting that God has His reasons, and waiting on Him is the key. Running ahead and doing your own thing is never the right response. It will always lead to tragedy—just ask King Saul!

Father, I want to learn to be patient and listen. Help me to trust You and Your plan even when You are silent. Amen!

SECTION V

PRAISE AND PRAYER

MONDAY

THE NECESSITY OF GRATITUDE

Having been firmly rooted and now being built up in Him and established in your faith, just as you were instructed, and overflowing with gratitude (Colossians 2:7 NASB).

When is the last time you told someone you were grateful for them? As a society we have become more ungrateful as the years have ticked off the clock.

Someone once said, "Every virtue divorced from gratitude will be stunted in its growth and therefore, won't last."

Gratitude would not be on most Christian's short list of godly virtues. In Colossians Paul says, *"overflowing with gratitude."* In the Greek this is a picture of a river overflowing its bank during flood season. A flood affects everything! It changes the landscape, it washes dead things away, and it refreshes the banks of the river so it can flow more freely. In short, fill your life with gratitude so that it affects every facet of your life. Let gratitude sweep away all the death and give you a fresh start.

Gratitude will produce three things in your life: joyfulness, appeal, and resiliency. Let's examine these three more closely.

1. Gratitude makes you *joyful.* So much of the time individuals produce the fruits of discouragement, despair, fear, and anxiety; and when you find these four bedfellows tagging along in life you *must* fill your life with gratitude. Choosing gratitude will naturally flood your life with joy. Choosing joy allows you to renew your mind on the Word of God, set your heart on savoring the gifts of God in your life and intentionally disciplining your tongue to speak the goodness of God.

2. Gratitude makes you *appealing.* To me, there is nothing more unattractive than an ungrateful person. Tell me what a person looks like when they are whining, murmuring, or complaining all the

time? Yep, ugly. Gratitude or ingratitude will be nothing more than the showcase of a person's heart. If you want to be appealing to others, you must be grateful.

3. Gratitude makes you *resilient*. In Psalm 73:1-3 Asaph says, *"Surely God is good to Israel* [His people], *to those who are pure in heart. But as for me, my feet had almost slipped; I had nearly lost my foothold. For I envied the arrogant when I saw the prosperity of the wicked."* He said he "almost slipped." Why? Because his eyes were on others and was filled with ingratitude; but he was resilient and recalled the goodness of God and he did not stumble.

Father, I repent of having an ungrateful heart toward You and others, and through Your strength I choose to be grateful and operate in gratitude. Amen!

TIME TO TAKE RESPONSIBILITY

Now no shrub of the field was yet on the earth, and no plant had yet sprung up, for the Lord God had not sent rain upon the earth, and there was no one to work [cultivate] the ground (Genesis 2:5).

Many years ago this one verse changed my life forever. I remember sitting in Cabin #2 at Restoration Ranch asking God to reveal to me what He was saying in this verse. After much prayer and fasting the Lord flooded my heart with His truth. If you take a careful look at the verse you will see a natural progression. *No shrub was in the earth, no sprouting of plants, God withholding rain,* this is the first three parts of the verse. The part that stuck out to me was part four, no one to take care of the ground.

I know God is a God of order. He never planned nor executed anything out of order. If we want to know God, we must know order. He never rushes. He's never late. He's always right on time.

So it was clear to me that in my life God was not willing to give me more ground until I took responsibility over the ground He had already entrusted me with. Know this dear reader, if you want more ground you *must* take responsibility over what you have already been given.

Over the years I have switched out the word "rain" with "reign." The greatest desire of my life is to have Christ reign in every area of my life. If there is an area in which He is not ruling and reigning, then it is my responsibility to submit those areas to Him. It is time to take responsibility.

What are some areas you need God to reign in? Starting today, I challenge you to submit to His rule and reign in your life. Start taking responsibility for the ground God has given you if you want to be given more ground. Being a good steward allows you to receive more and more. Stop taking responsibility and God will stop sending His reign into your life and the outcome will be nothing short of stagnation.

Heavenly Father, thank You for all you have blessed me with in this life. I confess that I have not been responsible for every area You have entrusted to me. Please forgive me and I commit to take responsibility for everything You have put under my care. Amen.

ENJOYING GODLY GROWTH

How blessed is the man who does not walk in the counsel of the wicked, nor stand in the path of sinners, nor sit in the seat of scoffers! But his delight is in the law of the Lord, and in His law he meditates day and night. He will be like a tree firmly planted by streams of water, which yields its fruit in its season and its leaf does not wither; and in whatever he does, he prospers
(Psalm 1:1-3 NASB).

Wow, what power-packed verses we have today. The preacher comes out in me when I look at these verses. There is a simple progression in the first two verses and then launches you into verse 3. There are multiple places in Scripture that give us a promise, but it comes with conditions. These verses happen to do just that!

IF we choose not to walk in the counsel of the wicked, nor stand in the path of sinners, nor sit in the seat of the scoffers, BUT rather we choose to delight ourselves in God's law and spend our days and nights meditating on them, something amazing happens. Our tree (life) will be planted (transplanted away from our own agenda) by God's streams of life and we will produce heaps of fruit in our lives without worrying about death. Thus, by having His streams of life coursing through our lives, we will live in prosperity.

Let's take a few seconds to talk about walk, stand, and sit. We should never walk in the counsel of godless men and women. Seek out for yourself godly men and women who will counsel you based on the Word of God, not out of their own selfish motives and intents. Don't be the one who stands in the same path as those who willfully choose to live a sinful life. Don't fall into the trap so many fall into. Matthew Henry states, "He does not associate with those that sit in close cabal to find out ways and means for the support and advancement of the devil's kingdom, or that sit in open judgment, magisterially to condemn the generation of the righteous."

We should have a passionate desire to live our lives planted beside the flowing canals of His love, life, and mercy. You do not have to worry about producing fruit; it will be a natural outcome of living planted in Him. Never be ashamed (letting your leaf wither) of the fruit God has blessed you with and your soul will prosper.

Father, give me the wisdom I need to avoid leaning on the counsel of godless men or women. Keep my feet from straying on any path of wickedness. I choose to be planted in You and call forth fruit and prosperity in my life because of what You have promised me. Amen.

SOVEREIGN PROTECTION

You prepare a table before me in the presence of
my enemies... (Psalm 23:5 NASB).

———————————

This verse comes alive when we look at the visual picture behind the words. Over the next few minutes let's journey together through this beautiful word picture.

Imagine with me a shepherd leading his flocks from pasture to pasture in ancient Israel. Every one of the sheep know his voice and respond when called. His beard is shaggy and not groomed, and oh the smell, just like the sheep he is tending. He has been around so long he has watched some of the sheep be birthed while others have died from age. This shepherd is extremely knowledgeable about the territory and knows firsthand the dangers of protecting his sheep.

As he enters the field he notices something; it is a vibrant green field with lush grass, but he knows there is danger lurking just below the surface. In the Middle East there are serpents living in burrows beneath the lush grasses in many of the valleys. These venomous serpents will slither their way to the surface when they feel the vibration of the sheep walking around grazing. Shepherds have lost many sheep to these deadly serpents. To protect the sheep from these deadly serpents the shepherds will keep the sheep away from the valley until they discover each and every hole.

Shepherds carried a flask of oil with them during their journeys. They would pour oil into and around the openings of every hole. The shepherds would then release the sheep into the pasture to graze. The snakes would feel the trembling of the ground and start working their way to the surface. When encountering the oil, the serpents could not make their way to the surface because it was too slippery, thus allowing the sheep to have supper without worrying about the enemies just below their hoofs.

In this colorful passage the Lord is letting us know He has gone before us and defeated the enemy so we can enjoy His table while the enemy looks on with no ability to touch us! Praise God!

With all that being said, we need to be willing to belly up to His table with no fear of what the enemy can do to us.

God, You are my great protector. I thank and praise You for Your protection. You have gone before me time and time again to hold back the enemy, allowing me to enjoy the fruits of Your table. My heart is filled with gratitude for all You have done for me. Amen.

THE REAL KING

The earth is the Lord's, and all it contains, the world, and those who dwell in it.
For He has founded it upon the seas and established it upon the rivers
(Psalm 24:1-2 NASB).

———————————⟡———————————

A well-known preacher in the 1970s named Ern Baxter once said in a message, "We would do well to rise every morning and quote Psalm 24:1." I would also like to add, we would be served well to remember, *"The earth is the Lord's and all it contains, the world, and those who dwell in it."* We are not in charge, God is. Pastor Wade Trimmer taught me a very powerful phrase, "God is large and in charge."

To know God and to know His attributes sets you free from the "self-centered existence" trap we all, at times, fall into. We are going to take a moment to look at just one of His many attributes.

God is omnipotent. Omnipotent simply means "all powerful, almighty, supreme or preeminent." A proper definition is given by Henry Thiessen: "God is all-powerful and able to do whatever he wills. Since his will is limited by his nature, God can do everything that is in harmony with his perfections."

Several verses to feast on:

1. God is Omnipotent in creation—Isaiah 44:24

2. God is Omnipotent in our salvation—Jude 24-25

3. God is Omnipotent in knowledge and understanding—Psalm 147:5

When you know you serve an all-powerful sovereign God, it is easier to handle the challenges of this life. Philippians 4:13 (NASB) says, *"I can do all things through Him who strengthens me."* God is the one that can give you strength when you are weak, courage when you are fearful and wisdom when you have no answers.

In the book *The Attributes of God*, Arthur Pink wrote, "Well may the saint trust such a God! He is worthy of implicit confidence. Nothing is too hard for Him. If God were stinted in might and had a limit to His strength, we might well despair. But seeing that He is clothed with omnipotence, no prayer is too hard for Him to answer, no need too great for Him to supply, no passion too strong for Him to subdue; no temptation too powerful for Him to deliver from, no misery too deep for Him to relieve." And I say, AMEN!

Sovereign Father, I ask You to reveal Yourself more fully to me. I want to know who You are and know Your attributes. Amen.

MONDAY

TRUE PRAISE

Praise the Lord! Praise God in His sanctuary; praise Him in His mighty expanse. Praise Him for His mighty deeds; praise Him according to His excellent greatness. Praise Him with trumpet sound; praise Him with harp and lyre. Praise Him with timbrel and dancing; praise Him with stringed instruments and pipe. Praise Him with loud cymbals; praise Him with resounding cymbals. Let everything that has breath praise the Lord. Praise the Lord! (Psalm 150 NASB)

Many believe freedom in worship is you worshipping the way they worship. "You are only free if you are as free as me" some Christians say. Well "bologna" is what I say! Every Christian will have to discover for themselves what freedom is for them. Every Christian in every generation has to do this for themselves.

The only thing I would challenge you to do in worship is follow closely and obey the Word of God. The Scripture you just read should give you a good indicator of how the King wants you to worship Him. It seems to me that the psalmist covers all types of worship in these powerful verses. The most powerful verse in this passage is verse 6: *"Let everything that has breath praise the Lord. Praise the Lord!"*

This short eleven-word verse encompasses every living thing on earth and then compels every living thing to give praise to God—and that includes you. True praise. One of the things we have done and would encourage you to do is put on live praise and worship music in your home. We believe God's Word is true when it says, "God inhabits the praise of His people." We have found that doing this brings peace and better attitudes in our home. It is amazing to see the results when we made the decision to change the atmosphere in our home by offering up praise to His name.

Father, I know You desire Your children to praise You in all of Your glory and majesty. I will determine to fill my heart and mind with Your Word and continually let Your praise be in my mouth! Amen.

GOD'S HOUSE

If it is disagreeable in your sight to serve the Lord, choose for yourselves today whom you will serve: whether the gods which your fathers served which were beyond the River, or the gods of the Amorites in whose land you are living; but as for me and my house, we will serve the Lord (Joshua 24:15 NASB).

First and foremost, we all need to be working on the same belief system to move God's kingdom forward. We are going to make sure we are clear in our understanding of what God's house really is and is not. It is not a building made of stone. It not located in a place but resides in a people. It is not a sanctuary but a submitted heart. In the Old Testament, God's presence dwelt in sanctuaries, tents, and to be precise, the Holy of Holies; but this is not His dwelling place any longer.

God the Father sent the Holy Spirit on the Day of Pentecost; God now takes up residency in the hearts of His people through the Holy Spirit. With this in mind, we need not think that because God dwells in us we are not responsible to do anything but just exist. On the contrary! We as Christians are held to an even higher standard with greater responsibilities.

As we continue, I have a question, "Who do you choose to serve today?"

Oh, some might say I serve God, but do their actions say the same thing as their mouths? When I was growing up my dad would always tell me, "Walk your talk or zip your lip." It seems to me that many people talk about loving God, serving God, and faithfulness to God's house, but talk is as far as it goes.

If we are going to say we choose the Lord, then we should "walk our talk or zip our lip."

Father, today my family and I choose to serve and honor You in our home. We also choose to make our walk and our talk match up with Your Word. Amen.

LIVING WATER

He who believes in Me, as the Scripture said, "From his innermost being will flow rivers of living water" (John 7:38 NASB).

———————————————————

Being a teenager in south Louisiana had its advantages. One of the advantages I enjoyed was water sports of all kinds. We would ski, tube, or float anywhere on anything in any body of water we could find. We explored bar ditches after a hurricane. Bayous, ponds, lakes, and rivers—every type of water source delivered its own unique experience. But none was more fun than the river. Bar ditches would dry up within a couple of days and bayous were full of alligators and who knows what else. Ponds typically held lots of snakes and stagnant water, while lakes were just big ponds with very little fresh water.

The rivers were so much fun because on the river things were always changing. We could sit on the bank of any river and the water we saw ten minutes earlier is gone forever and new water is coming. As adults, Melanie and I have had the privilege of driving up and down the Columbia River Gorge summer after summer on our way to Portland, Oregon. Every time I see the Columbia River Gorge, John 7:38 comes to mind.

John did not say out of your innermost being (belly) will flow lakes, ponds, or bayous, he said rivers! You have to ask; why did he use the word "rivers." He used the word because rivers are not still or stagnant. Rivers are constantly changing and constantly bringing new life.

As we believe and trust in Jesus, we will experience fresh, new life flowing out of our innermost parts to a world in desperate need of a change. One of the great consequences of having that river flow out of us is that we will experience that freshness for ourselves. If you find yourself living a dried up or stagnant life, remember that there is fresh, new life coming our way if we believe in Him.

———————————————————

Oh God, pour out Your sweet Holy Spirit and let it run like a river thorough my entire being! I know the world, the flesh, and the devil can never give the freshness I need to keep me from growing stagnant and dull. Amen.

DOERS OF THE WORD

But prove yourselves doers of the word, and not merely hearers who delude themselves (James 1:22 NASB).

———

I can't tell you how many times I have heard my dad preach on this verse. It seemed as though every church we went to with him, he would preach a message on this verse challenging the church to get off their "blessed assurances" and get to work for the kingdom of God. "Laziness" was not a godly trait, he would say. If you were privileged to see him preach when he was a younger man, you know there would be one of two responses from people: anger or repentance. Too many people get so caught up in hearing the Word, yet do nothing with it. What a waste to just be a hearer and do nothing with what someone is investing in you!

The word "hearer" in the Greek language is *akouó*. It is where we get the English word "acoustics" and leads us to the word "audit." This word "audit" has a particular meaning. The best way to use this word is in regard to a college student "auditing" a class. When students audit a class they go to each class, listen to the lectures, examine the information, but never get credit for having taken the class. What a waste!

This is exactly what happens when we hear the Word of God and do nothing with it. We go to the classes, hear the lectures, and examine the information; but until we put those words from God into practice, we are not getting credit for it in our lives. No, we can't earn favor with God by works. We do have the privilege of learning and growing as we are hearing and doing the words God gives us.

Today I strongly encourage you to be a doer of the Word and not just audit your way through life.

———

Father, I know that words and actions go together. My heart's desire is to put into practice the things that I read in Scripture and never, ever be a hearer only. I do not want to be an audience member—I want to be a full participant. Amen.

CHILDREN'S VALUE

Behold, children are a gift of the Lord, the fruit of the
womb is a reward (Psalm 127:3 NASB).

Melanie and I are so blessed to have four children and one grandson. Life is full! I remember when we were young in our marriage and trying to decide how many children we wanted to have. I wanted a lot and Melanie wanted two. As our family grew, my mind-set began to change. I was good when Emily arrived, then Demetri showed up, then Marlee Kaye changed our world, and once Zeke came around we believed we were done. We had no idea how incomplete our lives were until we met each one of our children. We could not imagine life without one of them. And now we have the most awesome grandson on planet Earth, Jaylen Carter Lewis. Just so you know he loves his Pappa and GiGi!

What a gift children are to all of us. God's Word says that they are a gift. You probably want to give that gift back to Him sometimes when they are breaking your heart, but God has given us the fruit of the womb for a specific purpose. Being a parent is one of the highest callings I can imagine—to raise our children to become bearers of fruit who bring glory and honor to God. God has entrusted you and me with the special privilege of launching these wonderful young men and young women into the world to be change agents for the kingdom of God. How are we handling these gifts God has given us? If you examine your heart and see you have missed the mark, repent and ask God and your children to forgive you. Get a copy of *Parenting with Purpose* by Paul and Billie Kaye Tsika to help equip you to become the parents you always wanted to be.

Start enjoying and investing in the fruit of the womb instead of just tolerating them.

Thank You, Jesus, for our children! Help us to lead, train, and equip these precious gifts You have so wonderfully bestowed on us. May we never take them for granted and always lead them in the "way they should go." Amen.

MONDAY

WHY SO SERIOUS?

A joyful heart is good medicine, but a broken spirit dries up the bones (Proverbs 17:22 NASB).

Our culture is pushing the belief that Christians are a bunch of stoic individuals who have no idea how to have fun or laugh. Well, if you believe that you have never been around the Christians I know. There is no way I could enjoy a greater life than the life I am living right now. Melanie and I make sure our home and life are filled laughter and joy. Life is too short to not enjoy it. Too many people take life way too seriously.

The Greater Westminster Catechism says, "The chief end of man is to glorify God, and to enjoy Him for ever." I love what John Piper said, "The chief end of man is to glorify God by enjoying Him for ever." I am not sure about you but I do not believe the word "enjoy" means "stoic." I firmly believe we are to enjoy God and enjoy those around us. God takes pleasure in me, why should I not take pleasure in what He has given me.

Can you laugh at yourself? To be honest, for years I took myself too seriously. I hated to be humiliated and laughed at. I was so concerned how people saw me; and then one day I realized no one was thinking about me at all. What a humbling revelation. I thought of myself more highly than I should have. Sound familiar? Welcome to the insecurity club. Learn to laugh, better yet learn to laugh at yourself. Quit being so serious.

The second part of this Proverbs 17:22 verse is heartbreaking. Even though we, at times, find ourselves with a broken spirit, we never want to remain in that condition for long. We can choose to have a joyful heart, and as we express that joyful heart we will restore the broken spirit that dries up our bones.

Choose joy!

Father, there are times when my life is filled with adversity. When I am faced with difficulty, never let me get bitter, but better. At the end of the day, I know You are in charge of my life, therefore I CHOOSE JOY! Amen.

HONOR BECAUSE IT IS RIGHT

Honor the Lord from your wealth and from the first of all your produce; so your barns will be filled with plenty and your vats will overflow with new wine (Proverbs 3:9-10 NASB).

Render to all what is due them: tax to whom tax is due; custom to whom custom; fear to whom fear; honor to whom honor (Romans 13:7 NASB).

The word "honor" has fallen on hard times in the past few decades. I believe those in my generation and younger have failed to give honor where honor is due. We have developed generations of selfish individuals with hearts flooded with the disease called entitlement. As you listen, you will be able to pick out those infected with this horrible disease. If you pay attention to what the entitlement generation is saying, you will hear words such as, "If my parents have it I should have it. I deserve something someone else has, or somebody owes me." There is too much entitlement and not nearly enough honor in our culture today. This disease has infiltrated every part of our society.

Both of today's passages of Scripture have everything to do with honor and nothing to do with selfish ambition. There is a solution for the disease of entitlement—GRATITUDE! The way we show honor is to live and express gratitude to those God has gifted us with in our lives.

Here is what I suggest:

1. Start listing all the people in your life you are grateful for. This should be a large list once you are completed. Take some time and think about all those your life collides with on a daily basis. Friends, family, coworkers—from anyone to everyone.

2. Once you have completed your list, start writing notes or verbally express gratitude to those you have listed and share with them why you are grateful for them. This, my friend, is a great way to start expressing honor.

Thank You, Father, for reminding me how important it is to honor people in my life. I will take steps TODAY to express my gratitude to each and every one who has made an imprint on my life and character. Amen.

PERFORMING BEFORE AN AUDIENCE OF ONE

Whatever you do, do your work heartily, as for the Lord
rather than for men (Colossians 3:23 NASB).

———————————————————

In my early twenties, Melanie and I were privileged to be youth pastors at a church in Irving, Texas. Boy did those students keep us on our toes. We were privileged to see many of these young men and women grow in God and in their destiny. I can't tell you how many times I preached messages in an effort to equip each of them to become all God wanted them to become. One of my favorite messages was entitled, "Performing Before an Audience of ONE."

Why is it that humanity has an insatiable desire to please others? The reason is because we so desperately want others to approve of us. We crave it and many will perform stupid acts just to get their approval. Many times we would rather please some person than God. We sacrifice our moral standards or give in to peer pressure just to get someone to accept us.

It is time to start *performing before an audience of ONE!* If God is pleased with our actions and the direction we are going in our lives, then who cares what others say? We were created for God's glory not human approval. Humankind's approval is fickle. God's love knows no bounds. He knows our sin and our depravity and continues to pour His love out for us. Our ultimate desire should be a desire to honor Him and have Him put His stamp of approval on our lives.

Whatever you do today or in the future you should ask yourself, "Is God going to be honored in this and am I performing before an audience of One"? Make this the cry of your heart today!

———————————————————

Lord, I know it's not what others think about me, it's only what YOU say about me that counts. I do not want other people's approval. My desire is to hear You say, "WELL DONE, GOOD AND FAITHFUL SERVANT!" Amen.

LIVING A STEADFAST LIFE

They were continually devoting [steadfast] themselves to the apostles' teaching and to fellowship, to the breaking of bread and to prayer (Acts 2:42 NASB).

Therefore, my beloved brethren, be steadfast, immovable, always abounding in the work of the Lord, knowing that your toil is not in vain in the Lord (1 Corinthians 15:58 NASB).

———◦———

Why is the word "steadfast" one of the most powerful words in the English language? The word "steadfast" conjures up the words "resolute, unbendable, unfaltering, unshakable, unwavering, committed, and devoted." Do these words describe you and the way you live your life? If someone was discussing you in a group, would they use these words to testify of you?

One of the greatest attributes of any man or woman is the attribute of being steadfast. This is a word I am passionately working to instill into my life. It is becoming an all-consuming pursuit. It is too easy for us to be tossed about by the waves of this life. To keep us from being tossed around, let us take a few moments and become familiar with how to start being steadfast and how to remain steadfast.

S - Start with a plan

T - Take into account the cost

E - Enjoy the process of planning

A - Accept the direction God is taking you

D - Develop strength for the journey

F - Fix your eyes on the prize

A - Acquire supporters of the plan

S - Stay steadfast to the plan

T - Trust the process

If you are going in the direction God is sending you, He will not leave you without a hope and a peace in the journey. Don't be half-hearted when you start or it will become extremely difficult to stay steadfast on the journey. Today commit to being steadfast in all you do.

Father, I will stay the course. I will refuse to be double-minded about my purpose and destiny. My eye is on the prize and I will not turn back. Amen.

VARIOUS TRIALS

James, a bond-servant of God and of the Lord Jesus Christ, to the twelve tribes who are dispersed abroad: Greetings. Consider it all joy, my brethren, when you encounter various trials, knowing that the testing of your faith produces endurance. And let endurance have its perfect result, so that you may be perfect and complete, lacking in nothing (James 1:1-4 NASB).

James had experienced various trials and was encouraging the twelve tribes to count the trials they were facing and those they were going to face with joy. WHAT? Count it all joy when I face trials? Yes, because the testing will produce faith and that faith will produce endurance.

The most colorful language ever used has been the Greek language. Throughout Scripture, words take on greater meaning and bring greater depth to the passage. One of those words in this passage is the word "various." In the Greek it is *poikilos*. We get the English word "polka dot" meaning "various" from the Greek word *poikilos*. To me this word translation opens up a crystal clear picture of what it looks like to live life.

As we walk in life we run into "various/polka dot" trials. Everyone has them, no one can avoid them, and I have never found a person who loves various trials. Oh yes, there are some who do a much better job at handling the various trials of life, but on the whole we have done a poor job of seeing God's hand at work in the trials.

Don't blame God for your bad decisions, just realize trials are part of every life. No amount of talent, skill, or money will make you exempt from trials in this life.

Remember, trials are going to come into every life.

Remember, you are never alone.

Remember, what this trial is producing.

Remember, God will never fail you!

Jesus, I know trials are going to come my way. Life's trials happen to everyone, and I know I am not exempt. Help me to remember it's not what happens to me, but what happens in me that matters. Amen.

MONDAY

FRUITFUL?

But the fruit of the Spirit is love, joy, peace, patience, kindness, goodness, faithfulness, gentleness, self-control: against such things there is no law (Galatians 5:22-23 NASB).

The fruits of the Spirit are traits God wants to work into our lives. What we want to do is take a minute and look at each one of these fruits of the Spirit. As we examine each, we must ask ourselves the hard question, "Are these traits being worked into my life?"

Love—Love primarily toward Him for all He has done for us, as well as love toward others.

Joy—Joy in the wonderful journey called life. Are we joyful for all God has done for us?

Peace—The peace Paul the apostle is referring to is a calm in the midst of a storm, knowing God is with us.

Patience—All I can say is, do not pray for patience, let it come on His schedule. Why, you may ask. Paul says in Romans 5:3, "tribulation works patience." So if you are praying for patience, you are asking God to bring tribulation into your life to build your patience.

Kindness—Do we express kindness to people? Are we kind to friends, family, the bagger at the supermarket? If we desire to express kindness, we should inform our face and put on a smile.

Goodness—When I see this word it makes me think of the passage in Genesis where God just created the world and He said, "It was good." The word "superior" comes to mind as well. Are we doing and acting in a superior way that will bring glory and honor to God?

Faithfulness—Following through with our commitments and being faithful in all we do is appealing. We should walk in our destiny with faithfulness.

Gentleness—Brash or harsh people are a big turnoff for most people. Tender-hearted people attract others.

Self-control—Last but not least! I think it's funny that Paul put this one last. If we have self-control, we can operate in all the other fruits of the Spirit.

Be fruitful!

———————————————

Father, I know when You are working in my life, the fruit of the Spirit will be produced. I understand it's not something I can work up, but something You display for Your honor and glory. I choose to be a willing vessel so others may see YOU through me. Amen.

WISDOM FROM GOD

But if any of you lacks wisdom, let him ask of God, who gives to all generously and without reproach, and it will be given to him. But he must ask in faith without any doubting, for the one who doubts is like the surf of the sea, driven and tossed by the wind. For that man ought not to expect that he will receive anything from the Lord, being a double-minded man, unstable in all his ways (James 1:5-8 NASB).

———————— ⟡ ————————

The source of all wisdom and understanding is found in God. God has a storehouse of wisdom waiting to be poured out on us if we ask for it. When you lack wisdom in any circumstance of life, all you have to do is ask God and He will give you all the wisdom you need. The key is asking in faith! When we do not ask in faith, we become an emotional roller coaster making ourselves sick as we ride the waves of disbelief.

James challenges us hard when he states that we should not expect anything from God if we are not going to act in faith. Who is a double-minded person? It is a person who believes God will give wisdom—then doesn't believe, then does believe.

When you ask God for wisdom, believe He is going to give it to you. Once you receive the wisdom in the situation, walk it out without doubting. Take, for instance, you are coming to Restoration Ranch for a visit. You call me and ask me to give you directions. I live at Restoration Ranch so I know how to get there—I have no doubt about it. I give you the directions and you start your journey and turn south on highway 71. You go thirteen miles on 71 and say, "I don't see the Ranch, Paul doesn't know what he's talking about," and you turn around and go the other direction. This is what James is talking about. When you get wisdom or direction, don't stop and turn back. If you keep going, you will reach His destination for you. Just as if you had kept driving, the Ranch would have been ahead only two more miles.

Ask and then do!

———————— ⟡ ————————

Lord, I need Your wisdom every single day. I know wisdom is more valuable than gold and more precious than silver. Without Your wisdom I am lost. Amen.

ABIDING IN THE VINE

I am the true vine, and My Father is the vinedresser. Every branch in Me that does not bear fruit, He takes away; and every branch that bears fruit, He prunes it so that it may bear more fruit. You are already clean because of the word which I have spoken to you. Abide in Me, and I in you. As the branch cannot bear fruit of itself unless it abides in the vine, so neither can you unless you abide in Me (John 15:1-4 NASB).

In the context of this passage the word "abide" gives no indication of a passive voice, it always implies action. God has called the Church to be a Church of action. *"Faith without works is dead."* We do not work for our faith, but work because of our faith. Ephesians 2:8-10 says, *"For by grace you have been saved through faith; and that not of yourselves, it is the gift of God; not as a result of works, so that no one may boast. For we are His workmanship, created in Christ Jesus for good works, which God prepared beforehand so that we would walk in them"* (NASB).

Of the twelve disciples, John was the closest to Jesus. John has a unique way of seeing things compared to the other Gospel writers. John gives us a window into the relationship we should have with Jesus.

There is a *pruning* process for everyone who is in Christ. Every Christian goes through times of pruning to help us grow spiritually. Do not despise these times as they are for your benefit. You will become more fruitful the more you get pruned. There is a *producing* season for everyone who is in Christ. God's plan for us is to be fruitful in every aspect of our lives. I believe there will be times in our lives when we can produce maximum amounts of fruit. Abide in Christ and let Him prune you so you can produce greater fruit.

Father, help me to never run from Your pruning shears. I desire maximum fruit, and I know the only way for that to happen is by allowing You the freedom to "cut the dead limbs." Amen.

NEW WINE, NEW WINESKINS

No one sews a patch of unshrunk cloth on an old garment; otherwise the patch pulls away from it, the new from the old, and a worse tear results. No one puts new wine into old wineskins; otherwise the wine will burst the skins, and the wine is lost and the skins as well; but one puts new wine into fresh wineskins (Mark 2:21-22 NASB).

A wineskin is a leather bottle made from a whole goat, sheep, oxen, or donkey, although other animal skins certainly were used when available. The longer the journey or bigger the party the larger the skin needed to make the bottle. The hair was left, only the inside was tanned and oiled for the purpose of protecting the contents of the skin. These skins are much better for traveling than clay pots. Skins are more pliable and fit for travel.

The animal that provided the skin had to give its life for the preparation to receive the new wine. The animal that once was alive, living for self, is now a wineskin created for the master's use. Someone had to die to be of use to the master. We are like the wineskin: we are grown, sacrificed, cleaned out, covered in oil, and prepared for new wine. We must be willing to give up our lives to gain the new life in the new wine.

Wineskins are "what we present to God." They are "old, cracked, brittle, new, limber, pliable" and are "ready to come, go, speak, hush, do, don't do, sit, stand, walk, stop, accept, reject." If and when there is ever a problem, it will be with the wineskin, not the wine. There are seasons in our lives in which we are in desperate need of the new wine to fill our empty wineskin. We must be ready! Be filled with the Holy Spirit—a command! We need to be READY.

R—Repent of the sin of powerlessness

E—Expect to get what you ask for

A—Ask in faith

D—Drink deeply

Y—Yield your whole self

Father, prepare my heart to receive the new wine of your Holy Spirit. Renew my "old skin" with fresh oil, that I may be ready to drink deeply from the well of Your abiding presence. Amen.

ADAPT OR DIE

And Samuel said to Jesse, "Are these all the children?" And he said, "There remains yet the youngest, and behold, he is tending the sheep." ...Now he was ruddy, with beautiful eyes and a handsome appearance. And the Lord said, "Arise, anoint him; for this is he." Then Samuel took the horn of oil and anointed him in the midst of his brothers; and the Spirit of the Lord came mightily upon David from that day forward (1 Samuel 16:11-13 NASB).

⌇

We all must expect the unexpected. If you are not ready for change, you will experience the heartache of apathy. A friend of mine once told me, "Anything that has life, grows and anything that grows, changes."

The following are a few quick keys to help you adapt to change.

- *There are challenges.* What is the main challenge you are facing right now? Sam Walton believed the problem was as simple as, "We should be the one offering the best bargains, always, on everything." Problems may exist in many levels in your life. If you focus on the low-level issues rather than the high-level issues, your life will never change.

- *You need a tactic.* We must do what Apollo 13 did when it was stranded in space. We should take a tactical inventory: What assets do we have? Who is with us? Who does not want to be on the team? (Actions speak louder than words.) Creating a tactical inventory should not be just a one-time effort.

- *Acquire proper thinking.* In top-down thinking, you start with your challenge and then develop methods for resolving it. In bottom-up thinking, your solutions come first. "Strategic thinking" involves using both approaches.

- *Stay focused on the objective.* Objectives can give us warning signs much like the instruments on the dashboard of a car. The dashboard tells us if everything is running properly as well as alerts us to potential challenges.

Like David, we all face changes and uncertainty in life. David knew God had a plan for his life and was not willing to let the challenges of being stuck in a pasture determine his future. David took an assessment and then employed the gift God gave him while training in the pasture of his father. David knew there was a challenge that needed to be addressed and was prepared to find a solution. David knew he was to be king over Israel. He checked the gauges and knew he must fix the problem.

We must work with the changes that come our way and discover the assets we have been equipped with while keeping our thinking properly focused on the objective of our life.

Father, I DON'T LIKE CHANGE, but I know it's part of Your process to get me to the next level. I realize I will never change the world before me, until I change the world within me. Amen.

MONDAY

FEAR OF FAILURE

For a righteous man falls seven times and rises again, but the wicked stumble in time of calamity (Proverbs 24:16 NASB).

There is no fear in love, but perfect love casts out fear, because fear involves punishment, and the one who fears is not perfected in love (1 John 4:18 NASB).

———————————————

Fear: **F**alse **E**vidence **A**ppearing **R**eal

Being raised in a preacher's house there were many rules that we were to follow. But the greatest and most important was that we were to have a healthy fear of dad. Fear is purposeful. For instance, we stop at stop signs due to the fact that the police will give us a citation or another automobile will crash into us. That type of fear is good and healthy.

There is another type of fear that will freeze us into inactivity. Our hearts scream, "Oh no, what will they say about me?" Many of us have been more concerned about what others will say instead of performing before an audience of One. This type of fear is not from God but from the enemy. The devil's desire is for us to be more concerned about self-preservation than honoring God in times of difficulty.

It is time to extract our heads from the sands of fear and trepidation and begin to operate full of faith and courage. Failing doesn't make you a failure! Being unwilling to get back up and move forward makes you a failure. So, if you have been bucked off, get back on now and stop worrying about what others might be thinking about you and start riding the waves of life again.

Failing miserably does not make you a miserable failure. Use failure as a stepping stone to greater achievement. Never let failure become your tombstone to mark your grave of regret for not giving it another try!

Thank You, Lord, for reminding me that failure is an event, not a lifestyle. I know that I have failed before, but I won't allow fear to keep me from trying again. Amen.

HOW TO HANDLE BUSY SCHEDULES

*Let us not become weary in doing good, for at the proper time we
will reap a harvest if we do not give up* (Galatians 6:9).

———————————

Oh my! This is not my favorite subject. Why, you may ask? Because I am
constantly guilty of being busy just to be busy. I know I am not the only one
who has ever overbooked and underperformed in this world. Well, if you too
are guilty of the same thing, there is hope for us. Don't be busy just to be
busy. Have a purpose to your busyness.

Let me suggest a few things that will help you with a busy schedule.

Improper delegation. If you want something done right, you have to do
it yourself. Does this sound like you? We must delegate to maximize our
valuable time:

- Decide what needs to be done.
- Select the best person to do the job.
- Make the assignment clear.
- Establish the level of authority granted.
- Anticipate problems.
- Build in checkpoints and reports.
- Evaluate and build on results.

Concerned what others think. We have a tendency to only work harder for
the approval of others. This mentality is performance-based, not relationship-
based. My dad has said for years, "The rewards in life are in direct proportion
to the problems you solve for others." Our ultimate desire should be to help
others and serve others. This will mean different things to different people
depending on your type of work. We should work as though we are performing before an "audience of One." When we perform before that audience of
One, we will not need to extol ourselves. God will move in on our behalf and
exalt us.

No rest, must work! God not only initiated work in the Garden, He started
the day of rest by not working on the seventh day. This was God's gentle way
of telling us we need to take time to rest. Every man and woman needs to
take time to relax and be refreshed. This can be done in many ways, such as
but not limited to, a nap, soft music, a gourmet meal, a night out, a weekend

away, or golf. Be systematic about your downtime and guard it because others will unwittingly eat into it. It is not only okay to rest, *it is godly!*

———————————————————

Father, help me to know the difference between the "urgent" and the "important" things of life. I want my life to be dictated by You, not by others. Amen.

PROGRAM MANAGEMENT OR PROBLEM SOLVER

In all your ways submit to him, and he will make your paths straight
(Proverbs 3:6).

Restoration Ranch lies fourteen miles off the Texas coast. We have seen some crazy hurricane seasons. Several years ago we had a near miss of a large hurricane named Ike. Watching the aftermath and destruction of Galveston and part of Houston, our hearts went out to those hit hard by the storm. As I watched the interviews, most every person interviewed did not care about the programs in place. They wanted someone to solve their problems. It didn't matter what their problem was, they wanted it solved. No one wants to be a number. Everyone wants to be someone special, important, valuable. Program managers assign you a number, problem solvers use names.

Program managers are not bad and problem solvers inherently good, but people need help to solve what ails them—not stuck in a system or program.

A judge in Houston found out that a multitude of trucks full of supplies for Ike victims were sitting in a parking lot ready to go. The problem was that the program had multiple requests from the same area and it got everyone confused. This judge went to the parking lot where the trucks were and personally sifted through the requests and found the neediest areas and sent the trucks. People were helped because this judge solved the problem.

Our lives are full of Ike-type problems. Programs will many times fail. Be a problem solver! Each of us has the God-given ability to solve problems to help in times of crisis. Men, our families need problem solvers. Women, our families need problem solvers.

No matter who you are or what is going on in your life, God can solve the problems you are facing. He is the righteous Judge who can step onto your parking lot of life and start distributing help to the destroyed areas needing help the most.

God can give you the ability to solve problems for people, not just manage the program.

Father, today I will become a problem solver, not a program manager. I know it won't be easy, but I'm willing to lean on your wisdom to confront whatever may come my way. Amen.

PERIODS OF DRYNESS

Then he said to me, "Prophesy to these bones and say to them, 'Dry bones,
hear the word of the Lord! This is what the Sovereign Lord says to these bones:
I will make breath enter you, and you will come to life (Ezekiel 37:4-5).

Everyone goes through periods of dryness. Dry spells will be as long as you choose them to be.

Every man, woman, boy, and girl will have periods of spiritual dryness. This is an inevitable fact of life. These periods of dryness will look different for each individual. There is one thing we all know, and that is when we are in a period of dryness. The periods of dryness make the times of refreshing so wonderful. We would not enjoy the fresh, cooling rain nearly as much if we didn't have the periods of dryness in our lives.

We can make a choice to remain in our dry state or move to a place of refreshing. Once we realize we are dry and in need of refreshing, it is our responsibility to make a move toward God and into more refreshing pastures. Yes, it is our choice and our responsibility to take action. Hebrews 13:8 says, *"Jesus Christ is the same yesterday, and today, and forever."* So the truth is, He is the same, we are the ones who find our way into the deserts of life. If we are willing to move back toward Christ, He is waiting with refreshing.

Ezekiel 37:1-14 comes to mind when I think of periods of dryness. Ezekiel sees a valley of dry bones. Don't we from time to time step back from our lives and see dry bones. Oh, we could be there right now. Well, our God has some solutions for those dry bones.

Realize: We must to come to a realization that we are in a period of dryness. If we veil our hearts from the harsh reality of the truth, we will not see refreshing for some time. A truth check is what most of us need. We must be willing to tell ourselves the truth about where we are. Admitting where you are is the first step in the battle for true refreshing.

Respond: "Action" is our word for the day. James 2:20 (NKJV) states that *"faith without works is dead."* This means we are called to be a people of action. God wants us to take action in our situation. It is time to choose to start moving toward God. Here are some ways: pray, read the Bible, listen to Christian music.

Father, I know being in a period of dryness does not mean I am a bad person. The desert is not where I want to live. I choose refreshing over dryness. I receive it today. Amen.

BREAKING OUT OF LIFE'S RUTS

Then they came to Jericho. And as He was leaving Jericho with His disciples and a large crowd, a blind beggar named Bartimaeus, the son of Timaeus, was sitting by the road. When he heard that it was Jesus the Nazarene, he began to cry out and say, "Jesus, Son of David, have mercy on me!" Many were sternly telling him to be quiet, but he kept crying out all the more, "Son of David, have mercy on me!" And Jesus stopped and said, "Call him here." So they called the blind man, saying to him, "Take courage, stand up! He is calling for you." Throwing aside his cloak, he jumped up and came to Jesus. And answering him, Jesus said, "What do you want Me to do for you?" And the blind man said to Him, "Rabboni, I want to regain my sight!" And Jesus said to him, "Go; your faith has made you well." Immediately he regained his sight and began following Him on the road (Mark 10:46-52 NASB).

My dad always told me to choose my "ruts" carefully, you never know where they will take you.

Below are eight things Bartimaeus did to get out of life's ruts. Follow these eight tips and you will be able to break out of your ruts.

1. Stop waiting for ideal circumstances. Patience is great, but don't let it stifle you. Waiting could make you worry.

2. Assume responsibility for your own life. No one can do it for you. *You* will have to give an account ,not someone else.

3. Stop worrying about what other people will say. God is the One we should want to please. When we listen to negative voices, we operate in fear.

4. Get on board with what God is doing. Each of us tends to get onboard with what God is doing later in the process rather than earlier. Be a thermostat not a thermometer. You should set the temperature, not just reveal it!

5. Do something bold and dramatic. Change your routine. If you aren't making mistakes, you are sitting idle. The reasonable person adapts to the world; the unreasonable person persists in adapting the world to him or herself. Therefore, all progress depends on the unreasonable person. *Balanced people do not change history!*

6. Believe you can change. God wants to change you on a regular basis. Change is present in you. If Jesus asked you the question He asked the blind man, what would your response be?

7. Clarify what you really need. God knows, but He wants you to admit it and confess it in faith. Confession is liberating.

8. Do it now! Why are you waiting? This is the time, you are the person, this is the place and your task awaits.

Lord Jesus, I don't want to live in a rut! Help me to cry out like Bartimaeus and change my environment so that I can move to the next level of my assignment. Amen.

MONDAY

CONTENT VERSUS SATISFIED

Not that I speak in respect of want: for I have learned, in whatsoever state I am, therewith to be content (Philippians 4:11 KJV).

I have always separated the words "contentment" and "satisfied." Why? Because wherever God has placed me I will be content, but I know the destiny God has for me and I will not be satisfied until I walk in that destiny.

Paul the apostle was a wealthy man during his life. His business of building tents supported him and his entire team of young followers. He states in Philippians 4:11, *"I am not saying this because I am in need, for I have learned to be content whatever the circumstances."* Paul tells the church in Philippi that all his needs are met and he is content with where God has placed him at that time. He also tells the Philippians that he is content even if they choose not to support him, although he is not satisfied till they get to that same place of contentment. This can and should be true of us.

If your heart is content with where God has placed you and you still have a desire to stretch for more to *glorify God,* then that desire is from the Lord. If you are not content with where God has you and you desire more to *glorify yourself,* then your motives are not pure. Make sure you understand that contentment is a heart issue not a material issue.

As your heart grows in contentment, it will also grow into a place where you are not satisfied with anything less than what God has called and destined you for. Anything you do for the purpose of bringing honor and praise to yourself in discontentment.

I am personally content where God has me, but I am not satisfied if I know there is more of God's destiny for me to walk in. I have made a choice in my life to take as much ground as God will give me and be content with what is under my dominion, but I also desire to take more so that Christ will be glorified.

Jesus told His disciples to go into every nation and make disciples. Jesus was content with what the Father had called Him to do, but He is not satisfied if we do not do what He told us to do.

There is nothing wrong with working hard and going after financial success. God told Adam to work and take dominion over the whole earth; and the mandate God gave Adam was and is for you and me, today!

Father, keep reminding me of the difference between being satisfied and content. I want to be "content" with where You have placed me, but I will not be "satisfied" until I know You more. Amen.

ARE YOU ACCOUNTABLE?

So then, each of us will give account of ourselves to God (Romans 14:12).

And he [God] *has given us this command: Anyone who loves
God must also love their brother and sister* (1 John 4:21).

———⸝—————

In 1993 Charles Colson wrote a book entitled *The Body,* which had this powerful excerpt in it:

> John Wesley was so concerned with building a righteous fellowship
> that he devised a series of questions for his followers to ask each other
> every week. Some found this rigorous system of inquiry too demanding and left. Today, the very idea of such a procedure would horrify
> many churchgoers. Yet some wisely follow just such a practice.
>
> Chuck Swindoll, for example, has seven questions that he and a
> group of fellow pastors challenge each other with periodically:
>
> 1. Have you been with a woman anywhere this past week that
>   might be seen as compromising?
> 2. Have any of your financial dealings lacked integrity?
> 3. Have you exposed yourself to any sexually explicit material?
> 4. Have you spent adequate time in Bible study and prayer?
> 5. Have you given priority time to your family?
> 6. Have you fulfilled the mandates of your calling?
> 7. Have you just lied to me?

First and foremost, we must be accountable to God before we can be accountable to each other.

Far too often we blur the lines between love and permissiveness. We do not
express love to someone by being permissive of their wrong action. If we truly
love our friends, we should be willing to run the risk of hurting their feelings
in order to help them by holding them accountable. Accountability is the truest
expression of true love in a relationship.

Accountable relationships can only take place between those who have
poured their lives into each other. This is not a place where we stand in judgment but a place where we love each other so much that we will share the truth.

Father, I desire to be accountable. I know it's the only way for me to grow into the mature believer You will be pleased with. Bring godly people into my life who I can trust to speak the truth in love. No more candy-coated Christianity for me. Amen.

EMBRACING YOUR LIMITATIONS

*Three times I pleaded with the Lord to take it
away from me* (2 Corinthians 12:8).

———————⟨⟩———————

I have heard my whole life that regardless of my limitations I can do anything. Well, that sounded good, but it's not true. I happen to be a 5'11" white guy with no real ability to jump over six inches high. I have a good outside jump shot, but as much as I practiced I was never even worthy to be a ball boy for John Stockton. So, my hopes of playing in the NBA were shattered by my limitations. There is no doubt in my mind that God created me the way He wanted me. He gave me the parents He gave me with the DNA that He wanted to pass on to me. So I have a limitation, a limitation given to me by God for a purpose. If I did not embrace the limitation, I would be stuck living in the past. I needed to embrace the fact that God created me for something and He has equipped me for that purpose.

Paul the apostle had a limitation and he asked God three times to remove it, but God never did. The only reason that I can think of is that God wanted to keep Paul cast on His mercies. The reason for our limitations is to keep us cast on God's mercies. If you can accomplish anything in your own strength, then you don't need God.

Take an honest look at your life to see the limitations in the light of God's purpose and design for you. If you are not willing to see your limitations as God's protection, you will constantly be disillusioned and disappointed in where He has you in life.

Over the past year Melanie and I have started running. We love spending that time together as a couple. When I started I could barely run a mile. I was limited by my lung capacity as well as the conditioning of my legs and body. I had to again embrace my limitations. Those training me said, "Start small and embrace your limitations. If you do that you will decrease your limitations." Within five months we ran our first half marathon and two months later we completed our second one. We noticed that when we embraced our limitations, God gave us the capacity to decrease our limitations as we cast ourselves on His mercies.

Today, embrace your limitations and cast yourself on God's mercies and let Him expand your capacities.

Father, today I place myself at Your feet. You have created me just like You wanted me, limitations and all. I accept that, without reservation. I will strive to be the best "me" I can "be" for Your glory. Amen.

TAKE COURAGE AND BE COMFORTED

Therefore, since we have so great a cloud of witnesses surrounding us, let us also lay aside every encumbrance and the sin which so easily entangles us, and let us run with endurance the race that is set before us, fixing our eyes on Jesus, the author and perfecter of faith, who for the joy set before Him endured the cross, despising the shame, and has sat down at the right hand of the throne of God (Hebrews 12:1-2 NASB).

In the early 1990s Bryan Lee Swift died, one of my dearest friends. I will never forget the day I received the news of his passing. I was standing in my sister's apartment in Irving, Texas. The news hit me like a ton of bricks falling out of a ten-story building. My heart was crushed. During this time in our lives we were youth pastors at Hilltop Drive Baptist Church. The day after hearing of Bryan's death my pastor took me to hear John Wimber at a church in Fort Worth. In his message John preached from Hebrews 12. The following morning Melanie and I drove to south Texas for the funeral.

Now if you have never been in Texas during the summer, you have missed seeing the most beautiful billowing clouds known to man. As we drove down I-45 toward Houston, I saw enormous cloud formations stretching toward the heavens. The vision God gave me was of Hebrews 12:1-2. You see, Bryan and I were called to preach the same day as young teenage boys. I could see him and a multitude of others as that cloud of witnesses cheering me on. My heart was filled with the overwhelming sense of the presence of the Lord, knowing that my friend was in that cloud of witnesses encouraging me to lay aside anything that restrains me, and fix my eyes on Christ Jesus. I will never see clouds the same way again!

Today as you look outside at the clouds, know there is a great cloud of witnesses filled with friends and family members encouraging you to lay aside anything that restrains you, and fix your eyes on Christ Jesus.

Dear Jesus, it was hard to lose a friend like Bryan. But in his passing You not only comforted me, but showed me a divine truth about courage. I rejoice in that great cloud of witnesses who surround me and encourage me each day. I may not see them with my physical eyes, but I know they are there cheering me on. Amen.

PREPARE FOR ACTION

Therefore, prepare your minds for action, keep sober in spirit, fix your hope completely on the grace to be brought to you at the revelation of Jesus Christ (1 Peter 1:13 NASB).

Years ago I found this story and it brings to light what we are talking about today.

> Dr. J. B. Gambrel tells an amusing story from General Stonewall Jackson's famous valley campaign. Jackson's army found itself on one side of a river when it needed to be on the other side. After telling his engineers to plan and build a bridge so the army could cross, he called his wagon master in to tell him that it was urgent the wagon train cross the river as soon as possible. The wagon master started gathering all the logs, rocks and fence rails he could find and built a bridge. Long before daylight General Jackson was told by his wagon master all the wagons and artillery had crossed the river. General Jackson asked where the engineers were and what they were doing. The wagon master's only reply was that they were in their tent drawing up plans for a bridge.

Are you an individual of action? Don't misunderstand me, we should prepare! However, most people prepare, prepare, prepare, prepare, and never act. I give you three steps for action—ACT:

A— Acknowledge something must be done. The first step is to acknowledge that action is needed. Too many times we never acknowledge that something is broken and needs fixing. If you are like so many, you will stand there and never fix the problem until the wheels come off.

C— Commit yourself to the task of an action plan. Commitment is in short supply in our culture today. Far too often those who have responsibilities over areas are not committed to the task because they are unwilling to develop an action plan. How often we hear people say somebody else will do it. Remember, there is nothing wrong with planning but you must execute the action plan.

T—Tweak your action plan as you are doing the task. There are always adjustments to action plans. We should not be stuck in neutral forever. We should engage and tweak things as we go.

Prepare your mind for action and then ACT.

Father, there are times when I would rather sit back and let others take action. Starting today, I will not hesitate when I know something needs to be done. You have given me all the tools necessary for success, and I will use them for Your glory. Amen.

MONDAY

FAITHFUL ALL THE WAY THROUGH

Moses built an altar and called it The Lord is My Banner (Exodus 17:15 NASB).

Israel had been delivered from slavery in the land of Egypt and was making their journey across the wilderness to their Promised Land of Canaan. Along the way they encountered many enemy nations that were intent on annihilating their nation. During one such time, Moses and the nation of Israel were fighting against the Amalekites.

Moses was not a warrior on the battlefield, but he was the leader and the liaison between the nation and God. Moses stood at the top of the hill, with the staff of God in his hand, where he had a ringside seat to observe the ensuing battle. As long as Moses held up the staff, the Israelites would prevail in battle; but when he lowered his hands they would suffer defeat. As the fighting lasted all day, Moses grew weary and could not hold up his arms for the extent of the battle. Aaron and Hur came beside Moses and held up his arms until Israel was victorious. He knew that because of the Lord fighting for them, Israel won the battle. Moses built an altar of thanksgiving to the Lord and proclaimed, *"The Lord is My Banner!"* (Exodus 17:8-16).

We have battles that we are fighting as we journey through our lives. When we are faithful to extend our hands toward God and follow His leadership, He is faithful to bring us through to the victory. Find some faithful friends who can hold up your arms when you are weary. These friends will encourage you to continue to depend on the Lord—all the way through each struggle. The Lord will bring you through to victory. You can say, "The Lord is My Banner!"

Father, I give You praise and honor because I know whatever battle I face Your faithfulness will bring me through. Even in my fear and doubt of the outcome, You will provide a way of victory. Amen.

ARE YOU POURING?

What you heard from me, keep as the pattern of sound teaching, with faith and love in Christ Jesus. Guard the good deposit that was entrusted to you—guard it with the help of the Holy Spirit who lives in us (2 Timothy 1:13-14).

———◆———◆———

Think about the great things you have learned in life from those whom God has placed around you. Learning to ride a bike, fish, cook, swim, and so many other great things that set the stage for memories that will always last.

Grandparents and parents have the privilege of impacting many others through the things they instill in their young loved ones. When I was a young child, my grandmother would read to me as she read the Word of God each morning. This faithful act developed a love and longing for the Word in my life from a very young age. God used this act of love to start my foundation as a believer. I couldn't even read yet, but I could tell you about things that God had done!

When I hear the story of Timothy, it reminds me of my grandmother teaching me about God and His love. Timothy's grandmother and his mother taught him just like mine had taught me. The apostle Paul wrote to his son in the faith, Timothy, and encouraged him to follow the pattern of sound doctrine that had been set before him and to guard the good deposit of the gospel that was entrusted to him.

Whether or not we have our own physical children or grandchildren, we have been entrusted with the good deposit of the gospel. Paul also wrote in Romans 1:16, *"I am not ashamed of the gospel, because it is the power of God that brings salvation to everyone who believes."* God has changed our hearts through Jesus, and others need to know about this change for themselves! Be aware of the individuals God has placed in your life and be faithful to pour God's love on them to affect change in their lives. They need to have this love in their life. Will you be faithful to tell them?

———◆———◆———

Thank You, Jesus, for those who have made a rich deposit in my life. Help me to never take them for granted. Now, I will turn around and make the same deposit of the gospel to those You have entrusted me with. Amen.

TIME TO SCHEDULE A TIME OUT

But seek first his kingdom and his righteousness, and all these things will be given to you as well. Therefore do not worry about tomorrow, for tomorrow will worry about itself. Each day has enough trouble of its own (Matthew 6:33-34).

We tend to make time for things that are important. We mark our calendars with dates we don't want to miss; we set alarms for times that we want to be sure are not overlooked. Are we setting our times with God as priorities? We are reminded in Jeremiah 17:21-23 in The Message version to *"Be careful, if you care about your lives, not to desecrate the Sabbath by turning it into just another workday, lugging stuff here and there. Don't use the Sabbath to do business as usual. Keep the Sabbath day holy...."*

He shows us the pattern to live our lives. It is written that the Sabbath day would forever be a sign between God and His people that the Lord made the earth in six days, and on the seventh day He rested and was refreshed (see Exodus 31:17). If the Creator of the universe rested and was refreshed, how much more important is that for our human frames?

As believers, we ought to guard these times with our Savior. Our days of worship with our spiritual family bring refreshing to our souls. Focusing on God and what He is communicating to us through our worship services will bring the balance to our lives that we are searching for in all other areas of life. When we take the time away from the hustle of life, we have time to be grateful and realize the abundant blessings that our Father has been waiting to cover us with.

Our lives are very busy and filled with things that are impacting the world for good. Make sure you are reserving times that God has declared as holy. God will make sure that you are equipped to accomplish all He has called you to when you honor Him by placing priority on His time. When you mark aside time for Him, He will be faithful to recharge, refresh, and reenergize you for those other six days!

Father, may I never get too busy that I neglect time with You. I want my schedule to be in alignment with Your purposes—not the other way around. You are my comfort and strength. I praise You and rejoice in Your goodness. Amen.

LIVING A 5-STAR LIFE

Their work will be shown for what it is, because the Day will bring it to light. It will be revealed with fire, and the fire will test the quality of each person's work (1 Corinthians 3:13).

———————⁘———————

Our family enjoys taking trips together. Flights are an important part of our travel experience. We fly on an airline that has great ratings for being on time, has good service records on their planes, and friendly staff. Could you imagine flying an airline that was perpetually late, always breaking down, and had grumpy staff? We certainly want to fly the friendly skies!

On our trips, we usually enjoy one really nice meal in each city. I love to plan for these times and have found that the Internet is so very helpful in my planning. I look for the type of food we want and see what is available in that city. The restaurants have to have a four or five-star rating for me to consider taking our family to eat there. I definitely want their sanitation rating to be excellent! People don't usually share good things about a 1-star dining experience.

If we are so intent on excellence when we travel and eat and other experiences throughout our daily lives, shouldn't we be intent on living our lives with excellence? Just think about this, a young believer is intently searching on the Internet for someone to pattern life after. They are looking for someone who starts the day out in the Word of God to hear from Him. They are searching for a person who works with integrity and excellence, not just to bring honor and success to an earthly employer, but desires to please and honor the heavenly Boss! This person they are searching for also has lots of excellent results in all areas of life that show God is blessing his or her efforts.

Would your name and bio turn up in the search? Don't despair if it would not, but determine to put habits in place that will bring your name up the next time the search for such a person of integrity takes place! Strive to live a life that has a five-star rating.

———————⁘———————

Father, I desire a five-star life. Show me what changes I need to make to live a life of excellence filled with integrity. I may not be at the top of the search list on earth, but may it rise to the top in Heaven. Amen.

YOU CAN DO THIS (WITH HELP)!

You, however, must teach what is appropriate to sound doctrine.
Teach the older men to be temperate, worthy of respect, self-controlled,
and sound in faith, in love and in endurance (Titus 2:1-2).

There are some traits that are not a favorite among society members to incorporate into their lives. I am certain that self-control would be included in that list. While waiting in grocery checkout lines, I have not seen any magazines with a list recommending "Five Easy Steps to Self-Control!" Yet the apostle Paul felt it was very important and listed it as a requirement for men and women in Titus 2. If Scripture requires it of every Christian, then God will certainly give the grace to attain it. The good news is that He has given us the power to overcome!

We fight a tough battle: we have sinful desires within our hearts and temptations before us. God promises to give us the grace of self-control to withstand the desires and temptations and maintain the victory. We must choose to be dependent on Him (see John 15:5).

We have to first realize that we have a problem. You may not be able to live without the latest gadget, but once purchased you realize it has a hefty payment that comes with its purchase. You may not be able to resist the cupcake shop, but your clothes refuse to zip after the weekend of splurging! Scripture acknowledges that sin brings pleasure, but warns that it is short-lived. It brings negative consequences when we follow those desires. Self-control spares us from these negative results.

Having a great reserve of truth on hand is vital to be able to maintain our control when we are attacked by unhealthy desires and temptations. Make sure you have taken the time to gather your weapons. Two of my most important weapons are Scriptures that remind me of the truth that I struggle with, and friends who will speak this truth and remind me of the negative results of my fleeting pleasures. You can do this, but you need His help! (See Philippians 1:6.)

Lord, I know I can do all things through Your help and strength. So many times I have failed to exercise self-control. It has cost me more than I am willing to spend. Holy Spirit, guard my tongue, surround my mind and heart so I will win the battle over my lack of self-control. Amen.

BENEFITS AND BLESSINGS

MONDAY

BENEFITS OF THE FEAR OF GOD

The angel of the Lord encamps around those who fear him, and he delivers them. Taste and see that the Lord is good; blessed is the one who takes refuge in him. Fear the Lord, you his holy people, for those who fear him lack nothing. The lions may grow weak and hungry, but those who seek the Lord lack no good thing. Come, my children, listen to me; I will teach you the fear of the Lord
(Psalm 34:7-11).

As a young child, I would hear of someone getting the fear of God struck into them. It never was clear to me what that meant, but it did not sound like something that I wanted to happen to me! When I was a teenager, I learned that the fear of God was the beginning of wisdom (see Proverbs 1:7), and so I considered that this fear was something that I definitely wanted to have. In fact, if you do a Bible search on the fear of God, Scripture is filled with great things that accompany people who have the fear of God in their lives.

Here are some things that people who fear God do: walk in the ways of God; stand in awe of His laws; put hope in God's unfailing love; keep His covenant; obey His precepts; are forgiven—the list continues for a very long time. Some of the great results for people who fear God are: walk in blessings and prosperity; eat of the fruit of their labor; the Lord delights in them; great is the Lord's love for them; their children are mighty; their generation is blessed because of them; they have health and nourishment; the Lord hears their cries; they are saved when they are in need; and the list of blessings continues without end.

After reading so many Scriptures, I have found that the fear of God in my life does not mean that I am afraid of God; it means that what is important to Him is important to me! When He shows me the right way to live, I strive to live that way because I know that the results are good things! God is pleased with me and blesses me, just as earthly parents bless their children when they do as instructed. *"Fear the Lord, you His saints, for those who fear Him have no lack!"* (Psalm 34:9 ESV).

Father, thank You for showing me that the fear of the Lord is not something to run from, but to run toward. For years I thought it was a negative thing, but now I know it is a healthy part of our relationship. Amen.

FAILURE TO LAUNCH

Flee the evil desires of youth and pursue righteousness, faith, love and peace, along with those who call on the Lord out of a pure heart. Don't have anything to do with foolish and stupid arguments, because you know they produce quarrels (2 Timothy 2:22-23).

It seems this generation of children has trouble launching into life as adults. Parents are supporting their children for years after the children are legal adults. Children expect so much more from their parents than their parents ever received from theirs. Churches are experiencing this same problem as believers are failing to mature past childhood.

There is a time when a person should put aside the things they did as a child. Paul encouraged Timothy to run away from the things that he used to be passionate about as a child. *"Flee youthful passions and pursue righteousness, faith, love, and peace, along with those who call on the Lord from a pure heart"* (2 Timothy 2:22 ESV).

How do you start to grow spiritually? Start doing things that promote growth. If you want a plant to grow, you have to put it in the right environment for growth. You make sure it has the proper light, food, and water. You are no different. You have needs, that when met, will guarantee growth.

Look for others who have the traits that you want to see in your life and attach yourself to them. Pursue righteousness, which means right living. Make choices that will bring good results. Work to build a strong faith with a community of believers that push you to grow, not hide out and soak off those around you. Mentors from within your church community can recommend great books to help you grow in specific areas.

God has big plans for your life. Prepare and get launched into the great future He has for you!

Father, You have given me all the advantages I need to grow and become a fruitful believer. I will not throw away all the things You have provided for me. Show me those around me who will add wise counsel to my growth and maturity. Amen.

WIN THE PERSON

As iron sharpens iron, so one person sharpens another (Proverbs 27:17).

———⌇———

I love today's Scripture that talks about iron sharpening iron. It is such a vivid description of how the Lord uses those around us to make us more effective. Sparks usually fly through the air during this process, so there are sometimes little burnt places on the ground. Most times this is used in reference to men; they are guys, after all!

God uses great times of discussion to build us and instruct us if we are listening with open hearts. There are times, though, when someone will take the opposite viewpoint in a discussion just to argue a point. All you desire is to have a great time together with friends or family, and a topic comes up in the conversation that has everyone mounting their soapboxes and taking their defensive positions. Times of sharpening are beneficial, but we need to examine our motives and protect those who are modeling their lives after ours.

In 2 Timothy 2:22-26 (MSG), Paul encourages us to *"Run away from infantile indulgence. Run after mature righteousness—faith, love, peace—joining those who are in honest and serious prayer before God. Refuse to get involved in inane discussions, they always end up in fights. God's servant must not be argumentative, but a gentle listener and a teacher who keeps cool, working firmly but patiently with those who refuse to obey. You never know how or when God might sober them up with a change of heart and a turning to the truth, enabling them to escape the Devil's trap, where they are caught and held captive, forced to run his errands."*

Realize that others are always watching you to see how you respond to situations. Pursue righteousness. Avoid discussions that have no purpose and don't add value to another's life. Be aware that those who need the Lord are taking note. My desire is to constantly edify my Lord in the eyes of those who do not yet believe. Live life in such a way that you "win the person," not the argument!

———⌇———

Father, my heart's desire is to always speak to others in such a way as to glorify You. I reject any notion of winning an argument in order to make me look good. I don't want to turn anyone away from You by anything I might say or do. Amen.

LIVE IN PEACE WITH ALL

If it is possible, so far as it depends on you, live at peace with everyone (Romans 12:18).

A sailor happened upon what appeared to be a deserted island with three huts on it. After he landed on the island, he discovered there was a lone inhabitant. The sailor was so curious about the huts and why there were three for just one person. "Oh, that's easy to explain. This one is my house and this one is my church," said the islander. "So what is the other building?" he asked. "Oh, that was my old church!"

Sometimes it seems that life would be so much easier if we lived all alone on an island so we didn't have to deal with so much turmoil. But even if you were the only person, you would find that you would change your mind about something you used to like!

The Lord uses relationships to get ugly things out of us. Sometimes it seems a strange way to go about things, but it teaches us lots if we will pay attention. God really uses family to get ugliness out of us. Our families are the people who are usually closest to us and able to irritate us by pushing all the right buttons to make things crazy! Isn't it ironic that you can be raised in the same household with others and turn out so very different?

Almost twenty years ago, Paul and I realized that there are some relatives we will never agree with on certain issues, but because we want to be able to impact their lives, we have to be mature enough to overlook or tolerate those things. We are strong believers in Jesus and our whole lives are dedicated to spreading the gospel and letting others know that Jesus loves them so much. We have relatives who do not worship God and do not want us "pushing our religion" on them. We love them but disagree with the lack of faith in their lives. We know that the only way we will ever have the possibility to minister life to them is to make sure that we leave the doors of our relationship open. This means that even if we don't agree with them about topics, we are mature enough to tolerate and endure the fact that we will not talk about those things. We have to agree to disagree and love each other anyway.

Keep the relationship open so that you may be able to share Christ's love with them. Romans 12:18 says it very well—*If possible, so far as it depends on you, live peaceably with all* (ESV).

Father, teach me how to love others as You love them. I am open to Your instruction because I know "peace with all" is missing in most relationships. I can never be at peace if I am constantly at war. Amen.

BUILDING CONFIDENCE IN YOUR MATE

*Do nothing out of selfish ambition or vain conceit. Rather, in
humility value others above yourselves* (Philippians 2:3).

———————————————

Jealousy is an ugly trait and we can all choose to struggle with it to some
degree. If you think about it, in a way it is a pretty high compliment for the
person of whom you are jealous. But it can be stifling to a relationship if not
brought under control.

My first questions when I hear that there is jealousy within a relationship are:

- What are you doing as a spouse to build the assurance of your
  mate so that he/she is your one and only?
- Are you doing things to assure him/her of your love?

In our busy society, it is easy to get distracted from giving our mates the
attention they deserve and need. Think of your mate's need as a gas tank in a
car. When the tank is filled up with love and confidence of your love, does your
mate seem less jealous during these times? If your mate has experienced infidel-
ity in past relationships, he or she might be prone to feelings of insecurity in this
area of your relationship.

If you are aware of areas of weakness in confidence, make sure you are building up in this area. Jealous people will have to deal with this in their personal
walk with Christ, but you can do these things to help: Make sure you are putting in effort each day to let them know how important they are in your life
and as you do this on a daily basis, you will see their confidence in this area get
stronger. Love notes, texts, dates, and verbal encouragement are all very important in the rebuilding of confidence. Jealousy can suffocate a relationship, but
can be overcome! Find mentors for your marriage within a local Bible teaching
church; this will make a HUGE difference in your life.

———————————————

*Father, teach me to build confidence in my spouse. I desire to do the things that are
positive and encouraging. Amen.*

MONDAY

ARE YOU EVER ALONE?

How precious to me are your thoughts, God! How vast is the sum of them! Were I to count them, they would outnumber the grains the sand... (Psalm 139:17-18).

Look around when you are out and about. There are so many people surrounding us in life. It has even been said that earth is overpopulated. I think whoever made that statement hasn't been to Wyoming or other less-settled states! Even in the midst of so many people in the cities of our country, you may feel terribly alone. It may seem that nobody is even thinking of you or your needs. I am reminded of song lyrics that asked "Is anybody out there?"

Psalm 139 tells us otherwise. God is there; He has been from your very beginning. There is nothing about you that God does not know before you even know it. He completes your sentences before you even start saying them. He goes before us and He is also behind us protecting our backs. There is nowhere you can go that you can get away from Him. There is never a point in time that you are alone.

"How precious also are Your thoughts to me, O God! How great is the sum of them! If I should count them, they would be more in number than the sand..." (Psalm 139:17 NKJV). You are valuable to God. He thinks of you constantly. Imagine going to the beach and just grabbing one handful of sand. Now try counting the grains of sand in your hand. What? You say that's impossible? Your handful of sand does not start to equal the thoughts God has of you.

Today, ask your heavenly Father to show Himself to you through things you read, see, and hear. Pay attention to the ways He is letting you know that you are not alone. It may be through a gorgeous sunrise or sunset; it may be through an act of kindness from a total stranger. It may be by finding money on the ground. He cares deeply for you and wants you to know that you will never be alone!

Father, thank You for reminding me how precious I am to You. Just to know how much You think about me gives me hope and encouragement. Amen.

GET AHEAD IN THIS WORLD

...Be wary of the shrewd advice that tells you how to get ahead in the world on your own. Giving, not getting, is the way. Generosity begets generosity. Stinginess impoverishes (Mark 4:24-25 MSG).

———————————————

People are on a mission to succeed in life. I haven't run across anyone whose mission in life is to fail. There have been so many books written, seminars taught, and methods put into practice for success in all areas of life. Lots of these are very productive and certainly bring results in the lives of those who participate.

Jesus said to listen carefully to what He said, *"Be wary of the shrewd advice that tells you how to get ahead in the world on your own. Giving, not getting, is the way. Generosity begets generosity. Stinginess impoverishes."* This is great truth and when put into practice, you see it unfold right before your eyes.

Remember the Christmas story of Ebenezer Scrooge? Mr. Scrooge is too concerned about how much money he has and working those around him to the bone to get every cent squeezed out of them; he is more concerned about his prosperity than the well-being of those around him. He was a miserable man even though he had more money than anyone else in town. Unhappiness does not equal success in my book. In the end, Scrooge discovered that when he was generous with his blessings to those around him, he enjoyed his life so much more!

We find this to be true in our present-day situations. How do you feel when someone pays for your drive-through order? Even better, how do you feel when you meet a need in someone else's life? *"Give, and it will be given to you. ...For with the measure you use, it will be measured to you"* (Luke 6:38). Live generously and see the success that abundantly abounds in your life!

———————————————

Father, I desire to live a generous life. I know that is contrary to the world's view, but I don't care about that. I want to be a giver not a taker. Show me places where I can make a difference in someone's life. Amen.

WHO CAN YOU TRUST?

*Let us hold fast the confession of our hope without wavering, for
He who promised is faithful* (Hebrews 10:23 NKJV).

It is hard to know who or what to put our trust in during these insecure times. Relationships are tried more than ever because people change the direction they are headed. Job situations are not as secure as they seem and are dependent on how the economy is doing in that specific arena. Families are more easily dissolvable with divorce being a mere matter of paperwork. Friendships are based on whether both parties are committed to working through difficulties. Who can you trust during these times?

When I was a teenager, I struggled with whom I could trust. I knew that both my parents loved me and wanted the best for me, but they were walking through their own difficulties. Both of them loved God and made sure that I was in the right environment to learn of His love for me. I am so grateful that they took me to church. It was in church that I learned that God loved me and wanted to have a relationship with me.

My relationship with God was different from any other relationships in my life. He had laid all the groundwork. He sent His Son Jesus to live a perfect life and give His life so that I could have a relationship with Him. All I had to do was trust Him. I found that God keeps His promises. I started reading the Bible and learning the promises He gave to me. There are so many, but here are just a few. He promised that He will finish the work He has started in my life (see Philippians 1:6); He will never leave me or forsake me (see Deuteronomy 31:8); draw near to Him and He will draw near to me (see James 4:8); and trust Him with all your heart and He will direct you (see Proverbs 3:5-6).

I know you face hard decisions when deciding whom to trust. I encourage you to put your trust in God. He desires to show you how much He loves you, and you can bank on the fact that He is faithful to keep the promises He makes to you.

Father, teach me Your ways and show me how to trust You more. While others may let me down, I know You will always be faithful and trustworthy. Amen.

DO WORK THAT MAKES YOU PROUD

Do your best to present yourself to God as one approved, a worker who does not need to be ashamed and who correctly handles the word of truth (2 Timothy 2:15).

When I was in elementary school, I loved art class. I took lots of time choosing the beautiful colors I would use to create my masterpiece. I was very careful to pay close attention and do my very best work. As I was working, I could just imagine my teacher admiring my finished work of art. It was very important to me that I did my very best because I wanted to hear the praise of my teacher.

As I have grown as a student in the Word, I have realized the importance of putting the same high value on my knowledge of the Word of God. Paul instructed Timothy, his son in the faith, to *"Do your best to present yourself to God as one approved, a worker who does not need to be ashamed and correctly handles the word of truth correctly."* My heart is to please God in what I do with His Word that He has entrusted to me. In the same way that I wanted to hear my art teacher praise me for my excellent work, I desire to hear God's praise for what I did in the life He has given me.

What does this look like practically in my daily life? I make time to read the Word of God. There are many guides for reading the Bible. Some use a yearly Bible that has a portion each day from the Old Testament, New Testament, and Psalms/Proverbs. Some choose one book of the Bible and then start another after finished with that one, until they read through. Another practical way to be your best is to get involved with a community Bible study or one within your local church. Also be sure to take advantage of opportunities to attend retreats or special meetings where you can learn more about how God would have you live. It is important that we put into practice the knowledge that we are gaining.

My desire is to live out the principles that I learn when I study the Scriptures so that God will give me His approval. I want to do excellent work in my life for God. My goal when my life is done is to hear Him say, *"Well done, good and faithful servant"* (Matthew 25:23).

Father, my joy is to study Your Word. It is food for my soul and drink for my thirst. My goal is to hear Your precious words that I have been a faithful servant. Amen.

WHAT IS THE THEME OF YOUR LIFE?

Trust in the Lord and do good; dwell in the land and enjoy safe pasture. Take delight in the Lord, and he will give you the desires of your heart (Psalm 37:3-4).

———————————————

Have you ever taken the time to figure out exactly what it is that God has for you to carry out during your time on Earth? Some parents are masters at observing their children and helping them walk in the theme that God has for their lives. If your parents couldn't do this for you, it may be that God puts others in your life that could help you observe and figure it out.

Here's a good start. What brings you to tears? What really gets you angry? What makes you happy? Look back through your personal history and see what things make you emotional. Events and activities that really bring peace and satisfaction to your life point to what it is you should be putting your most amount of effort into. I love hearing people's stories—how they were raised, what they enjoy doing with their free time. If you listen to someone talk for just five to ten minutes, you can hear what the person's heart desire is. *"Delight yourself in the Lord and He will give you the desires of your heart"* (Psalm 37:4 NASB). God gives us things that we want when we seek Him and walk in His ways. He is an amazing Father who gives His children good gifts. He wants us to enjoy our lives and will orchestrate circumstances to make it a reality for us.

As God is helping you recognize the theme of your life, look for Scripture that is consistent with that theme. Write these verses down and put them in places that you will see throughout your day. Memorize these words of God so that they are always on your mind. Pray these Scriptures and remember that God does not go back on His Word. God will be faithful to show you where you should go and what you should be doing. He loves you, His child, and wants to do good toward you.

"For I know the plans I have for you…plans to give you hope and a future" (Jeremiah 29:11). Look and listen and discover the theme of your life!

———————————————

Thank You, Father, for being a great Dad! You lead me, teach me, and provide everything I need—even much more than a generous earthly father who loves his kids. Amen.

MAKE TIME FOR WHAT MATTERS

But Martha was distracted by all the preparations that had to be made. She came to him and asked, "Lord, don't you care that my sister has left me to do the work by myself? Tell her to help me!" (Luke 10:40)

We all have the same amount of time in a day. How is it that one person seems to be able to accomplish so much more than another? Time management and organization adds to the number of things we can complete in a day.

Jesus was visiting Mary and Martha and both were each doing what was most important to them. Both things were good things; Mary loved to worship, while Martha loved to serve. Martha was upset because there were many things to be done in preparing the meal for Jesus and the men who traveled with Him, as well as the local friends who came to hear what Jesus had to share. Martha was appealing to Jesus, for Him to tell Mary to come and help. His reply, *"You are worried and troubled about many things. But one thing is needed, and Mary has chosen that good part, which will not be taken away from her"* (Luke 10:41-42 NKJV).

The one thing that Mary chose was to make worship of her Lord her priority. It was the one thing she was going to be sure to do. Martha was making sure that the meal was served. I'm sure that everyone raved about Martha's cooking and great countenance while serving, but those accolades would die down and go away. Jesus pointed out to Martha that worshipping Him was necessary and that the results of it would not be taken away from her. Serving is necessary, but worship is vital.

I believe that when you are faithful to give honor to the Lord by setting aside the first portion of your day to worship and spend time with Him, He will make the rest of your time more efficient and you will accomplish more. Let Him help you set priorities with your time. Scheduling time to read His Word and worship Him will add to the accomplishments you have at the end of your day.

Father, help me never to be too busy to spend time at Your feet. I choose to worship before I work, and never to choose the voice of others over hearing Your words. Amen.

PLEASING THE LORD

When the young man heard this, he went away sad,
because he had great wealth (Matthew 19:22).

———————⟡———————

There was a rich young ruler who came to Jesus and wanted to know what good thing was necessary for him to do to be able to have eternal life. He shared all that he had done by keeping each of the Ten Commandments and wanted to know what he was still lacking. At that point, Jesus told him to go and sell all he had and give it to the poor, and then he could enter the kingdom of Heaven. The young ruler left Jesus very downcast because he owned a lot of property and was very wealthy. Jesus shared with His disciples that it is very hard for a rich man to enter Heaven. They asked then who can be saved? Jesus said, *"With people this is impossible, but with God all things are possible"* (see Matthew 19:16-26 NASB).

Jesus makes it possible for us to obtain eternal life. He paid the entire price. So it is not by anything that we can do; there are not enough community service projects and random acts of kindness. He wants us to trust Him, not our works or our money, to get us into Heaven. These things are important, but not the necessary price to be paid to put us in right standing with God.

Scripture tells us that many believe that what they do for others will be enough to get them into Heaven and save them from hell. Donations to help orphans and church ministries that reach out to those in need are great things that we need to be part of, but not enough to make salvation possible for our souls.

So what does God require of us since He has done this great work on our behalf? What will please Him for us to do with our lives that He has given us? Micah 6:8 says, *"What is good. And what does the Lord require of you? To act justly and to love mercy and to walk humbly with your God."* He wants us to be lawful, fair and right to our neighbors. Be a good citizen; follow the laws that our government officials have put in place to ensure order and safety for others. Be compassionate and loyal as you show God's love in practical ways to those He puts in your path. Look for ways to serve those in need in your life. Be humble; don't stomp on those around you on the way to the top. Let God promote you in the eyes of others. In God's society, the last will be first and the first will be last. He will bless you and prosper you when you walk in His ways. With God, all things are possible!

Father, I know You are righteous and full of compassion. Help me to demonstrate the same to everyone with whom I come in contact. I know the way up is down. Amen.

WHERE IS YOUR FOCUS?

Don't fret or worry. Instead of worrying, pray (Philippians 4:6 MSG).

———◦———◦———

Observing all that is occurring around us and recalling what has happened during this lifetime could send a person into deep depression. World tragedies, constant war, environmental disasters, poverty, incurable diseases, and many other horrific events fill our newscasts and conversations on a daily basis. Closer to home, we could be stopped in our tracks by things happening in our families: loss of a job, marriage difficulties, rebellious children, or terminal illness. How does a person continue to be positive in the face of such difficult times in life? Where is God and why is He allowing this?

We have to remember that we are living in a fallen world that has sin and sinful people operating around us. It is also necessary to remember that God is still in control and will use all that is happening around us and to us for our good and to His glory. What can we do as His children who have to live in the midst of these things that seem to constantly bombard us from all directions? Where is your focus? Are you only looking at the negative?

One of the Scripture passages that brings me consistent consolation is Philippians 4:6-9 in *The Message Bible:*

> *Don't fret or worry. Instead of worrying, pray. Let petitions and praises shape your worries into prayers, letting God know your concerns. Before you know it, a sense of God's wholeness, everything coming together for good, will come and settle you down. It's wonderful what happens when Christ displaces worry at the center of your life. Summing it all up, friends, I'd say you'll do best by filling your minds and meditating on things true, noble, reputable, authentic, compelling, gracious—the best, not the worst; the beautiful, not the ugly; things to praise, not things to curse. Put into practice what you learned from me, what you heard and saw and realized. Do that, and God, who makes everything work together, will work you into His most excellent harmonies.*

Quit letting the problems that you are in the middle of consume your being. Trust in God because He is the only one who can change the situation. Fill your mind with truth about what God can do to make things right and know that He will do it!

Father, I will fill my mind with truth. Every time I allow the negative to enter my mind, I know it will only cause me worry and a loss of focus. My eyes are on You. Amen.

HIS HEART IS FOR US

Jonah began by going a day's journey into the city, proclaiming, "Forty more days and Nineveh will be overthrown." The Ninevites believed God. A fast was proclaimed, and all of them, from the greatest to the least, put on sackcloth (Jonah 3:4-5).

Nineveh was a seaport city whose people were exceedingly godless. The people of Nineveh did what felt good and right in their own opinion. God sent His prophet Jonah to proclaim to this city that in forty days it would be destroyed because of its state of sinfulness. As a result of Jonah's message from God, the entire city went into mourning and repented of the way they had been living. The king of Nineveh cried for a nationwide fast from food or drink of any kind. He decreed that everyone turn from their evil ways and from the violence that they were involved in. They cried out mightily to God to change His mind so that they might live.

When God saw what they did, how they turned from their sins, He relented the decision that He had made to destroy their nation, and He did not destroy them. Isn't it amazing that their unified decision to do right was able to do in change God's mind? Our God is a compassionate Father. He wants to bless us. He wants us to turn from our sinful ways so that He can bless us. He changed His plan to destroy them when Nineveh repented (Jonah 3).

Your Father God wants to bless you. His heart is for His children. He is so grieved when we live a lifestyle that is not in accordance with His Word. Scripture says that God has many blessings in store for us when we are obedient to His Word. Imagine what He has to wait to give us because we walk contrary to Scripture. How encouraged I am to read that God changed His mind when Nineveh confessed their wrong and chose to follow His precepts.

Stories are shared in the Bible so we know how God dealt with His children in the past. Our God never changes, so if He was faithful to bless Nineveh when they changed their ways, He will be faithful to bless us when we walk in His way. Be encouraged, child of God, His heart is for you!

Father, my heart overflows with joy that You respond to my pleas for forgiveness. What a comfort to know that You bury my sins in the depths of the ocean. Amen.

BELIEVE TRUTH

"What is truth?" retorted Pilate. With this he went out again to the Jews gathered there and said, "I find no basis for a charge against him" (John 18:38).

It has become increasingly more important that a person have a college degree to obtain desirable employment. Without a degree, it is hard to get a job that will provide enough income to support a household or a family. Most people are not satisfied with just a bachelor's degree in their major and continue on to earn a master's degree or a doctorate.

Could you imagine what their education would be worth if the professors who were teaching at the university only taught what the students wanted to hear and not the truth of the subject matter? Their education would be a farce and not worth the thousands of dollars spent to receive their degrees. Students pay huge tuition prices to receive the truth in their field of study.

Most believers are not paying money to learn the truth of God. We choose what church we attend based on criteria that we establish on our personal convictions. The church's worship, pastor's preaching style, flavor of the service, and denominational background are typical characteristics that church attenders consider when looking for a place to worship. One thing that should be extremely important in making this decision is whether the truth of the Word of God is being taught. Second Timothy 4:3-4 states that *"The time will come when people will not put up with sound doctrine. Instead, to suit their own desires, they will gather around them a great number of teachers to say what their itching ears want to hear. They will turn their ears away from the truth and turn aside to myths."*

God's words of truth are not condemning to His children; rather, He brings conviction in areas where we are not walking in His truth. We should make sure we are placing ourselves in the environment to hear His truth, believe His truth, and apply that to the area in our life that needs it. If we are just hearing what we want to hear, then we won't be growing to be more like Christ. Be sure that your faith walk is not a farce, but that you are earning a degree in *truth!*

Father, I desire truth from You, not from the world. I choose to put my face in Your Book and not get truth from a worldly system dedicated to twisting and distorting Your words. Amen.

MOVING FORWARD

Then the Lord said to Moses, "Why are you crying out to me? Tell the Israelites to move on. Raise your staff and stretch out your hand over the sea to divide the water so that the Israelites can go through the sea on dry ground (Exodus 14:15-16).

Moses and the people of Israel had just left Egypt and were faced with an immediate dilemma. The Egyptian army was pursuing them with Pharaoh leading the charge—their demise seemed eminent. Turning back would have been a pretty reasonable response. As a leader, Moses was faced with a difficult decision so he cried out to God. God's reply was simple, "Go forward."

How do we do that? When the circumstance seems hopeless, how can we still go forward? I think the first step is to believe in God. The people of Israel had just witnessed the ten plagues, and all that God told them had come true. Why would they have not believed in the ability of God to save them from the army? The same is true with us. Given the knowledge and experiences we have, why would we ever doubt.

We also need to receive and follow God's instruction. Psalm 32:8 states that God *"will instruct you and teach you in the way you should go; I will counsel you with my eye upon you"* (NASB). This takes realizing that God does not lead us into anything in which He has not given us His instruction. After the instruction, He continues to guides us along (remember the cloud by day and fire by night).

Last, we must trust God completely. Trusting Him means that we look past our circumstances. Moses and the people of Israel would naturally have had incredible fear and a lack of trust. They had nothing fit to battle the enemy so their trust had to be in the Lord alone. As believers, our ultimate confidence cannot rest in what we do. This is not to say that we don't put forth effort; it does not mean that we do not work hard, or that we don't plan or prepare. What it means is that we do all those things and we leave the result to God and MOVE FORWARD!

Father, lead me, teach me, and show me the way You want me to go. When the enemy is coming after me, give me courage to trust in Your provision and strength. Amen.

A BLESSED LIFE

Blessed is the man... (Psalm 1:1).

As you read those words today, do you truly feel that you are a blessed person? Those few words can be some of the most comforting or disturbing words you'll ever read. Certainly anyone who has trusted Jesus Christ as your personal Lord and Savior has already been blessed. No matter what your past, your sins have been forgiven and your future is secure for all eternity. So, do you feel like a blessed person today? I think for the Believer the sense of being blessed experientially comes from the next three phrases. The Psalmist goes on to say that the blessed man:

1. Walks not in the counsel of the ungodly.
2. Stands not in the way of sinners (literally is not a trouble maker).
3. Sits not in the seat of the scornful (does not judge others)

So instead of ungodly counsel or being a troublemaker and judging others they delight themselves in loving God and serving others. What a contrast in the way so many of God's people live their life and whether or not they have a sense of being blessed. Today would be a great day for you to start believing that God has already blessed you in Heavenly places in Christ Jesus. But those blessings in everyday life are contingent upon your willingness not to walk, stand or sit in ungodly ways but instead love God and serve others.

Father, today I pray you'll help me not to walk in any ungodly counsel, be a troublemaker or judge others. But instead you'll help me love YOU and serve OTHERS.

WISDOM FOR THE JOURNEY

These are the wise sayings of Solomon, David's son, Israel's king—written down so we will know how to live well and right, to understand what life means and where it's going; a manual for living, for learning what's right and just and fair; to teach the inexperienced the ropes and give our young people a grasp on reality. There's something here also for seasoned men and women, still a thing or two for the experienced to learn—fresh wisdom to probe and penetrate, the rhymes and reasons of wise men and women (Proverbs 1:1-6 MSG).

I love to read the book of Proverbs. It helps me in my Christian walk. After all, it's counsel from Solomon, and God said Solomon was the wisest man who ever lived (see1 Kings 3 KJV).

Solomon, as a young man with great responsibility (probably in his twenties), knew he needed God's wisdom in order to rule as king (see 1 Kings 3). We as ordinary, everyday people need God's wisdom and counsel too. Why? As you read earlier, it's a manual for living—right living before God.

How do we know how to treat people? How do we know how to do business? How do we know what life really means and who we are? We know these things by reading God's words of wisdom in the Bible.

I am amazed how much I have learned in my Christian walk as I've read Proverbs. However, it's not just reading the words—God graciously allows me to come face to face with situations where I can live out the teachings of His Word. It's one thing to read God's Word, it's another to *do* His Word, so God gives us opportunities every day to practice *doing* (obeying) His Word.

I don't know about you, but I want to be wise, righteous, and equipped for every challenge God brings my way. God's Word is available to give wisdom for each and every situation we face.

Father, give me a hunger and desire to spend time in Your Word every day. I need Your wisdom! Amen.

OUR HEARTS—GOD'S DWELLING PLACE

That Christ may dwell in your hearts by faith...
(Ephesians 3:17 KJV).

The God of creation wants to live His life in and through us. I remember when our daughter, Gretchen, was six years of age and she asked me a question at the dinner table. We were having one of Paul's favorite "Yankee" meals—beans and franks. Gretchen asked, "Mama, where does Jesus live?" I said, "He lives in our hearts." She thought for a while, then she stuck a hot dog on her fork and said, "Here comes a frank, Jesus." I believe this is the faith of children. They believe He's that real! That He's right here! That He's really living in them!

> *But without faith it is impossible to please him: for he that cometh to God must believe that he is, and that he is a rewarder of them that diligently seek him* (Hebrews 11:6 KJV).

> *Verily I say unto you, Whosoever shall not receive the kingdom of God as a little child, he shall not enter therein* (Mark 10:15 KJV).

Even though I told Gretchen that Jesus lives in our hearts, a few years passed before I really knew this myself. I thought of Him as way off somewhere beyond the blue. I didn't really understand or believe He was living in me. The God of creation living in me! What a revelation! What a joy! God set up His kingdom in the likes of me. Just to think He knew me before I was formed. He loved me from the foundation of the world. He paid the price for my sin. He is making intercession for me right now before the throne of God. All I can say is... Hallelujah!

> *He lives, He lives, Christ Jesus lives today,*
> *He walks with me, He talks with me*
> *Along life's narrow way.*
> *He lives, He lives, Salvation to impart.*
> *You ask me how I know He lives,*
> *He lives within my heart.*
> *("He Lives" by Alfred H. Ackley, 1887-1960)*

Lord, thank You for revealing Yourself to me. Thank You for sending Your Holy Spirit to live in me. Amen.

GOD'S MASTERPIECE

I will praise You, for I am fearfully and wonderfully made, marvelous are Your works and that my soul knows very well. My frame was not hidden from You, when I was made in secret and skillfully wrought in the lowest parts of the earth. Your eyes saw my substance, being yet unformed, and in Your book they all were written when as yet there were none of them (Psalm 139:14-16 NKJV).

God has a purpose for my life—and yours.

I find these verses in Psalm 139 so fascinating. To think that God didn't make us by mistake or as an afterthought, but that He made us on purpose, is a reason to be grateful. It should cause us to worship and praise our Father and Creator for everything. As author T. T. Munger wrote, "There is no road to success but through a clear and strong purpose—nothing can take its place—a purpose underlies character, culture, position, attainment of every sort."

There are many people who think they are the only ones on planet Earth made without a purpose in life. They wander around thinking that some-how God didn't know what He was doing when it came to them. NOT TRUE! Everything and everyone is made with purpose and destiny, and that includes you.

Stop and think! He was there in the lowest parts of the earth...wherever that is...when we were being made in secret. He saw our substance when we were unformed—amazing! And all our days are already known by Him, ordained by Him. He's not surprised by what we do. Nothing "slips up" on Him.

He made us on purpose for a purpose. I believe our main purposes are to glorify Him, live for Him, love Him, praise Him, be thankful to Him. It's all about HIM!

Father, I thank You for loving me and giving me life. I thank You for the ultimate sacrifice You paid for me to have life and life abundantly in Christ. I know you created me on purpose and I will determine to live it out. Amen.

MONDAY

BOUGHT WITH A PRICE

Flee fornication. Every sin that a man doeth is without the body; but he that committeth fornication sinneth against his own body. What? know ye not that your **body is the temple of the Holy Ghost** *which is in you, which ye have of God, and ye are not your own? For ye are bought with a price: therefore glorify God in your body, and in your spirit, which are God's* (1 Corinthians 6:18-20 KJV).

Surrender your rights to the One who bought and paid for you.

The world has made fornication an acceptable sin, and the Christian world has bought into the lie. These verses in First Corinthians are for the good of all Christians…not to harm us but to help us.

Many couples live under shame, guilt, and condemnation because of this lifestyle before marriage—and even after marriage (adultery). God doesn't condemn or bring shame. He convicts a Christian's heart about loving Him and obeying His Word rather than buying into the world's (Hollywood movies/TV) lifestyle of what's right. God's Word is truth, and it's for our good to give us blessed lives.

Forgiveness is God's way of making us clean and pure and whole. Hallelujah for forgiveness and love that's unconditional. Remember, when you trusted Christ and asked Him to save you, you ceased to belong to yourself anymore or have any rights when you repented and turned from your old life.

It says in First Peter 1:18-19, *"For you know that it was not with perishable things such as silver or gold that you were redeemed from the empty way of life handed down to you from your ancestors, but with the precious blood of Christ, a lamb without blemish or defect."*

And it says in Second Corinthians 5:17, *"Therefore, if anyone is in Christ, the new creation has come: The old has gone, the new is here!"*

You were purchased on the cross. A high price was paid for you at Calvary. Surrender your rights to the One who bought and paid for you. He is standing with open arms to receive you and forgive you.

Father, help me make the right choices for my life—choices that please You and bring blessing into my life. Amen.

HEAVEN, OUR ETERNAL HOME

But our citizenship is in heaven, and from it we await a Savior, the Lord Jesus Christ, who will transform our lowly body to be like his glorious body, by the power that enables him even to subject all things to himself (Philippians 3:20-21 ESV).

Our home is in Heaven with our Lord and Savior, Jesus Christ. He is our hope.

When my sister was dying from leukemia, our eleven-year-old daughter crawled up into bed beside her and said, "Bye, Aunt Kim, I love you very much." Kim raised herself up and said, "Love you too, and I'll see you soon."

Even with an almost-morphine-induced coma, Kim knew she would see Shelby again and wanted to declare it! That is our hope! Not only will we live eternally with our Creator and Savior, we will once again be united with our friends and family in faith, praising God all of our days. Isn't that exciting?

When it comes to death, believers have nothing to fear. The Bible makes it clear the last enemy of humanity is death, and Jesus did something about that. He conquered death, hell and the grave for us—therefore we have nothing to fear.

The writer of Hebrews put it this way: *"Since the children have flesh and blood, he too shared in their humanity so that by his death he might break the power of him who holds the power of death—that is, the devil—and free those who all their lives were held in slavery by their fear of death"* (Hebrews 2:14-15).

In the English Standard Version, Revelation 21:4 says, *"He will wipe away every tear from their eyes, and death shall be no more, neither shall there be mourning, nor crying, nor pain anymore, for the former things have passed away."*

The Living Bible says in Philippians 4:8, *"Fix your thoughts on what is true and good and right. Think about things that are pure and lovely, and dwell on the fine, good things in others. Think about all you can praise God for and be glad about."*

Father, thank You for providing a way for us to live with You eternally. Amen.

FILL YOUR MIND WITH GOD'S WORD

According to my earnest expectation and hope that in nothing I shall be ashamed, but with all boldness, as always, so now also Christ will be magnified in my body, whether by life or by death (Philippians 1:20 NKJV).

———

God's Word gives us hope. If there is anything our world needs right now, it is HOPE!

My son was singing a song to himself around the house. It was a praise song. My heart leaped as he sang it over and over. I love how the Father can put a song in our minds, and if it's the right song, it can ***give us hope****: "For thou art my hope, O Lord God: thou art my trust from my youth. By thee have I been holden up from the womb: thou art he that took me out of my mother's bowels: my praise shall be continually of thee"* (Psalm 71:5-6 KJV).

It can ***build our strength****: "The Lord is my rock, and my fortress, and my deliverer; my God, my strength, in whom I will trust; my buckler, and the horn of my salvation, and my high tower"* (Psalm 18:2 KJV), ***and enhance our faith****: "Therefore being justified by faith, we have peace with God through our Lord Jesus Christ: by whom also we have access by faith into this grace wherein we stand, and rejoice in hope of the glory of God"* (Romans 5:1-2 KJV).

The world our children are living in is totally different from the one you and I grew up in. They are facing challenges we never had to face. So encourage your children to learn the songs that glorify God and encourage their hearts to live the right way and do the things that will glorify God and strengthen their faith. They need encouragement every single day.

Psalm 119:147 says, *"I rise before dawn and cry for help;* ***I have put my hope in your word."***

———

Father, let my heart and my mouth be filled with Your praise as I go through my day. Keep reminding me of Your steadfast love. Amen.

UNCONDITIONAL LOVE

But God shows and clearly proves His [own] love for us, by the fact that while we were still sinners, Christ (the Messiah, the Anointed One) died for us (Romans 5:8 Amplified Bible).

———❧———

Isn't it wonderful to know that God's love doesn't depend on us! No matter what we have done in our past, God has shown mercy and grace by giving us something we desperately needed. Even though we weren't searching for Him, He was searching for us. Before the foundation of the world, I was on His mind. Apostle Paul explained it this way in Ephesians 2:4-5: *"But because of his great love for us, God, who is rich in mercy, made us alive with Christ even when we were dead in transgressions—it is by grace you have been saved."*

This verse in Romans should cause every Christian to have a truly thankful heart. God loved us while we were still going our own way, doing our own thing, not giving Him a thought, and living selfish, self-centered lives. This reminds me of a song Dallas Holm wrote many years ago that says, "He knew me then, He knows me now, and He died for me; He loved me then, He loves me now, Oh, how can it be? He saw my face; He knew the place I would be today. He knew me then, He knows me now and He loves me." He knew me, yet He loved me! He knows me and still loves me. Can I get an "Amen"?!

How amazing is this: His love never changes; He loved us when we were yet sinners; He loves us still. Yes, even when we don't make right choices, He loves us. When we are faithless, He remains faithful. Hallelujah! *"If we believe not, yet he abideth faithful: he cannot deny himself"* (2 Timothy 2:13 KJV).

———❧———

Thank You, Father, for loving me when I was unlovely. My heart rejoices to know Your love never changes—it's unconditional, unfailing, and everlasting. Amen.

THY WORD HAVE I HID IN MY HEART

*Teach me, O Lord, the way of thy statutes; and I shall keep it unto
the end. Give me understanding, and I shall keep thy law; yea, I shall
observe it with my whole heart. Make me to go in the path of thy
commandments; for therein do I delight* (Psalm 119:33-35 KJV).

Have you hidden God's Word in your heart so you will not sin against Him?
Do you have a hunger to meet with Him through His Word and prayer? Do you
want to have God's wisdom as you walk through this life? If so, you *must* spend
time with Him.

Psalm 119 (the longest chapter in the Bible) reminds us how vital God's Word
(law, precepts, commandments, judgments, statutes, testimonies) is to our lives.
Second Timothy 3:16 says God's Word is sufficient to make us wise, train us in
righteousness, and equip us for *every* good work.

So as Christians, why do we neglect His Word? Why do we try to figure things
out on our own?

Do we get too busy? Is it that we don't want to do what He says but are determined to do what we want to do? Are we just too lazy? YES! We can answer yes to
all of these questions at one time or another in our Christian walk. At least, I can.

However, my heart hungers for His Word. I find myself getting irritated, emotional, touchy, and frustrated when I've neglected spending time with my Savior.
My family can tell when I've gone too long without meeting with God. I get selfish and self-serving.

How do we spend time with Him? We talk to Him. We spend time in His
Word (love letters from God). We listen to praise music and worship Him. We
acknowledge Him as our only hope and the only One who can meet every need of
our lives.

*Father, give me a hunger and desire for You and Your Word. Help me make time
each day to seek Your face and acknowledge You as my sufficiency in every area of
my life. Amen.*

MONDAY

THE POWER OF FORGIVENESS

*And you, being dead in your trespasses and the uncircumcision of your flesh,
He has made alive together with Him, having forgiven you all trespasses,
having wiped out the handwriting of requirements that was against us, which
was contrary to us. And He has taken it out of the way, having nailed it
to the cross. Having disarmed principalities and powers, He made a public
spectacle of them, triumphing over them in it* (Colossians 2:13-15 NKJV).

Christ forgave us and nailed our sins to His cross.

Are there people in your life you haven't forgiven? You may say, "I won't forgive; I was hurt too badly. They destroyed my life." The list could go on and on; however, whatever reasons are on the list, they are covered by the blood of Jesus. As Colossians 2:14 reads in The Message version, *"Think of it! All sins forgiven, the slate wiped clean, that old arrest warrant canceled and nailed to Christ's cross."* Hallelujah! We can forgive. Why? Because we have been forgiven. All our sins have been nailed to the cross. We will never have to meet them again. God has put them away—as far as the east is from the west, as far as the sunrise is from the sunset, never will the two meet. Why do we harbor unforgiveness in our hearts when we have been forgiven much?

"To forgive is to set a prisoner free and discover the prisoner was you." —Unknown

Why not write down on a piece of paper all of the pettiness, anger, bitterness, hurt feelings, jealousy, unforgiveness, hatred, prejudice…anything that keeps you from being right with God and walking in freedom and joy. In your heart, nail them to the cross! He got rid of them for good. Burn the paper! Write on a balloon all your unforgiveness and let the wind take it to the heavens. Why don't you walk in freedom, dear friend? You hold the key to unlock your prison.

Father, I am so tired of holding on to all of the mess in my life. I ask that You give me the courage to nail it to Your cross, knowing You have done this for me. Set me free from the prison I have locked myself in. Cleanse me from all unrighteousness. Search my heart, oh God. Let me see if there's anything that is displeasing to You, and give me grace to repent. Amen.

KINDNESS—GOD'S WAY

I tell you, love your enemies. Help and give without expecting a return.
You'll never—I promise—regret it. Live out this God-created identity the
way our Father lives toward us, generously and graciously, even when we're
at our worst. Our Father is kind; you be kind (Luke 6:35 MSG).

When we treat people with kindness, we are not only obeying God's Word, we are teaching people how to treat us. Treat others the way we want to be treated!

When we show kindness to someone we think doesn't deserves it, we are imitating Christ by; obeying His Word. Paul tells us in Romans 12:9-21 how imitators of Christ put love into action. We are to bless our enemies, not cursing (speaking evil) them under our breath. God, who can't be fooled by any pretense on our part, always knows a person's thoughts. When friends are happy, we should rejoice with them; when they are sad and feeling down, we should weep with them. If someone says bad things about us, we don't get-them-back by saying bad things about the person. Don't just befriend people you think are the "somebodies"; rather, make friends with everyone—the somebodies and the down and out.

Don't insist on getting revenge, that's not for us to do, leave it to God. If we see people we think are enemies and they are hungry, feed them; if they are thirsty, give them a drink. God says this will surprise them with goodness. Who knows, we may make a new friend or two or three. I read this statement a while back, "The best way to get rid of your enemy is to make them your friend." Sounds like a great idea to me. Let's not let evil rule our lives—let God's kindness be the rule we live by day in and day out.

Lord, help me show kindness to everyone I come in contact with. Help me make the
right choice when someone does wrong to me. Let me respond with Your love and
kindness. Amen.

BEING CONFORMED TO LOOK LIKE CHRIST

*And we know that **all things work together for good** to them that love God, to them who are the called according to his purpose* (Romans 8:28 KJV).

If God works everything for our good, does that mean I will never suffer? Does it mean I will be healthy, wealthy, and wise all of my life? Does it mean tragedy will never strike my family? What is the "good" God intends for my life?

When God says all things work together for our *good,* does that mean we will never have problems or heartache or trouble? No! Scripture says, *"Many are the afflictions of the righteous"* (Psalm 34:19 NKJV) and *"In the world you will have tribulation"* (John 16:33 NKJV). "Good" means that God is using everything that happens in our lives (heartache, trouble, problems) to conform us to the image of His Son. Conform means to be or become similar in form, nature, or character. This is the good that is working in our lives: We are being made to be like Christ, we are being conformed to His image. This promise, that all things work together for our good, is not for everyone, it is for *"the called,"* those who belong to Him, those who love Him.

We know that we are saved by grace! We know it's through faith in Christ! We know it's not by works or any good deeds we perform, because everyone of us would definitely boast and brag about all we've done to merit salvation. *"For by grace are ye saved through faith; and that not of yourselves: it is the gift of God: Not of works, lest any man should boast"* (Ephesians 2:8-9 KJV). We are totally, 100 percent dependent on God to not only redeem us but to make us like Christ. So be encouraged, dear friend, when God allows a storm to come blowing into your life, His promise is to use it for your good and His glory.

Father, thank You for calling me, redeeming me, conforming me, and using everything that comes my way to make me more like Christ. I praise You for Your Holy Spirit who lives in me to give me courage, wisdom, and strength to yield to Your conforming work. Amen.

GOING THE SECOND MILE

And whosoever shall compel thee to go a mile, go
with him two miles (Matthew 5:41).

This passage of Scripture is a great reminder to me not to settle for less than God's best. He is The God of the second mile. Or to put it another way, He is The God of "and then some."

I really believe that success in any area of our lives is found in "and then some." Often times we just want to skim by whether it be in our ministry or the market place where God has placed us. But true success lies in the "second mile" the "and then some." So my question today is, are we just getting by, doing the minimum or are we second mile people who read the Word of God and then some? People who pray and then some? People who witness for Christ and then some? Those who give financially to the Lord's work and then some? In terms of your business in the market place are you just getting by, or are you going the second mile? Are you willing to do what unsuccessful people are not willing to do? My friend, those who are willing do the "and then some" of life and go the second mile will succeed in ways they only dream about now. Today is your day to begin a life of abundance, a day of excess and a day to make whatever sacrifice necessary to achieve your God given purpose.

Father, in Jesus name I commit today to go the second mile and do the "and then some" of life that I may hear from you, "Well done."

THE WAY WE ARE

I praise You, for I am fearfully and wonderfully made; marvelous are Your works, and that my soul knows very well (Psalm 139:14 NKJV).

God is in control of every aspect of our lives. Nothing is a surprise to Him.

When I was born I had some major difficulties: I arrived a month early and immediately had a hard time breathing. The doctors told my mom and dad that if I didn't breathe through my nose right away, I would pass away. This is due in part to that fact that I have what is called Mid-facial Hypoplasia. This makes it difficult to breathe through my nose, so I have to breathe through my mouth most of the time. I was also born with a disorder, a disability called 18p-Chromosome Deletion which brings about its unique challenges. So I have had difficulties throughout my entire life.

So fast-forward ten years. I was at a Kid's Camp at the church we attended when I was saved, but I realized later that I went forward for the wrong reasons. Everyone was going forward, so I went too because I didn't want to be different. But, I am different. This had me asking me a lot of questions of God: "Why me? God, why did You make me this way? Why am I not normal? What is my purpose in life?" I just kept asking those questions, and you know what God spoke to me? That I didn't trust Him. I was very down on myself and taking it out on my family. That is when I had to realize something VERY important.

The point to my story—trust God. He's in control!

Here are some of my favorite verses that remind us to be yourself, love yourself, take care of yourself, and know that God loves you.

> *But the Lord said to Samuel, "Do not consider his appearance or his height, for I have rejected him. The Lord does not look at the things people look at. People look at the outward appearance, but the Lord looks at the heart"* (1 Samuel 16:7).
>
> *...by his wounds we are healed* (Isaiah 53:5).
>
> *She is clothed with strength and dignity; she can laugh at the days to come* (Proverbs 31:25).

Lord, help me be content and praise You for who I am. I am Your child, and You love me unconditionally...just like I am. Amen.

RELAX AND REFRESH

MONDAY

CHANGE

And be not conformed to this world: but be ye transformed by the renewing of your mind, that ye may prove what is that good, and acceptable, and perfect, will of God (Romans 12:2 KJV).

———————————

How do I act when changes come into my life? Do I fuss and complain, or do I ask God to show me what His plan is in this change? Change is a very hard thing for me. I am one of those people who like a very stable life. When my parents came to me and my sisters about moving to Texas, it took me a little bit to processes it, because I am so used to being in California. It's stable! My friends are here! My church is here! Everything is here in Cali and it has been for fifteen years. Why does there have to be change?

However, when I was praying about it, I asked God, "What am I doing here in Cali? I can't find a job. I'm sitting at home with nothing to do. I could be working for my grandfather in Texas. So Lord, why am I so hesitant to move?" CHANGE!

I called my grandma and asked her if it was okay for me to come to the ranch earlier than planned. I talked to my mom and dad and told them I had a change of heart and a change of mind. So my point? Let God take control of your life! Let Him lead you and guide you. As God worked in my heart, I had to make up my mind what I wanted to do. I had to make a decision. I had to have the right attitude and spirit about this change.

Even though it may be hard, when you are trusting God, the changes He makes in your life will be for your good and His glory. *"But he is singular and sovereign. Who can argue with him? He does what he wants, when he wants to. He'll complete in detail what he's decided about me, and whatever else he determines to do"* (Job 23:13-14 MSG).

———————————

Lord, continue to work in my life to conform me to look like Christ. I want to be an obedient and trusting child who knows You bring changes into my life for my good and Your glory. Amen.

GREEN PASTURES

He makes me lie down in green pastures, he leads
me beside quiet waters (Psalm 23:2).

———————

Green pastures is such a beautiful image. You see it was the shepherd's responsibility to provide for the basic needs of the sheep, which were very simple, just grass and water. I can picture in my mind a flock of sheep bedded down in green meadows, having eaten their fill and now totally satisfied. Then I can see the good shepherd leading the flock by still waters. What an awesome picture of calm and tranquility.

But I am sure there were times when the sheep had to travel through unpleasant places. I am sure they would have traveled through areas where the pasture would have been less than restful.

At times, we too travel into restful and not-so-restful places. I can only speak for myself and there are times when I have tried to find rest in the wrong places; however, it goes deeper than that. As I have gotten older I realized that these times have always been a result of choices that I made. As someone told me, "You are nothing more and nothing less than the choices you have made in your life." Don't blame others, just look in the mirror.

Life can be deceptive at times. It tries to make us think that rest (green pastures) is in the places where it really is not. It tries to make us think that rest is when we have enough money or possessions, or when all seems to be going our way. While rest can be there, it is not exclusively there. True rest is not dependent upon anything or any person.

True rest only comes through the leading of the Shepherd. For the Christian, true rest can only be found in the presence of the True Shepherd. The True Shepherd who declares, "My burden is light and My yoke is easy."

———————

Lord, please help me to see that true rest comes only in Your presence and through what only You provide. Help me to never substitute the glitter for the gold! Amen.

THE SHEPHERD

The Lord is my shepherd, I lack nothing (Psalm 23:1).

Psalm 23 could arguably be the most popular chapter in the entire Bible. It is quoted oftentimes when difficulties, especially death and illness, affect someone. I cannot even count how many funerals I have been to in which this chapter is read for the purpose of granting comfort to those who are grieving. When I look at each verse of this psalm, as well as the psalm as a whole, there are several things that always catch my attention.

The first thing I see in verse 1 is the person of the Shepherd. Psalm 23 starts not with man, but with the Shepherd, who is identified simply as *"The Lord."* It is wise to have some understanding of the role of the shepherd. Keep in mind that David, the author of the Psalm, was himself a shepherd, and the son of a shepherd. He is later known as the Shepherd King of Israel. He knew what he was talking about from personal experience.

The shepherd becomes a shepherd by demonstrating four key characteristics. The first characteristic is that of *provider*. The shepherd provided the needs of the sheep to keep them content and healthy. The second characteristic is that of *protector*. Shepherds were the ones who stood as warriors between the sheep of the fold and anything or anyone who would cause the sheep harm. The third role was that of *guidance*. Shepherds guide the sheep in the right direction, ensuring their safe passage. The last role was that of *correction*. If any one of the flock went astray or got out of line, the shepherd was there to bring it back where it belonged—safe and sound within the flock under the shepherd's care.

Those are the exact roles that our Savior Jesus Christ plays in our lives. He is our Provider, Protector, Guide, and Corrector. He does all this for His glory and our good.

My Savior Shepherd, I praise You for who You are, for what You do in my life. I pray that the true desire of my heart is You! Amen.

RELAX

He makes me lie down in green pastures, he leads
me beside quiet waters (Psalm 23:2).

Everyone can become overwhelmed in life. I believe that absolutely no one is immune to this fact. The encouraging thing, though, is that God knows this very well. We see this in vivid form in Matthew 11:28 (NASB) when He says, *"Come to Me, all who are weary and heavy-laden, and I will give you rest."*

In Psalm 1 it says *"He makes me lie down."* It is up to the Shepherd to free His flock from harmful distractions and influences. The strange thing about sheep is that their very makeup does not lend itself to being relaxed unless four requirements are met:

1. They must be free from fear.
2. They must be free from friction with the other sheep.
3. They must be free from flies or parasites.
4. They must be free from hunger.

One of the hardest things about being overwhelmed is allowing ourselves to relax. I have seen many children go and go and go until they literally cannot go anymore. During this time when you try to get them to rest, it is very difficult. They don't want to relax. When our children were smaller, there were times we used strong discipline, saying to them, "Enough is enough, it is time to take a break and relax."

This is the mind-set that I have when reading this verse in Psalm 23. I know there are times when I do a great job of telling God that I am okay and don't need His help. It is at those times when the wrestling can become unpleasant. It brings me back to when I was a child and I needed a parent to tell me, "Enough is enough, time to relax."

That is when the words of this Psalm ring the loudest, *"He makes me...."* In the midst of life and all the storms thrown my way, *"He makes me...."* What a great comfort in three simple but profound words.

Jesus, Rest-giver, please help me to see that my rest comes from You! Amen.

ROAD TO BETTER PASTURE

*He makes me lie down in green pastures, he leads
me beside quiet waters* (Psalm 23:2).

What leads to the wanting of green pasture? There are times when I take a spiritual inventory of my life. Often the cause that brings on these times is spiritual dryness. I want to communicate clearly that I am not saying that there are no signs of spiritual life. In fact, the opposite is often the case. It is the Holy Spirit abiding in me who is prompting me to ask this question of myself. I have found that there are four things that I can attribute bad pastureland to:

1. Lack of prayer time (communication) with the Shepherd is a habit that, if ignored, can very quickly lead to spiritual wasteland for the believer.

2. When I hunger for other things rather than feeding on the Word of Life. There are some disciplines that are necessary for feeding on the Word. I feed on the Word through hearing, reading, studying, memorizing, meditating, and applying.

3. True fellowship with God's people is so crucial. This for me is usually not too much of an issue from the outside looking in. What I mean by this is that for people who are observing me, they would think that I have this down pat. After all I am in church regularly, leading Bible studies, etc. The sobering fact of the matter is this, I can do all those things and still not be in fellowship with the people of God.

4. We have been saved to serve. The Dead Sea is called the Dead Sea because water flows into it, but nothing flows out of it. The opposite should be true of the Christian life—a life dedicated to giving rather than just receiving.

Father, I desire to lie down in pastures that are green. I pray that with Your help I will always be found doing the things necessary to experience them. Amen.

MONDAY

FACT OVER FEELING

*He makes me lie down in green pastures, he leads
me beside quiet waters* (Psalm 23:2).

David, when he wrote this beautiful psalm, was looking at life from the standpoint of sheep. When he wrote, *"He leads me beside quiet waters,"* he was telling us the Good Shepherd knows where the still, quiet, deep, clean, pure water is to be found. He doesn't want His sheep drinking unfit water.

What are we being led by? Is it our thoughts, feelings, emotions, or are we being led by truth? I believe that this verse gives some insight into how we can tell. When the Spirit is truly leading us, it grants a sense of calm.

What I am saying is that God does not always work to the benefit of our thoughts, feelings, and emotions. I catch myself telling the Lord often that I don't feel this way or that. The great thing about God is that He is not worried about our feelings. He is concerned with His truth. Feelings and emotions don't always tell the truth or line up with God's Word. Circumstances change and that will affect how we feel. God's Word is unchanging!

Here are some truth statements that often contradict feelings:

I will never leave nor forsake you.

No one can pluck you from My hand.

While in the womb I knew you.

Not one sparrow falls....

He knows the number of hairs on my head.

Cast your cares upon Him because He cares for you.

He leads me beside still waters.

What this tells us is that the results of God's leading are always to our benefit. I may not see the benefit at first, but it is always there. The river of life may seem like a torrent, but the reality is that as a Christian the river of our lives is always quiet water.

Lord, please help me to see life though the truth of Your Word. Please help me to be driven by that truth, not by my thoughts, feelings, or emotions. Amen.

LET GO AND LET GOD

*Trust in the Lord with all your heart, and lean not on your
own understanding; in all your ways acknowledge Him, and
He will direct your paths* (Proverbs 3:5-6 NKJV).

Trust at times can be a commodity that is sorely lacking in our world. In
these times, it seems like distrust is more readily available and at a cheaper price.
In the Christian life however, trust is not something we earn completely on our
own, because God is there to help us build trust in Him. Trust is also something that is not without incredible promise or guarantee. Our trust is rooted
deeply in the truth of God and His Word. It was bought for us through the
sacrifice of God's only Son, Jesus, and is secured for us through the giving of the
Holy Spirit.

This is not to say that trust comes easily. The reason that this statement is
true is because trust demands that we are to let go, which at times is a very difficult thing for us. We try to hold on tight! We want to be in control! The truth
is that we cannot have it both ways. We cannot grasp onto God and still hold
on to ourselves. It is very much like the monkey who tried to get the candy from
the jar. He stuck his hand in through the mouth of the jar that was just large
enough for his hand to fit. When he grabbed the candy his fist became too large
to remove unless he let go of the candy. He refused to let go of even some of the
candy in order to be free.

Our lives are so much like this. God has great things in store for us but they
require us to let go in order to receive them.

*Lord, there are so many things in this world that I hold dear. Please help me realize
that in order to receive what You have for me, I must let go of what You don't have
for me. Amen.*

STAY ON THE RIGHT PATH

...He leads me in the paths of righteousness for His name's sake
(Psalm 23:3 NKJV).

I remember going on a hunting trip with my dad when I was a child. I was too young to hunt so all I could do was follow my dad. It was winter in Colorado and we were in the middle of a snowstorm. When we woke up the next morning we had to force the door of the camper open because the snow had blocked it. Of course I did not want to go out because the snow was almost to my waist.

I remember my dad telling me to follow closely behind him as he walked—to literally place my steps in the same place as his. When I did this, the going was not too bad. It was only when I stepped outside of his steps that the going was tough.

I believe this is the heart behind what David is saying in Psalm 23:3. David was speaking from firsthand experience. He knew that no other class of animals required more careful handling, more detailed direction than do sheep. David knew for a flock to flourish the shepherd had to maintain control and give the right kind of guidance.

Let's face it, the Word points out that most of us are like stubborn sheep (see Isaiah 53:6). We prefer to follow our own paths and do our own thing. Just as sheep will follow one another along the same trails until they become ruts that lead to disaster, we humans will cling to the same habits that will ruin our lives.

But if we stay on the right path, the going is easier. To me there are four keys to staying on the right path.

1. Stay close to the Shepherd.
2. Avoid taking wrong turns.
3. Pay close attention to directions.
4. Realize that ultimately you are headed to His destination.

Father, please find me sticking close to You as I walk through this life. When I stray (and I know I will), please help me to get back on track. Thank You for leading and guiding me in the way that is for my good and for Your glory. Amen.

DIRECTIONS

...He leads me in the paths of righteousness for His name's sake
(Psalm 23:3 NKJV).

———————————

As we go through this life, it is important to know that the Shepherd we are following holds the key to the destination we are all heading toward. It is also important to know that as we are on this journey of the Christian life, we are going to need to ask for and be willing to receive directions.

Asking for directions should be a familiar practice for us. When trying to get directions, it is important to ask someone who knows the area, who can tell you where to go, what hazards to avoid, etc. There is nothing worse than getting inaccurate directions. Wandering around aimlessly is not fun. The opposite is also true. When we get accurate directions from a solid source, it is very comforting.

I love what David says in Psalm 50:15: *"and call on me in the day of trouble; I will deliver you, and you will honor me."* Whether it's in times of trouble, distress, or we have just lost our way, we can call on Him 24/7!

This is certainly the case with the Shepherd we are following. The Guide we are following is a Shepherd who is more than qualified. He knows the destination and the path that will take us there. He will not lead us astray or give us misguided directions.

The practical application for us is that we need to be humble and willing to ask for directions and then follow them specifically. We cannot try to navigate the course on our own and depend upon the Shepherd at the same time. The encouraging part is if we ask, He will answer. He is never too busy, on vacation, or unavailable.

———————————

Father, I admit that at times I try to navigate this life without Your help. I confess this and ask for Your help. I pray that I will be found obedient in asking for and following Your directions. Amen.

GOD'S PASSION

...for His name's sake (Psalm 23:3).

When thinking about God's passion, I am left with a question. Is His passion more for me or is His passion more for Himself? I believe the answer to this question is tucked away in this Scripture passage. The answer is that the Shepherd is doing all His work—saving, refreshing, providing, restoring, guiding, etc.—*for His glory!*

Sometimes a challenging thing for us is the truth that God's passion for God always outweighs God's passion for me. It is funny that this psalm, a psalm often used to comfort people and make them feel better about themselves, declares that the reason we have this comfort and can overcome stress is not to make our life easier or to ease our pain. He does it all for His glory.

There are several additional passages in Scripture that validate this truth as well. Please read Psalm 79:9; First Samuel 12:22; Second Samuel 7:23; Psalm 31:3; Psalm 25:7,11; Psalm 106:8; Isaiah 63:12; Ezekiel 20:9,14,22; Isaiah 48:9-11; Psalm 109:21; Jeremiah 14:7; Matthew 19:29; Romans 1:5; Third John 7; Revelation 2:3; First John 2:12.

Some may ask, "Is God an egomaniac?" The answer to that is an emphatic NO! Let me share with you a quote from Sam Storm, "Your greatest good is in the enjoyment of God. God's greatest glory is in being enjoyed. So, for God to seek His glory (the fame of His name) in your worship of Him is the most loving thing He can do for you. Only by seeking His glory preeminently can God seek your good passionately."

I pray, Lord, that I will be able to see my good in the midst of Your glory, knowing that as You work things out for my good that You are glorified. Amen.

MONDAY

THE STRUGGLE IS REAL

Beloved, do not be surprised at the fiery ordeal among you, which comes upon you for your testing, as though some strange thing were happening to you
(1 Peter 4:12 NASB).

"The struggle is real." This is a statement that many young people are using today. Of course it is usually attached to some kind of First World problem like not being able to find a place with free Wi-Fi or the problem of an inflight movie being longer than the actual flight. These "problems" are so very trivial compared to the life-and-death, larger struggles that exist in the world.

When Peter was writing his first letter, the people of God were experiencing real struggles. Their struggles were to the point of severe persecution and in some cases death. It was about this reality that he wrote to encourage people in the struggle. He tells believers to not be surprised but to expect to struggle. What encouragement is there for this?

The encouragement is that the Lord is with us during these struggles. We may not like to admit it, but all of us have struggles. The size of your bank account or how many names of important people you have in your phone book do not exclude you from life's difficulties. All of us, from time to time, need encouragement. The up and the in and the down and out are all in a single class when it comes to trouble and pain.

But what do you do when it seems like encouragement is not there? That is when we need to rely upon the truth that God is always present!

Father, I know that struggles are part of life and what You use to mature me. Find me keeping my eyes on You in the midst of them. Amen.

TIMING IS EVERYTHING

While he was yet speaking, there came also another, and said… (Job 1:6 KJV).

"Timing is everything." I am sure you have heard that statement at some point in your life. It is a statement that is very true and also very challenging. The reason I make this assertion is because we want everything to work according to our timing. Living in our microwave world has caused us to want what we want when we want it. This also rings true of difficulties that we face. We want to know when they are coming and we want to determine when they leave.

Something that helps me a lot in this area is some basic understanding in knowing that trials are going to come. To some this may be the most encouraging truth because some think that trials should never come to Christians. The truth is, we would love it if difficulties stayed away from us. But trials are inevitable.

Another basic understanding is that trials seem to come when we least want them. This cuts at the very core of many of our struggles. We want to be in control! We want to have the right to tell God when trials are welcome and when they are not. This mentality causes God's purpose to be put on hold or to be subverted altogether. God has a purpose for every trial we face and we must allow Him to use us for His purpose—even it if means accepting trials and difficulties.

The true reason for trials in our lives is that God uses them to make us into His image. This happens as we go through trials and overcome difficulties; we learn that God is doing His work in us.

Lord, I truly desire to see Your work through all the aspects of my life. At times it is easy to see You in the good things, but please help me see them in the bad times as well. Amen.

DIFFICULTIES ARE DECEPTIVE

Yea, though I walk through the valley of the shadow of death, I will fear no evil;
for You are with me; Your rod and Your staff, they comfort me
(Psalm 23:4 NKJV).

I remember hearing a great story about the deceptive reality of difficulties. After a little research I discovered that the story was from Dr. Donald Grey Barnhouse. Dr. Barnhouse was the pastor of the Tenth Presbyterian Church in Philadelphia. God gave Him this insight on the day of his first wife's funeral. She had died of cancer.

> He, with his children, had been to the funeral service, and as he was driving home, Dr. Barnhouse said that he was trying to think of some words of comfort that he could give them. Just then a huge moving van passed them. As it passed, the shadow of the truck swept over the car, and as the truck pulled out in front of them, an inspiration came to Dr. Barnhouse. He said, "Children, would you rather be run over by a truck, or by its shadow?" The children said, "Well, of course Dad, we'd much rather be run over by the shadow! That can't hurt us at all." Dr. Barnhouse said, "Did you know that two thousand years ago the truck of death ran over the Lord Jesus in order that only its shadow might run over us?"[14]

Even though this story is about what could possibly be the most difficult situation in life—death—it also grants incredible comfort in all the difficulties we face in life. I don't know how many times Psalm 23:4 has been read, quoted, or used to comfort those who have lost loved ones. For the child of God, death is not the end but merely a door into an eternity of joy and delight in the presence of God.

Father, I am asking for the strength to see my difficulties in reality. I praise You for the fact that You paid the ultimate price for my sin so that all that touches me now is just a shadow. Amen.

THIS TOO SHALL PASS

And after you have suffered a little while, the God of all grace, who has called you to His eternal glory in Christ, will Himself perfect, confirm, strengthen, and establish you (1 Peter 5:10 NASB).

It seems sometimes like the trials of this life never stop. I know for me, when trials occur I want them to leave. My prayer is often, "God, please make this stop." At times I am a wimp and cry uncle very quickly. It is during these times that my comfort rather than God's will in the trial is what really matters to me. I would rather live in what appears to me to be comfort rather than go through the struggle. This is a very me-centered response to the trials I face.

A provoking question is this, "What if God's purpose in the struggle is not over?" Do I want it to end, which I think is good for me, or do I want God to let the trial complete the work that He has for me? Oftentimes the answer to these questions is a reflection of our faith and trust in God. Our faith is great as long as the boat is not rocking. When it begins to rock and our faith is tested, our faith stumbles.

It is during these times when we hear that still, small voice whisper in our ear, "This too shall pass." There is light at the end of the tunnel. Whatever affliction we are facing will ultimately come to a conclusion. That conclusion should be that our faith in God and His love for us is strengthened for the journey ahead.

I do not desire to cut short anything that You have for me. Whether it be good or bad, I pray that I will be found enduring and growing! Amen.

THE PRODUCT OF TRIALS

Count it all joy, my brothers, when you meet trials of various kinds, for you know that the testing of your faith produces steadfastness (James 1:2-3 ESV).

We live in a world that wants to see the product. It is a very hands-on culture. I will believe it when I can see it, touch it, smell it, etc. This mentality is prevalent in every corner of our present world. In today's world when we talk about "faith" we generally see a blank stare in response. We are so accustomed to being able to "have it our way" that we don't see the value of trusting anything "by faith."

The problem with this mentality in light of the Christian life is that sometimes it seems difficult to see. This starts at the very moment of our salvation due to the fact that the very essence of the Christian life is rooted in trust. This trust is founded in the truth of the gospel in which we are granted the faith to believe.

When it comes to trials, we are no different. Besides wanting the trials to go away, we want to know what they are for. What is their purpose? This is something that you cannot touch, see, smell, or taste. It is not observable through our senses. How then can we know that faith is producing something?

The Word of God says in James that trials are to strengthen our faith. Faith is like a muscle and only grows through testing it (working out, exercising). In the same way, our faith grows when tested. When tested, we have a history of past trials proving how God has been faithful to see us through. In many ways this is God's on-the-job training for His children.

Father, please help me to always see the product of the trials that come my way through the faith that is growing in me. When I am tempted to doubt, find me looking at a life of walking through trials with You! Amen.

MONDAY

MONDAY

RIGHT RESPONSE TO TRIALS

And behold, I am with you always, to the end of the age
(Matthew 28:20 ESV).

When difficulties come, how should we respond? When we don't understand that God has a royal purpose for trials and difficulties, we are in danger of getting bitter instead of better. As one Christian author wrote, "Everything, including trials, must first be Father-filtered before it gets to us." What he is saying is nothing happens in our lives that is not first approved by the Father.

Knowing that difficulties are to help grow our faith is part of the solution. It always helps to have an end goal in mind, but what is the means to the end? What specifically can be done to ensure that God's purpose in the difficulty will be accomplished in our lives?

The first thing is to not let difficulty lead to defeat. The enemy would love nothing more than for the difficulty to lead us to the point of throwing in the towel. He would love it if we forgot that in Christ we are already victorious! In Christ we have won! A great reminder that we should repeat to ourselves daily is *the gospel is not a message of do but done!*

Another thing we should remember is that God is with us. He cannot forsake us, because in doing so, He would forsake Himself. He is ALWAYS faithful and always with us. When we stumble, He is always there to pick us up and carry us as needed.

Last, it is great to remember that God is protecting us. In Psalm 23 He tells us that when we face life's trials, He is there. He is there as our mighty Protector keeping watch over us always.

Thank You, Lord, for being with me through all the storms and trials of this life. I give You praise for the fact that You cannot be unfaithful! Amen.

COMFORT WHEN FACING OUR ENEMY

*You prepare a table before me in the presence of
my enemies...* (Psalm 23:5 NKJV).

In this verse from Psalm 23 we see something quite incredible. David had been pursued by Saul, even to the point that Saul tried time and again to kill him. It is from this context that Psalm 23 is written. Up to this point in the psalm David has expressed great confidence in the Lord's ability to lead, guide, provide, and protect. Now we see that David is taken to the banquet room where the one who oppressed him is sitting before him.

In writing about this verse, the great theologian F. B. Myer wrote: "This is a very significant addition—in the presence of mine enemies. We surely are to understand by it all around us may stand our opponents—pledged to do us harm; to cut off our supplies; to starve us out. But, they cannot cut all supplies that come our way from above. They cannot hinder the angel ministers who spread the table and heap it up."

We see David partake in a feast in which the enemy is forced to watch. The enemy is also forced to look on while the Shepherd lavishes His mercy, grace, and goodness onto David. What a great scene this is. Isn't there a part of us that would love that scenario? Basking in the goodness of God while our enemy looks on, incapable of doing any form of evil against us.

The great part about this—this is exactly what God has done for us in the face of our enemy, satan. Satan knows he has been defeated and is forced to watch as God lavishes His love and grace upon us over and over and over! This is a constant reminder to satan that Christ is victorious and that he is defeated!

Wow! Lord, what a great comfort it is to know that in Christ our enemy has been defeated and that You don't just save us to leave us to ourselves. You save us and daily lavish Your love and grace upon us! Amen.

KNOW THE ENEMY

Be sober-minded; be watchful. Your adversary the devil prowls around like a roaring lion, seeking someone to devour (1 Peter 5:8 ESV).

I think virtually everyone at some point has had an archnemesis. Someone who just seems to be at odds with everything we do and is against everything that we stand for. I remember as a kid there was a school bully, and he always got under my skin. It seemed that everything I did he tried to thwart. When I thought I was gaining ground, he was always one step ahead of me. There were even times when I wished I could just stay home or go to another school to get away from him.

It was not until I was much older (probably the ripe old age of thirteen) that I realized that the guy who I thought was the problem was really not my problem. The Word of God is very clear that our struggle is against the ultimate enemy.

This enemy is very cunning. Peter uses a lion to describe him. I love nature shows and remember watching one about lions. It was fascinating to watch the lions stalk their prey. One interesting truth—that is so true for us as well—is that the lion will stalk the weakest, not the strongest. They will seek the young, hurt, and weak rather than the strong and mature. Applied to our lives this means that the enemy is always looking for our weak spot.

To combat our weakness, God gave us tools such as prayer, the Word, other believers, etc. He gave us these tools so we can stand firm and resist the enemy and overcome every challenge.

Lord, I pray that I will always be able to see the attacks of the enemy. Find me using your strength to stand. Amen.

BATTLE STRATEGY

Submit yourselves therefore to God. Resist the devil,
and he will flee from you (James 4:7 ESV).

———⌁———

The enemy is very strategic and is relentless in his assault on us. For us to walk in the victory that is ours, we must employ an effective battle strategy. An effective battle strategy against the enemy is one in which we know what is important and exactly what not to do. There are many things we try, oftentimes with no success. These become ineffective strategies in our struggle with the enemy.

At times we hope the enemy will leave us alone. This finds us trying to hide from the enemy, hoping that if we lay low, maybe he won't pay attention to us and just leave us alone. We also try at times to run from the enemy. This is very deceptive thinking. As hard as we try, we cannot run away from the strategies of the enemy. The last thing we do is worry about the enemy. We fret and become afraid of what the enemy can do, not realizing that in Christ we have great power against him.

James 4:7 gives us a simple but effective strategy. It tells us that the real key lies in submitting ourselves to God. After submitting to Him, then and only then, do we have the strength to resist. The success is seen immediately in the enemy's reaction.

Instead of submitting to our fears and doubts, we must trust in the effective strategy of the One who lives inside us. Remember in times of struggle the words of John, *"You, dear children, are from God and have overcome them, because the one who is in you is greater than the one who is in the world"* (1 John 4:4).

Submission and resistance chases the enemy away!

———⌁———

Father, I submit myself to You today! Please help me to stand firm and resist what satan throws my way. I will praise You while watching the enemy flee! Amen.

GOD'S GOODNESS RUNS DEEP

So that in the coming ages he might show the immeasurable riches of his grace in kindness toward us in Christ Jesus (Ephesians 2:7 ESV).

———————

Stuart Townsend put these words to song, "How deep the Father's love for us, How vast beyond all measure, That He should give His only Son, To make a wretch His treasure. How great the pain of searing loss, The Father turns His face away, as wounds which mar the Chosen One, Bring many sons to glory."

Often I have been in awe and wonder of the truth that God's goodness runs so deeply. My belief in the truth of Scripture leads me to this awe and wonder. In His Word it is clear that the depth of His goodness is seen in the fact that it is universal. In Matthew 5:45 His Word declares that God sends rain on the just and unjust alike. God is not a respecter of persons and loves people in spite of themselves.

It helps to know that this love extends from His very character. I believe that the single character trait of God recognized in a virtually universal way is love. People may struggle with the justice or wrath of God, but people cling tightly to the truth that God is love. His love is most manifest in His willingness to forgive.

It is beneficial to take the truth that God's love extends past our feeble understanding by personalizing this truth. To do this we can chose to believe that it runs deeply for each of us!

———————

Lord Jesus, I cannot describe my deep gratitude for the fact that Your goodness runs deeply and that it runs deeply for me! Please find me never taking this for granted in my life. Amen.

MONDAY

CONSTANT COMPANIONSHIP

Surely goodness and mercy shall follow me all the days of my life...
(Psalm 23:6 NKJV).

In the Old Testament we find the Hebrew word *chesed*, which is often translated as goodness, faithfulness, mercy. The meaning behind the word is a covenant-keeping God. The richness behind the word is the demonstration that when God enters into relationship with us, it is a covenant-based relationship. A relationship that is not dependent upon anything we do, but one that rests in what Christ has done for us.

In the New Testament there is a Greek word that tends to mirror the meaning behind the Old Testament word *chesed*, which is the word *charis*. This word is translated into the English language as the word "grace," which carries the idea of God's covenant relationship that He enters into because of His divine will and favor. Through grace we clearly see the goodness, faithfulness, and mercy of God on vivid display!

It is with this in mind that David pens the powerful words of Psalm 23:6. He says that God's *chesed* and His *charis* will follow us all the days of our lives. We cannot run from it, it will never run from us! His goodness and mercy are new every day of our lives. Our inner joy and peace has as its basis an unshakable reliance on His ability to do what He said He would do. He is our constant, faithful Companion.

Father, I am speechless when it comes to praising You for Your goodness, faithfulness, and mercy. I know that I did nothing to merit Your favor, but You lavished it on me regardless! Amen.

MOVING FORWARD

The steadfast love of the Lord never ceases; his mercies never come to an end; they are new every morning; great is your faithfulness (Lamentations 3:22-23 ESV).

Sometimes it may seem to us that it would be easier if life had a pause button. In fact, if truth be known, it may be even more realistic if life had a rewind button. At times, we try to correct the problems of yesterday. But this is an impossible task. No matter what Hollywood wants us to think, time travel is not a reality. While this may dash certain hopes we have of correcting former problems, in reality it should be incredible comfort to us.

The reason for this comfort is that while we cannot change yesterday, we are given the privilege of living each day fresh and new. All of us have things in our past we wish we could change. It is time to determine not to allow our past to become an anchor dragging us backward.

In Philippians chapter 3 the apostle Paul gives us a charge to push forward. He tells that he has let go of the past and with assurance he presses forward because of the reality that God has made him His. What a comfort to know that God does not deal with us according to our past, rather He lives with us in the present. Greater yet, because of the resurrection, He has secured us in the future.

It is because of this that we can say, *"his mercies never come to an end; they are new every morning."* Each day can then be lived as though it is the first day of the rest of our lives.

Your mercies are new, Father! What an incredible promise we have from You, Lord! I pray that You will find me living each day fresh and new, moving forward in the grace that You have so richly supplied for me. Amen.

THE HERE AND NOW

The thief comes only to steal and kill and destroy. I came that they may have life and have it abundantly (John 10:10 ESV).

Where are you headed? This question is asked of many travelers. The truth is that we are all headed somewhere. There is no neutral position in life. All who are in Christ are heading to a destination where we will live eternally in His presence. That is great for eternity, but what about now. It is dangerous for the Christian to focus on the life hereafter. Doing so finds us gazing upward, neglecting the life we are living now in this world and neglecting the journey.

One thing that helps our everyday focus is to see that Jesus promises that in this life He grants abundance. This is not just meant for the hereafter, it is also meant for the here and now. In the here and now we have God's presence. The Holy Spirit, who is God, dwells in us! We also have God's protection. Isaiah 54:17 says that no weapon formed against us can stand. God hovers over His children, protecting them because they are His own.

In this life we also have God's peace. His peace is felt in a tangible way in the life of the believer. All hell can be breaking loose around us and we can say with confidence that peace that cannot be explained is a heavy presence in our lives.

The apostle Paul wrote the following words as a means of comfort and strength. Let it soak over your soul: *"Do not be anxious about anything, but in every situation, by prayer and petition, with thanksgiving, present your requests to God. And the peace of God, which transcends all understanding, will guard your hearts and your minds in Christ Jesus"* (Philippians 4:6-7).

Lord, I pray that I will not be so heavenly focused that I am no earthly good. Please help me to keep my feet grounded and firmly planted in Your truth! Amen.

THE ULTIMATE PROMISE

...and I will dwell in the house of the Lord forever (Psalm 23:6).

Death is a topic that many are not okay with. I have had the privilege of leading many funeral and memorial services. I say this with complete integrity—it has been a privilege to be entrusted to lead during these times.

Unfortunately, I have presided over a few of these services for people who did not demonstrate that they had ever surrendered their lives to Christ. This is not said in judgment because I am not God and would have no way of knowing anyone's eternal state. But I can say that these services had a certain somber tone. The tone came from a lack of hope.

A promise is only as good as the one who makes it. I am sure you have heard the saying, "If it sounds too good to be true, it probably is." For example, I may promise that if you will write me an email, I'll give you $10 million. Sounds great doesn't it? Only one problem with that promise, I don't have $10 million to give you. You see, it is important to never make a promise you can't keep. Hope for the Christian comes from the ultimate promise. Jesus said clearly that for those who have surrendered their lives to Christ, the promise of eternal life with Him is sure and certain.

In John 14 Christ Jesus states that He is the way, the truth, and the life, and that because of this He is the only way to receive the ultimate promise. The reality of this ultimate promise should put our minds and hearts at rest. That rest comes because He has prepared a special place for each one who is His child.

Jesus, I am humbled to be called Your child. I am also humbled that because I am Your child I am entitled to all that You have promised Your children. Please, Lord, may a response of love and obedience be my response to Your love for me. Amen.

BLESSED

Blessed are the poor in spirit, for theirs is the kingdom of heaven (Matthew 5:3 NKJV).

Jesus begins the Sermon on the Mount with what is well-known as the Beatitudes. The term "beatitude" is a fancy word for the simpler word "blessed." In this sermon preamble, Jesus introduces seven ways in which believers are blessed. Many have used this preamble to give Christians a new prescription by which to live their lives. However, these words are meant to be more descriptive of the Christian.

Jesus is describing characteristics that should be obvious in the life of Christians. Jesus says that the benefit of having these characteristics is being "blessed." As Christians we are blessed when our lives reflect the life Jesus calls us to live. The struggle is that we live in a world that has a warped view of what a blessed life looks like. The world's view is whoever has the biggest house, the fattest bank account, or most expensive cars is surely a blessed person. Nothing wrong with those things, but that is not the measure of God's blessings. The greatest treasure of all is the deposit of gold (the Holy Spirit) our heavenly Father has placed inside each and every believer.

Understanding the blessed life means that we must reject the world's view of blessing. The world views blessing as something that is temporary, while God's truth of blessing is what the believer receives and it never fades away. The world sees blessing as something driven by our situations, status, or our will, while God's truth of blessing is that it is not dependent upon us but upon Him. The world's view of blessing is rooted in emotions, while God's truth of blessing is rooted in the truth of His Word.

I am so blessed to be called Your child and to have the privilege of living a life that reflects Yours. Lord, please know that I am eternally grateful for what You have done for me. Amen.

MONDAY

SPIRITUAL WEALTH

Blessed are the poor in spirit, for theirs is the kingdom of heaven (Matthew 5:3 NKJV).

This verse in Matthew 5 may be very difficult for some to receive. I believe that is because many do not really understand what Jesus is saying here. Jesus is talking not about monetary poverty but spiritual poverty. The reason I believe I can make this assertion is because nowhere does Jesus condemn wealth. The only condemnation lies not in money itself but in the way in which we approach money.

It is with this in mind that we can see that Jesus is talking about spiritual poverty. Spiritual poverty would have been a hard subject for the people receiving this message. It would have been difficult because spiritual poverty was lacking in the religious leaders of the day. Religious legalism then, as now, was rooted in pride. Pride that caused them to believe that strict adherence to the law was the way to Heaven. Oftentimes that religious legalism then, as now, led to a false sense of self-pity. Self-pity was seen in how they would make a scene when fasting and in prayer. They would try to make themselves look pitiful in order to fulfill what they thought it took to achieve righteousness.

This is contrary to the message of this verse and the message of the gospel. The message of the gospel is received by the attitude of being poor in spirit. Being poor in spirit means that we have a complete rejection of self, instead we trust Christ only. Being poor in spirit means that we are completely surrendered to Him, letting go of ourselves and clinging only to Him.

I praise You, Lord, for the simple message of the gospel! That it is not a message of what I have to do, but what You have done. Amen.

TUESDAY

SPIRITUAL SORROW

Blessed are those who mourn, for they shall be comforted (Matthew 5:4 NKJV).

———————————◦———————————

What makes you sad? I can think of many things that make me sad. This may be because I am an emotional person and it doesn't take a lot to make me cry. I know, real men don't cry. I get that, but it has yet to stop me.

Of course I know and fully realize that there is vast difference between being sad and having godly sorrow. Oftentimes sadness comes and goes. Godly sorrow sticks with you because behind godly sorrow lies a biblical motive. The biblical motive behind godly sorrow is seen in Psalm 51 when David states clearly that his sin was against God and God alone. When looked at in light of the gospel, our sorrow is godly when it forces us to look at ourselves in the light of the perfection of our holy God. When we look at ourselves in the mirror of God's Word, we see the truth of what we really are—lost and undone without Jesus Christ. The truth of God's Word is not to condemn us but to lead us to make necessary changes.

Godly sorrow should lead us to be on a mission to act toward others as God acts toward us. As God has been gracious and forgiving, we too are to be gracious and forgiving. The fact that God has redeemed us to Himself should be a strong motive to go and do likewise.

The spiritual reward for spiritual mourning is comfort. This comfort, however, is not to be kept to ourselves. It is in this truth that we should be comforters because God has comforted us.

———————————◦———————————

Thank You, faithful God, for so richly pouring out comfort to my soul. I pray that I will be found returning this comfort to all with whom I come in contact. Amen.

SPIRITUAL MEEKNESS

Blessed are the meek, for they shall inherit the earth (Matthew 5:5 NKJV).

When you think of a meek person, what image comes to your mind? Is it an image of a warrior who is strapped with the most technologically advanced and strongest warfare weapons? This image is not the case when it came to King David. He was a simple shepherd boy, small in stature and simple in heart. When God was choosing the next king to serve Israel, it was probably a prevailing thought that someone of similar stature to King Saul would be the next in line.

When David was chosen, even his father questioned the decision, because David was the epitome of meekness. This same simple shepherd boy chose not to wear armor and instead went with a sling and five smooth stones to face the giant. This does not line up with the world's image of a warrior. When we think of David facing Goliath, what we really want is a picture of Rambo. Instead, God chose to use a boy, barely a teenager, to face the most experienced and fearsome combat soldier known at the time.

"Meekness is weakness" is a prevailing ideology in our world. The attribute of meekness is often viewed as someone willing to be walked on, as someone who is looked at as "less than." Isn't it great to know that this is a false assumption that is not backed up in Scripture? In fact, the meekest Person to have ever lived is Christ Himself. Christ was a "man's man," a Man who did not shy away from conflict, pain, suffering, and even death. We would all do well to emulate His form of meekness.

I confess, Lord, that there are oftentimes when I feel like meekness is not an attribute I want to display in the circumstances of this life. Help me to see meekness as a great gift of strength from You. Amen.

DELIGHTING IN RIGHTEOUSNESS

Blessed are those who hunger and thirst for righteousness,
for they shall be filled (Matthew 5:6 NKJV).

───────────────※───────────────

I have a confession to make. I love to eat. Before you get too judgmental, let me ask you a question, do you like to eat? Many people are like me. In fact, one of our first thoughts when we wake up in the morning is, "What's for breakfast?" Hunger is a human response to a basic human need. Thirst is somewhat different because we can live quite a while without food but die quickly without water. One thing is for certain—we become hungry and thirsty again and again.

When Jesus states that we are blessed when the hunger and thirst of our life is focused on righteousness, then and only then will we be filled. Of course He is not talking about physical hunger and thirst; rather, He is talking about spiritual matters. He is also stating that when our appetite is focused on righteousness we will be full!

So what is this righteousness that Jesus is referring to? It is not a righteousness that we can attain on our own. We cannot earn it, regardless of all our efforts. This kind of righteousness is actually not our righteousness at all. The righteousness He is referring to is HIS righteousness that justifies, sanctifies, and will ultimately glorify us. Our response is to receive this as a gift, walk in it, and ultimately set our hope on it.

Romans 5:9-11 says, *"Since we have now been justified by his blood, how much more shall we be saved from God's wrath through him! For if, while we were God's enemies, we were reconciled to him through the death of his Son, how much more, having been reconciled, shall we be saved through his life! Not only is this so, but we also boast in God through our Lord Jesus Christ, through whom we have now received reconciliation."*

───────────────※───────────────

The truth that I cannot and will not earn righteousness is a truth that sets me free! Lord, I thank You for gifting me with Your righteousness. Amen.

SHOWING MERCY

Blessed are the merciful, for they shall receive mercy
(Matthew 5:7 ESV).

In Luke's gospel chapter 10 we read the story of the Good Samaritan. In this story we see a traveler on his way from Jerusalem to Jericho. This was an indication that he was a Jewish man. On his way he is robbed, beaten, and left half dead. The first person passing by is a priest. The priest sees the man and offers no support. The second is Levite. He also sees the man and again offers no support. The third man who sees him is a Samaritan. This is significant because the Jews and Samaritans detested each other. To the Jew, Samaritans were an abomination. But the Samaritan man stopped and helped the man who was robbed and beaten, wrapped up his wounds, and took him to town. The Samaritan also paid to ensure that the man was provided for. There is little doubt that this Samaritan had nurtured a merciful heart.

We can learn some great lessons from this story. We can certainly understand that mercy has been shown to us. It is out of God's love that He has shown us mercy. Mercy is simply not receiving what we deserve. We deserve the very worst, but God has given us His very best. Because of this we are to be sowers of mercy in the lives of others. The reward for sowing this seed is that we in turn receive mercy!

Be merciful, just as your Father is merciful (Luke 6:36).

But because of his great love for us, God, who is rich in mercy, made us alive with Christ even when we were dead in transgressions—it is by grace you have been saved (Ephesians 2:4-5).

Lord, I do not deserve Your mercy. I am brought low in light of the reality that You have granted me mercy even though there is nothing in me that is deserving of this great mercy. Amen.

MONDAY

PURE IN HEART

Blessed are the pure in heart, for they shall see God (Matthew 5:8 NKJV).

What is the process to develop a pure heart? If a pure heart is a prerequisite to seeing God, then we should all be seeking the same answer. After all, as Christians, one of the base desires we should have is to see the God who saved us by giving His life for us. I believe the process is simple.

Developing in purity happens as we are faithful to the Word of God. The Word is pure and reveals what purity looks and acts like. This action is seen as we are faithful in our Christian walk. This walk is best lived in a very simple step-by-step walk—always moving forward, never looking back.

Purity is also nurtured and grown as we continue to live our lives with hearts of repentance. Repentance indicates that we are forsaking the old way of life and embracing the new.

Prayer is also import in growing in purity because it is through prayer we seek not to change God and His plan but to mold ourselves into what God is doing. Prayer is for us to get on God's agenda, not the other way around, which provides an atmosphere for purity to grow in us.

Growing in purity is also seen in the act of worship. Worship is, at its core, focusing all we are, all we have, and all we want to be on to God. He becomes the object of our affection. The natural result of this is that we become more like Him and less like the world.

Father, in this prayer I desire for You to find in me a heart that is developing in purity and that by doing so I will be able to see You clearly! Amen.

TUESDAY

DON'T FORGET TO REMEMBER

I am reminded of your sincere faith, which first lived in your grandmother
Lois and in your mother Eunice and, I am persuaded, now lives in you
also. For this reason I remind you to fan into flame the gift of God, which
is in you through the laying on of my hands (2 Timothy 1:5-6).

Have you ever been in a situation that appeared to be totally hopeless? And, can you think of a time in your life when God intervened and turned your situation into a miracle? I am amazed that when we are challenged with a new set of difficult circumstances we tend to forget God's faithfulness in our past.

The apostle Paul wrote a letter to his young protégé Timothy. The young man was facing a mountain of problems. People were dying for their faith. The fire of persecution was spreading throughout the Roman Empire. I am sure there were times when the people of God, including their leaders, were wondering if God was going to forget them.

Paul used this occasion to remind Timothy of two things:

1. *God's faithfulness was part of his heritage.* Timothy needed to remember his grandmother Lois trusted the Lord, as well as his mother Eunice. In times of stress and difficulty God had never failed Timothy's family, and he must not fail to remember that God would not abandon him now in his darkest hour.

2. *You must not forget to remember.* When Paul said, *"For this reason I remind you to fan into flame the gift of God,"* he is saying to "regather or to recollect memories." This means there are some things and some memories we must never forget! For example, we must never forget to remember and replay in our minds the times God demonstrated His faithfulness to heal us, to deliver us, and rescue us in times of stress and trouble.

When the devil speaks into your mind and tells you there is no way out, hit the rewind button in your brain and remember what God has done before, He will do again. Ask the Holy Spirit to help you to regather all of the memories of God's faithfulness in past events. As you remember those times, your faith will be strengthened and your confidence will rise to new levels.

Father, thank You for Your past faithfulness. May I never fail to remember Your goodness and grace! Amen.

PEACEMAKERS

Blessed are the peacemakers, for they will be called children of God (Matthew 5:9).

It does not take a rocket scientist to see that we live in a world that does not know peace. We are bombarded daily by stories that demonstrate a complete lack of peace. We lack peace in our world, in our families, and in ourselves. That is what makes this verse in Matthew 5 such an incredible challenge to us. Oftentimes people are revenge seekers rather than peacemakers. How can we ensure that this changes in us? How can we be peacemakers?

Someone who is a peacemaker first and foremost has experienced peace personally. Apostle Paul states in Romans 5:1 that the result of being justified by Christ is that we can experience peace. Of course this is not the peace that the world thinks will solve the problem, but spiritual peace that cannot be explained. It is that simple knowledge that God is sovereign and in control of all things. It certainly does not mean that storms in life will cease, but that God is there to see us through the storms. Then and only then can the Christian be about the business of helping others being at peace as well.

The great result of being a peacemaker is that by doing so we are called the children of God. Why is this? This is because when we are peacemakers we are directly reflecting the heart of God, our heavenly Father. It shows that we are God's children because we are doing what He wants us to do.

God promises His people a peace the world does not understand. Two of my favorite verses that speak volumes:

> *When the Lord takes pleasure in anyone's way, he causes their enemies to make peace with them* (Proverbs 16:7).

> *I have told you these things, so that in me you may have peace. In this world you will have trouble. But take heart! I have overcome the world* (John 16:33).

Father, in a world that knows nothing of peace, please find me relaxing in the truth that I have peace in Christ and sharing that truth with people who need to hear it. Amen.

PERSECUTED FOR HIS NAME

Blessed are those who are persecuted for righteousness' sake, for theirs is the kingdom of heaven. Blessed are you when others revile you and persecute you and utter all kinds of evil against you falsely on my account. Rejoice and be glad, for your reward is great in heaven, for so they persecuted the prophets who were before you (Matthew 5:10-12 ESV).

For the believer, the question is not if persecution occurs but when persecution comes. The reality of persecution can be a very sobering thought. Oftentimes we look at persecution as something that happens to other people in distant and far-off places. The problem with this thinking is that it does not line up with Scripture. Jesus does not use the word "if" in Matthew 5, He uses the word "when."

All who claim the name of Christ will be persecuted for claiming that very name. This persecution takes numerous including from physical abuse, social exclusion, monetary loss, etc. In the world we live in now, persecution of Christians seems to be an ever-increasing reality. This brings to a solemn reality the "when" of persecution.

Persecution is not a geographical, political issue; rather, it is an issue of the fact that the world hates Christ so it hates those who claim Christ. Jesus states this fact in John's gospel chapter 15 verse 18. If we claim the name of Christ we can expect a harsh response from the world.

It is such a comfort to know that Christ will have the last say. There will be a day when He removes the one who opposes Him and those who are His will be rewarded for enduring the hatred this world shows toward His children.

Father, I pray for those who are enduring extreme persecution in our world. I praise You for the fact that You WILL have the last word! Amen.

SALTY

You are the salt of the earth, but if salt has lost its taste, how shall its saltiness be restored? It is no longer good for anything except to be thrown out and trampled under people's feet (Matthew 5:13 ESV).

———————————————

Salt seems to have a bad reputation these days. It seems like there are regular reports of the dire consequences of salt consumption. My family is always telling me to cut back on my use of salt. When they do this, I tell them I am trying to fulfill what Jesus said in Matthew 5. I am trying to be salt in this world.

As Christians, Jesus tells us that we are the salt of the earth. This makes us distinct people who have a great responsibility. Our responsibility as people who are the salt of the earth can be seen in what salt was used for during this time. People used salt in that day to purify things. If someone had an open wound, oftentimes salt was put into the wound to clean it and guard against infection. People would also use salt to help preserve food. Refrigeration was not available so salt was commonly used to keep food edible. Another quality of salt was its ability to penetrate what it came into contact with. Because of these qualities and its many uses, salt was a very valuable commodity.

This leaves us with some questions to ask ourselves. Are we a purifying force in the world? Are we being used as a preservative to those around us? Are we making an impact in the world? Do people consider us a valuable commodity?

———————————————

Lord, I pray that the above questions are true of me! If not, please accept my confession and help me to be salt in this world. Amen.

MONDAY

LIGHT

*You are the light of the world. A city set on a hill cannot be hidden. Nor do people light a lamp and put it under a basket, but on a stand, and it gives light to all in the house. In the same way, **let your light shine** before others, so that they may see your good works and give glory to your Father who is in heaven* (Matthew 5:14-16 ESV).

Growing up in Colorado I remember going several times to the Cave of the Winds—a popular tourist destination. There was one spot in the tour where the tour guide would turn off all the lights in a particular section of the cave and it became pitch-black dark. When I say dark, I mean a dark that I could feel. We were several feet underground and no natural light was available. The lights were off for a few minutes and then turned back on. The result was an instant transformation. The light absolutely affected the entire section.

When I read that Jesus calls me light, it makes me think of these verses, which makes me think of the consequence I am supposed to have as light in this world. As light, one of my primary tasks is to declare the gospel. The gospel is literally the "good news" that the world is looking for! How and why could I ever not display that light?

Another consequence is by displaying this light, I bring glory to God. I do not let my light shine so that people will see me and all that I have done; rather, it points all the glory to the Lord who made the light possible in the first place.

Father, I pray that my light is being shown to all those I come into contact with. I pray that I will not hide it, but that I will let it shine until Jesus comes! Amen.

355

INFLUENCE

You are... (Matthew 5:13).

———————————————

Influence! There have been multitudes and multitudes of books written on this very important subject. I would suggest that everyone wants to live a life that matters, a life that has meaning, a life of influence. I would also suggest that literally everyone on this earth has influence at some level.

When it comes to the Christian life there are three important things to know in regard to influence. *The first thing* is that it is impossible to live the norms of the kingdom privately. The Christian life is not a life that is lived in a vacuum. It cannot be lived in seclusion and exclusion of others. It is meant to be a beacon of hope to the world.

The second thing is that Jesus' words mean nothing if the Christian's life is not different. We serve to validate the words of Christ by the way we influence others in this life. It is a true saying that "We are the only Jesus that some will ever see."

The last thing is that the world we live in is rotten to the very core and is in dire need of Christian influence. It is a scary thought to think what this world would be like if every Christian was removed. Unfortunately, this, in some cases, is exactly what has happened. Instead of being an influence in the world, we hide and render ourselves an ineffective influence.

———————————————

Jesus, thank You for being the greatest influence this world will ever know. I pray that my life will reflect Yours! Amen.

ARE YOU READY

Always be prepared to give an answer to everyone who asks you to give the reason for the hope that you have (1 Peter 3:15).

———————————

In 1980 the Lakers met the 76ers in the NBA Finals. In game five, Kareem Abdul-Jabar hurt his ankle so badly that he could not play in the crucial game six. Everyone was concerned because without him the chances of winning the championship were slim to none.

1980 was also the rookie season for one future NBA superstar, "Magic" Johnson. When he learned that Kareem would miss the game, he did not panic. He knew he was prepared and he knew they would be fine. That night Magic did it all—he scored a rookie record forty-two points in a playoff game, made fourteen of fourteen free throws, grabbed fifteen rebounds, dished out seven assists and had three steals. Magic was truly ready.

The apostle Peter tells us, *"Always be prepared to give an answer to everyone who asks you to give the reason for the hope that you have."* We become ready by staying close with God, reading His Word, talking with Him, and getting to know Him better. We are just part of His plan to further His kingdom here. It is important that we are ready to live out our faith. Doing this will make people wonder what makes us different; we can explain God's love and hope inside us. We don't do that by arguing with people, rather by allowing God to help us live lives of faith, devoted to Him, and being ready to give an answer to those who are asking.

———————————

Lord, please find me ready to give an answer to the hope that exists within me. I thank You for that hope and pray for courage to share it. Amen.

LOOK UP

You have been traveling around this mountain country long enough. Turn northward (Deuteronomy 2:3 ESV).

Anyone who has ever taken any kind of survival training knows that when you are lost, a key way to getting to where you need to go is to discover where north is. In the old days people used a compass that helped with determining this. Today, many "smart" phones actually have a compass you can use to find north.

In Deuteronomy 2:3, God tells the people of Israel to head north. He tells them they have been wandering too long and that north was the way to go. I believe there is a spiritual truth that can be applied here. North on a compass is always up. I believe that physically He was telling them to go up, and I also believe that He was telling them to spiritually look up.

God was not only giving them direction so they would not just wander aimlessly, He was also giving them a hint to where He is. He was telling them to look up, not down! This is still true for us today. Before Christ entered our lives, we wandered aimlessly, being mired in the past. Now we should be looking up—up into His glorious face of love for us. This direction is also reflected in John 14:6 when Jesus declares that He is the only way, and we need to look up to Him.

I praise you, Father, for providing THE WAY for me! I trust in You and ask that You continue to guide me as I look to You and You alone for direction. Amen.

BEAUTY FROM ASHES

And provide for those who grieve in Zion—to bestow on them a crown of beauty instead of ashes, the oil of joy instead of mourning, and a garment of praise instead of a spirit of despair. They will be called oaks of righteousness, a planting of the Lord for the display of his splendor (Isaiah 61:3).

True beauty must start on the inside. I am guilty of being the girl who was never satisfied with herself. I hated my smile, body, hair, face, etc. I struggled for years with a skin condition. Many nights I would just cry because I hated that this was happening to me. Many nights I would pray and ask God to "fix" me. I came to the realization that God didn't need to fix me, that I had to be satisfied with myself. As much as I hated my body, God *unconditionally* loved me and made me *perfect.* He created me, every part of me for a reason.

My all-time favorite story of the Bible is of Tamar, King David's only daughter. She is such an inspiration to me. She thought that she was the lowest of the low, that she wasn't good enough to be called his daughter. She grew up with two brothers, and one of her brothers, Amnon, desired her. He lusted after her so heavily that he eventually lured her into his room and raped her. After Amnon was done, she ran outside and plunged her hand into ashes and placed them on her disheveled hair. She staggered away and tore the front of her richly embroidered outer robe as a sign of her despair. With her hand on her head, the sign of a bereaved woman, she staggered through the palace corridors crying aloud.

She tore her robe because she felt ugly and unworthy. She drenched herself in ashes as a sign of feeling dirty. As I read this, I realized that as much as she despised herself for something she had no control over, God was still in control. No matter what had happened to her, she was just as beautiful and loved that day as the day God created her.

Lord, help me to see myself as a true, beautiful daughter of the one true King. I know that You make everyone different and in Your image. Please help me to not doubt Your perfection and the fact that You are God. I am Yours, and no matter what, You love me unconditionally! Amen.

MONDAY

FOREVER REIGN

No temptation has overtaken you that is not common to man. God is faithful, and he will not let you be tempted beyond your ability, but with the temptation he will also provide the way of escape, that you may be able to endure it (1 Corinthians 10:13 ESV).

One of my favorite worship songs is "Forever Reign" by Hillsong. The lyrics reveal how great and all-powerful God truly is. The following is an excerpt of this amazing song:

You are more, You are more
Than my words will ever say
You are Lord, You are Lord
All creation will proclaim
You are here, You are here
In Your presence I'm made whole
You are God, You are God
Of all else I'm letting go…

How powerful are those words? He is more than we could ever say and He is God of all else. It is a reminder that God can take it all. He is not just up there watching our pain, He is living it. When we hurt, He hurts; when we cry, He cries. He feels our aches and our pains. We need to remember this when we go through trials and tribulations.

For all the things that change in our lives, there is One who is *always* constant—God. Malachi 3:6 (KJV) says, *"I am the Lord, I change not."* He feels our pain and gets us through the roughest storms in our lives. He is here when we have no one. He reigns forever.

Father, it brings me great comfort to know that You are not distant and uncaring. As the song says, "In Your presence I'm made whole." Amen.

COVERED

If we claim that we're free of sin, we're only fooling ourselves. A claim like that is errant nonsense. On the other hand, if we admit our sins—make a clean breast of them—he won't let us down; he'll be true to himself. He'll forgive our sins and purge us of all wrongdoing (1 John 1:8-9 MSG).

I am not perfect! In fact, I am far from it. I try, just like everyone else, to glorify God; but just like the devil wants, I fail. The devil also wants us to believe that we can never be forgiven, which in all reality is 100 percent false. The blood Jesus shed on the cross was enough to cover our sin for all eternity. At times when we feel guilt or shame, we forget that Jesus knows all our steps because He planned them out for us.

The great thing about Jesus is, to Him we never fail. He is never disappointed because His love is greater than we can imagine. The feeling of failure is not something that comes from God. It is something that comes from the devil. The thing about temptation is, yes, God sees it on our path, but it *never* comes from Him. He saw it coming and has made a way of escape for us. Isn't God amazing? He always provides a way out and has already forgiven us.

The good thing about forgiveness is, no matter how many times we are tempted and sin, forgiveness is right there waiting for us when we ask Him to forgive us. How powerful is that? I have made a lot of mistakes, and the worst part—even though I was raised to know better, I believed I could never be forgiven. I recently reached my breaking point and realized that I truly am forgiven—because I am a beautiful daughter of Christ. I could not gain enough strength in the world to fight this battle but with God it is possible. This is the truth for all believers!

What a glorious reality that I am forgiven, my heart can't even come close to expressing the gratitude that I have for this truth! Amen.

GO AND MAKE DISCIPLES

Then he said to his disciples, "The harvest is plentiful but the workers are few. Ask the Lord of the harvest, therefore, to send out workers into his harvest field" (Matthew 9:37-38).

We all know the Bible has four Gospels—Matthew, Mark, Luke, and John. The reason there are four Gospels instead of one is because each apostle has a different viewpoint. The great thing about the Gospels is that, yes they are written from different viewpoints, but they are all the same in that they reveal Jesus' time on earth.

One important statement by Jesus that is contained in all four Gospels is the command to *"go and make disciples."* That is our calling. We are followers of Christ, so as followers of Him, are we doing what we are supposed to do? Luke 10:2 says: *"He told them, "The harvest is plentiful, but the workers are few. Ask the Lord of the harvest, therefore, to send out workers into his harvest field."* And John 4:35 says: *"Don't you have a saying, 'It's still four months until harvest'? I tell you, open your eyes and look at the fields! They are ripe for harvest."*

This is our job. Jesus does the saving and supplies the harvest. We are the workers who are being sent out. It is not just a one-time job, though. The harvest, like it says in John, is always there and it is our responsibility to go out and make those disciples and fill Heaven with *every* follower of Christ.

*Father, I pray that You find me always on the go for You, and as I am going, please strengthen me to share the **great news** of the gospel. Amen.*

HOW TO RESIST THE
SCHEMES OF THE DEVIL

*Be alert and of sober mind. Your enemy the devil prowls around like a
roaring lion looking for someone to devour. Resist him, standing firm
in the faith, because you know that the family of believers throughout
the world is undergoing the same kind of sufferings* (1 Peter 5:8-9).

Jeremiah 29:11 is one of my favorite verses. It contains the true heart of a
Father who is concerned for His children: *"For I know the plans I have for
you,' declares the Lord, 'plans to prosper you and not to harm you, plans to give
you hope and a future.'"*

Wow, those are some powerful words. Notice what it *doesn't* say, "For *you*
know the plans I have for you." A lot of the time we think that life is going
so well for us that we must be on the right path. There are times we get on a
"God high" where we are so on fire for Him that we feel nothing can touch
us. That is when the devil's schemes are the most powerful. This is the time
when we must be on guard, because the devil knows when to strike.

But at other times when things are not going our way, we sometimes feel
or think God loves everyone but us, is taking care of or putting everyone
else's needs before ours. Those thoughts come from the devil. When those
thoughts come, we must hold on to the Word of God and stand our ground.
It is the most powerful weapon we have against the schemes of the devil.
We have a weapon at our disposal that is more powerful than any weapon
on earth. What is that? It is the double-edged sword of the Word of God—
the Bible!

God has given us this weapon to use against the devil, not only did He
give it to us but God uses it as well. The Word is the only way to fight him
off. It is the only way to keep the thoughts of the world out. I encourage you
to daily spend time in the Word. Meditate on it, take a figurative Word bath,
and learn how this weapon will keep the devil away.

*Lord, the enemy is a formidable opponent, but I claim the truth that Your Word
is the power for me to live victoriously against any scheme he can throw my way.
Amen.*

STRENGTH FROM ABOVE

*You armed me with **strength** for battle; you humbled my adversaries before me* (2 Samuel 22:40).

Something God has shown me recently is that I really need strength. The funny thing about strength is that for the longest time I thought I could receive it on my own, that I did not need God to give it to me. I have learned, however, that this is not true. God is the One who gives me strength when I need it the most.

First Chronicles 16:11 says, *"Look to the Lord and **His strength**; seek His face always."* We must look to Him always! And Psalm 105:4 (ESV) says, *"Seek the Lord and **His strength**; seek his face continually."* The list of verses I could cite goes on, saying the same thing—our strength comes from seeking His face and His love. Real strength is not found in the gym or in taking a certain kind of pill. It is not in who can scream the loudest in an argument. NO! Strength is only found when we come before His presence, seek His face, and learn to wait on Him to provide the strength we need. It is only in this place that the believer can acquire any strength.

God is showing me that He knows I need Him and Him alone. He set me free and provides me everyday strength I need for the battle I fight with the enemy. Strength from God is so relieving, it allows you to know that you are truly never alone, and that God is always near to pick you up and put you on a solid foundation. I challenge you to trust His promises; spend time in prayer and watch what your heavenly Father will do the next time you are faced with a challenge. His strength is truly amazing!

Jesus, I seek Your strength this very day. I pray that I will draw upon that strength as I go through this day!

MONDAY

FORGIVENESS

*Be kind to one another, tenderhearted, forgiving one another, even
as God in Christ forgave you* (Ephesians 4:32 NKJV).

"Forgiveness is more than saying sorry." I know this is a line from a secular
song but to me it is so true. Forgiveness, true forgiveness, is saying, "I forgive you"
and never, and I mean never, bringing up the offense again. Bringing it up after
you have said that you have forgiven, means you did not truly forgive the person.

Paul states in Ephesians 4:32 that our forgiveness toward others should be
done in light of the forgiveness we have received from Christ. Every day God forgives us for our sins against Him. My sin is really against Him. David stated this
clearly in Psalm 51:4 when he wrote, *"Against You, You only, have I sinned, and
done this evil in Your sight"* (NKJV).

Jesus died on the cross to take away the sin of the world—our sin—and He
forgives us. He takes our sins and casts them as far as the east is from the west.
Why not the north to the south? Because there is an endpoint there, but the east
never meets the west.

Forgiving others at times is not easy because some offenses against us are great.
It seems that these offenses are so big that forgiving seems impossible. In those
circumstances, go to God because He is the only help. All you have to do is ask.
In Jeremiah He says to, *"Call to Me and I will answer you and show you great and
mighty things, which you do not know"* (Jeremiah 33:3 NKJV).

*Father, help me to forgive. In my flesh I don't want to. I would like to hold on to
the offense. It has become like a badge of honor of what someone did to me. I am
calling on You to help me forgive. Thank You for forgiving me! Amen.*

WHAT'S WORSE THAN BEING BLIND?

*Where there is no revelation, people cast off restraint; but blessed
is the one who heeds wisdom's instruction* (Proverbs 29:18).

One day an interviewer asked Helen Keller, "Is there anything worse than
being blind?" "Yes," she replied, "having eyesight but no vision!" In her mind
there was something worse than being blind, and that was living without
a vision!

Robert Fritz wrote, "It is not what a vision is; it's what a vision does." What
does a vision do? Vision is the ability to see a preferred future. Vision is the vivid
image of the compelling future God wants to create through you. People are
hungry for leadership. Not dictators or self-centered people who only care for
themselves. Genuine leaders see the future and empower others to go with them.

Mike Vance tells of being at Walt Disney World soon after its completion
when someone said, "It's too bad Walt Disney didn't live to see this." Vance
replied, "He DID see it—that's why it's here."

What kind of vision do you have?

- Are you nearsighted? It's called myopic vision. Myopic leaders
  are so terribly nearsighted that they live only for today. Their
  vision of the future is muddy. They can barely see beyond the
  fingers on their hands.

- Are you blindsided? This is living with peripheral vision. Leaders
  with peripheral vision are blindsided by side issues. They are
  easily distracted and pulled away by difficulties lurking in the
  shadows.

- Are you living in a tunnel? Leaders with tunnel vision can only
  see what is in front of them. Their worldview is shaped by the
  objects dead ahead. They never seem to have a clue that there
  are others around them. It's hard to lead living in a tunnel.

- Or, do you see the big picture? Leaders who see the big picture
  see beyond today. They see what is ahead of them. They have a
  basic understanding of the key ingredients of a healthy organization and know the steps that it will take to get them there.

Vision is perhaps the greatest need of leadership today. As someone said
regarding the church but it pertains to any organization, "Our preachers aren't

dreaming. That's why the church is such a nightmare." If you are trying to lead without a vision, your organization will be like an unbridled horse. With a God-inspired vision the organization will be focused, moving toward the fulfillment of the dream.

Father, give me Your vision. I want to lead with a clear direction for the future. I never want my dream to turn into a nightmare. Amen.

GOD REMEMBERS

"Can a mother forget the infant at her breast, walk away from the baby she bore? But even if mothers forget, I'd never forget you—never. Look, I've written your names on the backs of my hands" (Isaiah 49:15-16 MSG).

———————————⟋⟍———————————

Have you ever thought about this verse, *"I have written your name upon the palms of my hands?"* God has us tattooed on His hands!

Do you ever feel like God has forsaken you? That He's forgotten you? That He's forgotten where you live? You may cry out to Him in desperate times and ask, "Do You still know my address, Lord?" It may not be spoken out loud, but I'm sure you have been in this place at least one time during your walk with your Lord.

We've been desperate! We've felt abandoned! We've felt forgotten! We've felt unloved, unwanted and ugly. This is the time we must rely on the truth of God's Word and His promise to never forget us! We cannot always trust our feelings, but we can always trust God's Word.

There's a quote that says, "If God seems far away, guess who moved?" Dear friend, it's not God who moves, it's us! We walk away! We turn our backs! We stop praying, seeking, asking, worshiping, praising, and reading His Word. When we are faithless, He remains faithful (see 2 Timothy 2:13).

Yes, a mother may forget her child. However, God's promise to us as His children is that He will never leave us or forsake us. (see Hebrews 13:5). He is our Helper.

———————————⟋⟍———————————

Thank You, Father, for Your promise to never leave me or forsake me. I know I can trust You no matter what I'm feeling; no matter what the circumstances of my life. Lord, You are my hope and peace. Amen.

TRANSFORMING LOVE

Now the Lord saw that Leah was unloved, and He opened her womb, but Rachel was barren (Genesis 29:31 NASB).

⸺⸺⸺

This is a fascinating story. Here are two women: first, there is Leah. She was unloved by her husband but was loved by the Lord. Then there is Rachel. She was loved by her husband but had a barren womb. The Lord did not honor Rachel in the thing that began to matter more than her beauty, her brains, and everything else she had going for her.

This story points out the difference between having love from someone here below and receiving love from the Lord. Earthly love is only temporary and it focuses only on the here and now. But, love from above points to the future. Do you feel unloved because you don't have "everything going for you"? Do you feel "less than the rest" because you don't have a Master's degree or a high-paying job? Do you feel unappreciated because you have never won a beauty contest? Success in life is more than brains and beauty, my friend.

Here's the good news: No matter your station in life, you are loved by the Lord! You ask, "How can I know?" Well, to begin with, Hebrews 12:6 (ESV) says, *"The Lord disciplines the one he loves."* What does this mean? It means when God begins to deal with you He forces you to learn something in a way that is pretty tough.

It may be the Lord who has kept you from getting that job or from getting married. It may be the Lord who has brought you to a place where everything happening around you looks bad, and you wonder where God is. Sometimes God brings you so low that there's nowhere to look but up; and then, when you start looking at Him, He says, *"Oh, good, you're coming to Me. That is what I wanted."* And you begin to realize that the Lord loved you so much that He beckoned you in His direction. You see, those whom the Lord loves, He deals with; and those who are dealt with, are truly His. So be encouraged, God has not forgotten you or forsaken you. He will make something good out of every situation.

⸺⸺⸺

Thank You, Father, for using the tough things in my life to get my attention. Even when I don't understand what You are doing, each trial brings me closer to You. Amen.

THE REASON FOR THE SEASON

And being found in appearance as a man, he humbled himself by
becoming obedient to death—even death on a cross! (Philippians 2:8)

———————

If you were asked to describe the real meaning of Christmas, what would you say? You may think that is an easy answer, but I am constantly amazed at what I see and hear during the Christmas season. To some, Christmas is nothing more than a holiday from work and an excuse to party. To others it is the stress of crowded schedules and limited budgets. And to some, the holiday season is filled with sadness because of the loss of a loved one, or just reflecting on a year filled with unmet expectations.

The normal answer that people give when asked to describe the meaning of Christmas is that of a baby born in a manger. Of course the sweet scene of the Nativity warms our hearts and fills us with joy. But there is more to the story. The reality of His coming must move us beyond the baby in Bethlehem's manger to a rugged cross.

The apostle Paul goes behind the scenes and tells us the real reason for the season. He states in magnificent terms that the purpose of Jesus' coming was not to be remembered as a baby in a manger but as a Man who was born to die for the sins of the world.

Paul makes it very clear that when Jesus came to earth He set aside His glorious appearance and exchanged it for the clothing of human flesh. He took upon Himself the clothing of a servant, humbled Himself, and became obedient unto death, even death on a cross.

As you celebrate Christmas this year, be sure to remember the real purpose of His coming to earth. It isn't just a time to celebrate the birth of a baby boy, but to rejoice in the fact that Jesus humbled Himself and was willing to do whatever was necessary to redeem us from the slavery of sin. Redemption was and is the greatest Christmas gift ever given, and it is truly the "gift that keeps on giving."

———————

Father, thank You for coming to earth to redeem me. It fills my heart with joy and thankfulness. May I always remember the real reason for the season. Amen.

THINK LIKE A SNAKE!

I am sending you out like sheep among wolves. Therefore be as shrewd as snakes and as innocent as doves (Matthew 10:16).

I'm going to be honest, I'm not a big fan of snakes. I may not like them, but my dislike will not stop me from learning spiritual truth. In Matthew 10:16 Jesus commanded His disciples (and us) to be wise as serpents. He is not advocating "snake handling" but "snake thinking." The word "wise" literally means prudent, careful, cunning, discerning, thoughtful, intelligent or sensible. The word Jesus used perfectly fits the behavior and actions of the serpent.

For Jesus to command us to be *"wise as serpents"* means to be prudent, discerning, intelligent, thoughtful, and careful as snakes! This attitude applies to all of us in regard to our families, businesses, ministries, or any opportunities God places in front of us.

Consider for a moment how a snake behaves and how it relates to us and our conduct:

- Snakes always evaluate new territory.
- They never announce their presence.
- They stay low, quiet, and blend into the environment. We can walk right near a snake and never even realize it.
- They have a unique ability to stay invisible as long as possible.
- Snakes evaluate new situations to see what kind of opportunities are available.
- Snakes will identify shelter and the best hiding places to protect themselves from attack.
- They are patient to observe the easiest prey.
- They wait until all the facts are assessed before acting.

When God calls us to do something new or to move into new territory of opportunity, it is wise for us to move carefully and slowly. Acting hastily before all the facts are gathered can lead us to make decisions that we will later regret. It is better to lay low, and blend into the environment for a while, learning from the sights and the facts. If you are not sure when to "lay low," be sure that the Holy Spirit will lead you to be sensitive enough to know what to do. There is a time to observe and there is a time to strike.

Father, I ask You to help me to learn when to sit still and when to act. I will look to Your leadership. Amen.

GOD'S ODD CHOICE

Brothers and sisters, think of what you were when you were called. Not many of you were wise by human standards; not many were influential; not many were of noble birth. But God chose the foolish things of the world to shame the wise; God chose the weak things of the world to shame the strong (1 Corinthians 1:26-27).

If you have ever felt you were not smart enough, or wise enough to be used by God, then I have great news for you! The apostle Paul outlines exactly in whom God delights choosing and using to do mighty things in His kingdom: *"But God chose the **foolish** things of the world to shame the wise."* The word "foolish" means someone who is dull, dense, or foolish—hence, a fool. The word "foolish" comes from a Greek word from which we get the English word "moron." Yes, you heard it right. God will use (according to the world's view) morons to get the job done. The truth is no one is a moron or an idiot from God's viewpoint. The world often has a low opinion and a scathing denunciation of anyone who lives their lives dedicated to the Lord Jesus Christ.

It is simply a fact that to live as a Christian in today's society means to be ridiculed as being nitwits, mentally defective, or just plain idiots. Whom the world calls stupid or morons, God says He will use to "confound" the wise of the world. The word "confound" means to put to shame, to embarrass, to confuse or to baffle.

Here is what Paul is saying, "God calls people whom the world considers morons in order to put to shame, embarrass, confuse, frustrate, and baffle those who think they are smart!"

If anyone has ever called you stupid or foolish for serving Christ, it is time for you to rejoice. Why? It makes you a candidate—you are the kind of person God wants to use. It is time for Christians to stand up, speak up, and stop feeling badly because we have chosen to follow Christ. A lack of education, culture, or refinement has never stopped God from using people who have a willing heart to obey His voice. If your heart is right and you are willing for God to use you, then you are the very one God is seeking to change the world.

Father, thank You for choosing to use people like me. I may not have the refinement of the world, but I have a heart that is willing. Take me and use me. Amen.

AN INSIDE JOB

Come to me, all you who are weary and burdened, and I will give you rest.
Take my yoke upon you and learn from me, for I am gentle and humble
in heart, and you will find rest for your souls (Matthew 11:28-29).

Most of us really want to live in peace and demonstrate gentleness with others. It's one thing to want it, but another to achieve it. On our own it is just not possible to walk out of our door and force ourselves to be gentle. We can't manufacture gentleness, because inside we are still going to be under stress. It's got to be an "inside" job. It has to be the fruit of God's Spirit inside us.

When listing the nine different fruits of the Spirit the apostle Paul included gentleness: *"But the fruit of the Spirit is love, joy, peace, forbearance, kindness, goodness, faithfulness, **gentleness** and self-control. Against such things there is no law"* (Galatians 5:22-23).

Gentleness is an important quality for us to practice. It diffuses conflict with others. It disarms critics—don't be shocked, we all have them. Gentleness is persuasive. It's attractive. It communicates love. It is something worth fighting for!

Most importantly, gentleness makes you more like Jesus. Matthew 11:28-29 says, *"Come to me, all you who are weary and burdened, and I will give you rest. Take my yoke upon you and learn from me, for I am gentle and humble in heart, and you will find rest for your souls."*

Does this mean that the stress you're feeling is because you are not gentle? Without a doubt, it means exactly that. The Bible is very clear that the more gentle you become, the more Christlike you become and the more at rest you will be.

Do you want to be at peace? Do you want to be like Jesus? Jesus is gentle and humble. When you let Him share your burden, you will walk with Him in a close relationship. You will learn how to be more gentle and humble, and He will give you rest and peace, not stress and pressure.

Father, thank You for reminding me that I can be more like Jesus. When I am under stress, help me to give You my burden. Help me to demonstrate to others a gentle spirit. Holy Spirit, I lean on You. Amen.

THURSDAY

IT'S NOT WHAT YOU THINK

You were taught, with regard to your former way of life, to put off your old self, which is being corrupted by its deceitful desires; to be made new in the attitude of your minds; and to put on the new self, created to be like God in true righteousness and holiness (Ephesians 4:22-24).

Let me give you something to think about. And it may come as a shock to your system. God's goal for your life is not comfort, but character development! From the time that satan perpetuated his lie in the Garden that we can become "as gods," humanity has been trying to figure out how to control circumstances and events. Let's be clear about one thing—you and I will never become God! As created creatures, we will never be the Creator. It's not about becoming a god, but becoming godly. His desire is for us to take on His character, values, and attitudes. When we do that, then His character will come shining through our lives.

The apostle Paul said we are *to be made new in the attitude of our minds.* The kind of life Paul referred to is renewed from the inside, working its way to our conduct on the outside. God's ultimate goal is for you and I to grow up spiritually and become like Christ. God has created each one of us uniquely; He is not about trying to change our personalities, but He is definitely trying to transform our character. He is not looking for robots but men and women whose desire is to live a Christlike, God-centered life.

It is important to remember when we push character development aside and become concentrated only on our circumstances, the end result will be frustration and confusion. Never, ever confuse the abundant life promised by Jesus to mean a life free of painful circumstances and difficulties. Whether we want to admit it or not, difficulties and pain are what enable us to grow.

One final shock. Life is not about you. You and I were created for God's purposes, not the other way around. As one theologian put it, *"Why would God provide Heaven on Earth when he's planned the real thing for you in eternity? God gives us our time on Earth to build and strengthen our character for Heaven."* To which I say, "AMEN!"

Thank You, Father, for reminding me that it's not about comfort, but character. Give me the wisdom to know the difference. Amen.

I SHALL RETURN

*They were looking intently up into the sky as he was going, when
suddenly two men dressed in white stood beside them. "Men of Galilee,"
they said, "why do you stand here looking into the sky? This same
Jesus, who has been taken from you into heaven, will come back in
the same way you have seen him go into heaven"* (Acts 1:10-11).

Early in World War II, General Douglas MacArthur had to evacuate the Philippines because the islands were being overrun by the Japanese army. In answer to reporters' questions, the leader of America's forces in the Pacific war zone declared: "The President of the United States ordered me to break through the Japanese lines and proceed from Corregidor to Australia for the purposes, as I understand it, of organizing the American offensive against Japan, a primary object of which is the relief of the Philippines. I came through and *I shall return.*"

In October 1944, General MacArthur landed with his troops in the country he had left two years earlier and announced over a loudspeaker: "People of the Philippines: *I have returned.* By the grace of Almighty God we have come dedicated and committed to the task of destroying every vestige of enemy control over your daily lives." The Philippines were soon liberated and the victorious commander had returned in power.

In the midst of the world struggling against spiritual forces, men and women of goodwill seek peace, but instead face ever-increasing unrest and war. While we seek answers, there can only be the reassuring words of Jesus who said, *"I shall return."*

Jesus came to earth the first time as a servant and a lamb. He came to die as a sacrifice for the sins of the world. He is coming again as a conqueror of all evil and the King of the universe He created. His triumphant return is as certain as His first coming.

The theme of the second coming of Christ is the greatest theme in the Bible. While people may discuss and even disagree on the varying aspects of His second coming, there is one thing all agree on—He came the first time to liberate us from the chains of sin, and He's coming back a second time to gather us home! It is time for Christians to live every day with our hearts set on the soon return of the Lord Jesus Christ.

Father, I rejoice in truth of the second coming of Jesus. When I am discouraged, remind me of the precious hope I have in His soon return. Amen.

ENDNOTES

1. *Merriam-Webster Online*, s.v. "encourage," www.merriam-webster.com/dictionary/encourage.

2. Steven K. Scott, *The Richest Man Who Ever Lived* (New York: Doubleday/Random House, 2006).

3. Ibid.

4. "Billy Graham: I Know Where I'm Going," www.beliefnet.com/search/site.aspx?q=billy%20graham%20beliefnet (accessed January 18, 2016).

5. *Merriam-Webster Online*, s.v. "trust," www.merriam-webster.com/dictionary/trust.

6. Ray Stedman, "Hidden Faults," www.raystedman.org/daily-devotions/psalms/hidden-faults (accessed January 18, 2016).

7. Warren W. Wiersbe, *Be Transformed* (Colorado Springs, CO: David C. Cook, 1986).

8. Warren W. Wiersbe, *Be Faithful* (Wheaton, IL: Victor Books, 1983).

9. Kelly Benton, "Ain't Nobody God Time for That," www.sermoncentral.com/sermons/aint-nobody-got-time-for-that-kelly-benton-sermon-on-time-174291.asp?Page=2 (accessed January 18, 2016).

10. Todd Duncan *The Power to be Your Best* (Nashville, TN: Word Publishing, 1999).

11. Mike Fleischmann, "Endurance: It Matters How You Finish," July 31, 2012; www.mikefleischmann.net/?p=1236 (accessed January 19, 2016).

12. "The Amazing, True Story of D. L. Moody." http://nowtheendbegins.com/pages/preachers/dwight-moody.htm (accessed January 19, 2016).

13. Warren Wiersbe, *The Bumps Are What You Climb On* (Grand Rapids, MI: Baker Books, 2016).

14. Story by Lou Nicholes, missionary and author.

JOURNAL PAGES